NEOLIBERALISM

AS EXCEPTION

NEOLIBERALISM

as EXCEPTION

MUTATIONS IN CITIZENSHIP

AND SOVEREIGNTY

Aihwa Ong

DUKE UNIVERSITY PRESS

Durham and London

2006

2nd printing, 2007

© 2006 Duke University Press

All rights reserved

Printed in the United States of

America on acid-free paper ∞

Designed by Amy Ruth Buchanan

Typeset in Carter & Cone Galliard

by Keystone Typesetting, Inc.

Library of Congress Cataloging-in-

Publication Data and republication

acknowledgments appear on the last

printed pages of this book.

To

ALAN DUNDES,

dear friend

and colleague

CONTENTS

aCKNOWLEDGMENTS

The essays gathered in this volume have been part of an ongoing reflection on what might be called an anthropology of the global. My aim has been to pose big questions through an ethnographic investigation of the lines of mutation that shape diverse situations of contemporary living. I thank the many individuals and interdisciplinary programs that invited me to speak or to submit papers on these themes. Their enthusiasm and interest have stimulated me to revise work in progress and to pursue new lines of thinking. Some of the friends whose help, comments, and conversations have benefited me include Stephen J. Collier, Ching Kwan Lee, Ryan Bishop, Lisa Hoffman, Jesse Sanford, Dar Rudnyckyj, Donald Nonini, Andrew Ross, and Ken Wissoker. I also thank Shannon May for her suggestions and skillful editing. Part of the work was funded by a MacArthur Foundation grant to undertake research on risk and (in)security in Asian cities.

As always, my husband, Robert R. Ng, provided a nice balance of support and detachment, conditions that freed me to write in the midst of a busy family life.

Neoliberalism seems to mean many different things depending on one's vantage point. In much of the world, it has become a code word for America's overweening power. Asian politicians and pundits view "American neoliberalism" as a strategy of market domination that uses intermediaries such as the International Monetary Fund (IMF) to pry open small economies and expose them to trade policies that play havoc with these nations' present and future economic welfare. For example, in the decade of the emerging Asian economies (1980s–90s), Asian leaders proclaimed that "Asia can say no" to American neoliberalism. Such rhetoric became more vociferous after the "Asian financial crisis" of 1997–98.[1] In popular discourses, *neoliberalism* also represents unregulated financial flows that menaced national currencies and living conditions. South Korean anti-neoliberal protestors who lost their jobs due to imposed economic restructuring sported T-shirts that proclaimed, "IMF means I'M Fired!" In Latin America, the U.S. drive for open markets and privatization is called "savage neoliberalism." Since the invasion of Iraq, critiques of neoliberalism have included the perception that America would stoop to conquest in order to grab oil resources for major corporations. Thus, in the global popular imagination, American neoliberalism is viewed as a radicalized capitalist imperialism that is increasingly tied to lawlessness and military action. As we shall see below, despite such widespread criticism, Asian governments have selectively adopted neoliberal forms in creating economic zones and imposing market criteria on citizenship.

Neoliberalism at Large

In the United States, in contrast, *neoliberalism* is seldom part of popular discourse outside the academy. Rather, *market-based policies* and *neoconservatism* are the native categories that code the ensemble of thinking and strategies seeking to eliminate social programs and promote the interests of big capital. *Liberty* has become a word that designates "free economic action" rather than political liberalism, which has become a dirty word. In rather broad terms, one can say that the Democratic Party promotes itself as the defender of individual rights and civil liberties against the excesses of an unfettered, market-driven ethos, while the Republican Party relies on a neo-liberal (read neoconservative) discourse of individual solutions to myriad social problems. Both kinds of liberalism focus on free subjects as a basic rationale and target of government, but while the Democrats stress individual and civil freedoms, the Republicans underline individual obligations of self-reliance and self-management. For instance, the conservative columnist William Safire writes that "a Republican brain" chooses values that "include self-reliance over community dependence, intervention over isolation, self-discipline over society's regulation, finding pleasure in work rather than working to find pleasure."[2] In political life, both kinds of liberal rationalities frequently overlap and fuse, but Republicans have strengthened neoliberalism's hold on America by casting (political) "liberalism" as "un-American." Such partisan debates in fact highlight the chasm that is opening up between political liberal ideals of democracy and the neoliberal rationality of individual responsibility and fate.

Upon his reelection to a second term, President George W. Bush claimed a political "mandate" to transform life in the United States. In a raft of proposed new "market-based policies," he has proposed to dismantle fundamental aspects of American liberal democracy institutionalized since the New Deal, from the privatization of Social Security and health care to the abolition of the progressive tax code.[3] Bush calls his new vision the "ownership society," an explicit claim that American citizenship under his watch will shift toward a primitive, narrow vision of citizenship that includes only property owners, privileging "an independent and egoistical individual" in isolated pursuit of economic self-interest.[4] In his second inaugural address, President Bush was explicit about "preparing our people for the challenges of life in a free society . . . by making every citizen an agent of his or her own destiny."[5] This neoliberal view of citizenship also has the moral support of evangelical Christian groups.[6]

But presidential attempts to marketize politics and reengineer citizenship have not gone unchallenged. Close to half the citizenry has opposed such policies of privatization. For decades, a plethora of protest movements have defended the steady erosion of the civil rights of prisoners, workers, women, homosexuals, minorities, and aliens, to name only a few. They promise to continue the fight to protect individual liberty and the national patrimony. But the Bush administration continues to seek to reverse antipoverty programs, health coverage, environmental protection, and food safety, among other policies, in the spirit if not in the name of neoliberal reason. This cluster of neoliberal logic, religion, rights, and ethics has become the problem-space of American citizenship, with outcomes as yet unknown. Nevertheless, as I mentioned above, since the 1970s, "American neoliberalism" has become a global phenomenon that has been variously received and critiqued overseas.

Neoliberalism and Exceptions

This book argues that as a new mode of political optimization, neoliberalism — with a small *n* — is reconfiguring relationships between governing and the governed, power and knowledge, and sovereignty and territoriality. Neoliberalism is often discussed as an economic doctrine with a negative relation to state power, a market ideology that seeks to limit the scope and activity of governing. But neoliberalism can also be conceptualized as a new relationship between government and knowledge through which governing activities are recast as nonpolitical and nonideological problems that need technical solutions.[7] Indeed, neoliberalism considered as a technology of government is a profoundly active way of rationalizing governing and self-governing in order to "optimize." The spread of neoliberal calculation as a governing technology is thus a historical process that unevenly articulates situated political constellations. An ethnographic perspective reveals specific alignments of market rationality, sovereignty, and citizenship that mutually constitute distinctive milieus of labor and life at the edge of emergence.

I focus on the active, interventionist aspect of neoliberalism in non-Western contexts, where *neoliberalism as exception* articulates sovereign rule and regimes of citizenship. Of course, the difference between *neoliberalism as exception* and *exceptions to neoliberalism* hinges on what the "normative order" is in a particular milieu of investigation. This book focuses on the interplay of exceptions in emerging countries where neoliberalism itself is not the general characteristic of technologies of governing. We find neoliberal interventions in liberal democracies as well as in postcolonial, authoritarian, and post-socialist situations in East and Southeast Asia. Thus neoliberalism as exception is introduced in sites of transformation where market-driven calculations are bring introduced in the management of populations and the administration of special spaces. The articulation of neoliberal exceptions, citizenship, and sovereignty produces a range of possible anthropological problems and outcomes.[8]

At the same time, *exceptions to neoliberalism* are also invoked, in political decisions, to exclude populations and places from neoliberal calculations and choices. Exceptions to neoliberalism can be modes for protecting social safety nets or for stripping away all forms of political protection. In Russia, for instance, subsidized housing and social rights are preserved even when neoliberal techniques are introduced in urban budgetary practices.[9] At the same time, in Southeast Asia, exceptions to neoliberalism exclude migrant workers from the living standards created by market-driven policies. In other words, exceptions to neoliberalism can both preserve welfare benefits for citizens and exclude noncitizens from the benefits of capitalist development.

But there is an overlap in the workings of neoliberal exceptions and exceptions to market calculations. Populations governed by neoliberal technologies are dependent on others who are excluded from neoliberal considerations. The articulation of populations and spaces subjected to neoliberal norms and those outside the preview of these norms crystallizes ethical dilemmas, threatening to displace basic values of social equality and shared fate. The chapters that follow present diverse ethnographic milieus where the interplay of exceptions, politics, and ethics constitutes a field of vibrating relationships. New forms of governing and being governed and new notions of what it means to be human are at the edge of emergence.

In this approach, I bring together two concepts—neoliberalism and exception—that others have dealt with separately. Neoliberalism as a technology of governing relies on calculative choices and techniques in the domains of citizenship and of governing. Following Foucault, "governmentality" refers to the array of knowledges and techniques that are concerned with the systematic and pragmatic guidance and regulation of everyday conduct.[10] As Foucault puts it, governmentality covers a range of practices that "constitute, define, organize and instrumentalize the strategies that individuals in their freedom can use in dealing with each other."[11] Neoliberal governmentality results from the infiltration of market-driven truths and calculations into the domain of politics. In contemporary times, neoliberal rationality informs action by many regimes and furnishes the concepts that inform the government of free individuals who are then induced to self-manage according to market principles of discipline, efficiency, and competitiveness.[12]

The political exception, in Carl Schmitt's formulation, is a political decision that is made outside the juridical order and general rule. Schmitt has argued that "the sovereign produces and guarantees the situation in its totality. He has monopoly over this last decision. Therein lies the essence of the state's sovereignty, which must be juridically defined correctly, not as the monopoly to coerce or to rule, but as the monopoly to decide."[13] The condition of exception is thus a political liminality, an extraordinary decision to depart from a generalized political normativity, to intervene in the logics of ruling and of being ruled. The Schmittian exception is invoked to delineate friends and foes in a context of war. Giorgio Agamben has used the exception as a fundamental principle of sovereign rule that is predicated on the division between citizens in a juridical order and outsiders stripped of juridical-political protections.[14]

In contrast, I conceptualize the exception more broadly, as an extraordinary departure in policy that can be deployed to include as well as to exclude. As conventionally understood, the sovereign exception marks out excludable subjects who are denied protections. But the exception can also be a positive decision to include selected populations and spaces as targets of "calculative choices and value-orientation"[15] associated with neoliberal reform. In my formulation, we need to explore the hinge between neoliberalism as exception and exception to neoliberalism, the interplay among technologies of governing and of disciplining, of inclusion and exclusion, of giving value or denying value to human conduct. The politics of exception in an era of globalization has disquieting ethicopolitical implications for those who are included as well as those who are excluded in shifting technologies of governing and of demarcation. This book will explore how the market-driven logic of exception is deployed in a variety of ethnographic contexts and the ethical risks and interrogations set in motion, unsettling established practices of citizenship and sovereignty.

Interrelationships among exceptions, politics, and citizenship crystallize problems of contemporary living, and they also frame ethical debates over what it means to be human today. For instance, neoliberal exceptions have been variously invoked in Asian settings to recalculate social criteria of citizenship, to remoralize economic action, and to redefine spaces in relation to market-driven choices. These articulations have engendered a range of contingent and ambiguous outcomes that cannot be predicted beforehand. Neoliberal decisions have created new forms of inclusion, setting apart some citizen-subjects, and creating new spaces that enjoy extraordinary political benefits and economic gain. There is the Schmittian exception that abandons certain populations and places them outside political normativity. But articulations between neoliberal exceptions and exceptions to neoliberalism have multiplied possibilities for moral claims and values assigned to various human categories, so that different degrees of protection can be negotiated for the politically excluded.

The yoking of neoliberalism and exception, I suggest, has the following implications for our understanding of how citizenship and sovereignty are mutating in articulation and disarticulation with neoliberal reason and mechanisms. First, a focus on neoliberalism recasts our thinking about the connection between government and citizenship as a strictly juridicallegal relationship. It is important to trace neoliberal technology to a biopolitical mode of governing that centers on the capacity and potential of individuals and the population as living resources that may be harnessed and managed by governing regimes. *Neoliberalism* as used here applies to two kinds of optimizing technologies. *Technologies of subjectivity* rely on an array of knowledge and expert systems to induce self-animation and self-government so that citizens can optimize choices, efficiency, and competitiveness in turbulent market conditions. Such techniques of optimization include the adherence to health regimes, acquisition of skills, development of entrepreneurial ventures, and other techniques of self-engineering and capital accumulation. *Technologies of subjection* inform political strategies that differently regulate populations for optimal productivity, increasingly through spatial practices that engage market forces. Such regulations include the fortressization of urban space, the control of travel, and the recruitment of certain kinds of actors to growth hubs.

As an intervention of optimization, neoliberalism interacts with regimes of ruling and regimes of citizenship to produce conditions that change administrative strategies and citizenship practices. It follows that the infiltration of market logic into politics conceptually unsettles the notion of citizenship as a legal status rooted in a nation-state, and in stark opposition to a condition of statelessness.[16] Furthermore, the neoliberal exception articulates citizenship elements in political spaces that may be less than the national territory in some cases, or exceed national borders in others.

The elements that we think of as coming together to create citizenship — rights, entitlements, territoriality, a nation — are becoming disarticulated and rearticulated with forces set into motion by market forces. On the one hand, citizenship elements such as entitlements and benefits are increasingly associated with neoliberal criteria, so that mobile individuals who possess human capital or expertise are highly valued and can exercise citizenship-like claims in diverse locations. Meanwhile, citizens who are judged not to have such tradable competence or potential become devalued and thus vulnerable to exclusionary practices. On the other hand, the territoriality of citizenship, that is, the national space of the homeland, has become partially embedded in the territoriality of global capitalism, as well as in spaces mapped by the interventions of nongovernmental organizations (NGOs). Such overlapping spaces of exception create conditions for diverse claims of human value that do not fit neatly into a conventional notion of citizenship, or of a universal regime of human rights. In short, components of citizenship have developed separate links to new spaces, becoming rearticulated, redefined, and reimagined in relation to diverse locations and ethical situations. Such de- and re-linking of citizenship elements, actors, and spaces have been occasioned by the dispersion and realignment of market strategies, resources, and actors.

Second, neoliberalism as exception refines the study of state sovereignty, long conceptualized as a political singularity. One view is of the state as a machine that steamrolls across the terrain of the nation, or that will eventually impose a uniform state bureaucracy.[17] In actual practice, sovereignty is manifested in multiple, often contradictory strategies that encounter diverse claims and contestations, and produce diverse and contingent outcomes. In the course of interactions with global markets and regulatory institutions, I maintain, sovereign rule invokes the exception to create new economic possibilities, spaces, and techniques for governing the population. The neoliberal exception allows for a measure of sovereign flexibility in ways that both fragment and extend the space of the nation-state. For instance, in Southeast and East Asia, zoning technologies have carved special spaces in order to achieve strategic goals of regulating groups in relation to market forces. The spatial concentration of strategic political, economic, and social conditions attracts foreign investment, technology transfer, and international expertise to particular zones of high growth. Market-driven strategies of spatial fragmentation respond to the demands of global capital for diverse categories of human capital, thus engendering a pattern of noncontiguous, differently administered spaces of "graduated" or "variegated sovereignty." Furthermore, as corporations and NGOs exert indirect power over various populations at different political scales, we have an emergent situation of overlapping sovereignties.

For instance, technologies of optimization are repositioning the metropolis as a hub for enrolling networks of resources and actors, making the metropolis the hub of a distinctive ecosystem. Saskia Sassen has proposed an influential model of a few "global cities" — New York, London, and Tokyo — that control key functions and services that sustain global circuits. This transnational urban system dominates "cities in the global south which are mostly in the mid-range of the global hierarchy."[18] The explosive growth of Shanghai, Hong Kong, and Singapore suggests the rise of a different kind of space-time synergy prompted by neoliberal exceptions. Market-driven calculations create novel possibilities for combining and recombining external and internal elements to reposition these cities as the sites of emergence and new circulations.

Situated mobilizations of strategic knowledge, resources, and actors configure vibrating webs of interaction, that is, space-time "ecosystems" that extend the scope of hypergrowth zones. This governmentality-as-ecology strategy does not seek to fit emerging Asian centers into a preexisting transnational urban system. Rather, the logic is to reposition the hometown (*oikos*) in its self-spun web of symbiotic relationships among diverse elements (ecosystem) for the strategic production of specific material and social values.[19] This Microsoft-like approach creates "platforms" — "services, tools, or technologies — that other members of the ecosystem can use to enhance their own performance."[20] It is a hub strategy that uses capital not to perform conventional city functions but to leverage their relationships for innovative collaborations with global companies and research institutions that become intertwined with the future of the site.

Third, the calculative mechanisms of open markets articulate new arrangements and territorializations of capital, knowledge, and labor across national borders. Michael Hardt and Antonio Negri's influential book, *Empire*, contends that economic globalization has produced a uniform global labor regime.[21] But the complex interactions between diverse zones and particular networks challenge sweeping claims about a unified landscape of labor regulation. Rather, I argue, different vectors of capital construct spaces of exception — "latitudes" — that coordinate different axes of labor regulation and of labor disciplining. Lateral production systems permit the stretching of governmentality as well as coercive labor regimes across multiple sites. Latitudinal spaces are thus formed by a hybrid mix of regulatory and incarceral labor regimes that can operate with little regard for labor rights across far-flung zones. Nevertheless, the latitudinal controls are subject to unexpected and unbidden challenges that rise intermittently from mobilities of labor among various sites.

Fourth, neoliberalism, as an ethos of self-governing, encounters and articulates other ethical regimes in particular contexts. Market rationality that promotes individualism and entrepreneurialism engenders debates about the norms of citizenship and the value of human life. For instance, in Southeast Asia, the neoliberal exception in an Islamic public sphere catalyzes debates over female virtue. *Ulamas* resist the new autonomy of working women, while feminists claim a kind of gender equality within the limits of Islam. Contrary to the perception that transnational humanitarianism replaces situated ethics, questions of status and morality are problematized and resolved in particular milieus shaped by economic rationality, religious norms, and citizenship values.

Indeed, different degrees of political and moral claims by the politically marginalized can be negotiated in the shifting nexus of logics and power. There are conceptual limits to models that pose a simple opposition between normalized citizenship and bare life. Giorgio Agamben draws a stark contrast between citizens who enjoy juridicallegal rights and excluded groups who dwell in "a zone of indistinction."[22] But ethnographic study of particular situations reveals that negotiations on behalf of the politically excluded can produce indeterminate or ambiguous outcomes. Indeed, this is the complex work of NGOs everywhere, to identify and articulate moral problems and claims in particular milieus. At times, even business rationality may be invoked in seeking sheer survival for those bereft of citizenship or citizenship-like protections. Humanitarian interventions do not operate in a one-size-fits-all manner but must negotiate the shifting field of crisscrossing relationships.

Neoliberalism as exception articulates a constellation of mutually constitutive relationships that are not reducible to one or the other. Rather, ethnographic exploration reveals novel interactions between market-driven mechanisms and situated practices in space-time interrelationships through which problems are resolved. Technologies of self-governing articulate elements of citizenship, self-enterprising values are translated into movable social entitlements, and mobile entrepreneurial subjects can claim citizenship-like benefits in multiple locations. Meanwhile, the neoliberal exception in governing constructs political spaces that are differently regulated and linked to global circuits. Such reflexive techniques of social engineering and the reengineering of the self interact with diverse ethical regimes, crystallizing contemporary problems of citizenship and ethical living.

The rest of this introduction is divided into the following sections. First, I review theories of neoliberalism and discuss why neoliberalism as a technology of governing is a useful concept for ethnographic inquiry into contemporary mutations in citizenship and sovereignty. Second, I propose a concept of citizenship as an ensemble of elements that can be delinked and relinked to market-based rationalities. Third, the neoliberal exception is a crucial analytic for rethinking sovereign power as neither a singularity nor a simple opposition of normativity and exception but a shifting and flexible ensemble of heterogeneous calculations, choices, and exceptions that constitute security, life, and ethics. The final section discusses how articulations of neoliberal projects and moral economies can both strip human beings of citizenship but also become realigned in the interests of protecting bare life.

Modalities of Neoliberalism

Let us briefly review the genealogy of neoliberalism as a concept. An analytical discussion of neoliberalism should begin with Karl Polanyi's warning in the early twentieth century about letting the free market mechanism be the sole director of the fate of human beings and of mother earth. Polanyi famously argued that modern society is characterized by a "double movement," whereby the free circulation of capital is met by a counterforce: political demands for self-protection against the disruptive and polarizing effects of free markets on contemporary life.[23] Polanyi had faith that state legislation could regulate markets and thus protect society.

But Polanyi's opponents were skeptical that laws and social norms could ensure the best use of resources for society. Friedrich von Hayek, an Austrian philosopher, proposed an alternative economic theory at the subjectivist level, identifying individual actions that aim to maximize self-interest as the key mechanism for making sure that public resources are allocated efficiently. At the center of Hayek's liberalism is the *Homo economicus*, an instrumentalist figure forged in the effervescent conditions of market competition.[24] Hayek's ideas influenced Milton Friedman[25] and Gary Becker,[26] two of the leading proponents of the Chicago School of neoliberalism in the 1960s. This doctrine came to be associated with Thatcherism and Reaganomics as a first wave of neoliberalism in the 1980s. At home, the neoliberal doctrine was used to attack "big government" and the bureaucratic welfare state. The focus was on restructuring the public state sector in order to increase corporatization and privatization and introduce "efficiency." Abroad, economic liberalization was promoted to open up access to overseas markets. These policies were referred to as the "Washington consensus" when exported to the Eastern Bloc, as a set of "adjustment" strategies to restructure socialist economies for engaging economic competition.[27] Overseas, such policies of privatization and open economies were also referred to as "American neoliberalism," or economic globalization, that is, policies supporting a global shift in economic planning from the national to the regional level, through the formation of trading blocs.

By the nineties, neoliberalism came to be understood by a new generation of economists such as Francis Fukuyama and Jeffrey Sachs, as the inevitable endpoint in the evolution of market economy. Public figures such as Joseph Stiglitz and Jürgen Habermas lament the social consequences of economic globalization and urge political defense against the ravages of the freely roaming market. But while debates have weighed the pros and cons of neoliberalism, most agree that neoliberalism is "the expression of a specific kind of progressive modernization."[28] In this second wave of neoliberalism, individual internalization of neoliberal traits was stressed, based in a new way on technologies of subjectification. Under the Clinton administration, "individual responsibilization" became the new norm in previously subsidized domains such as health and education, and it was used as the rationale for "workfare" programs.[29] In short, the main elements of neoliberalism as a political philosophy are (a) a claim that the market is better than the state at distributing public resources and (b) a return to a "primitive form of individualism: an individualism which is 'competitive,' 'possessive,' and construed often in terms of the doctrine of 'consumer sovereignty.'"[30] It is important to note that neoliberal reasoning is based on both economic (efficiency) and ethical (self-responsibility) claims.

In the human sciences, there is widespread agreement that neoliberalism has become the number one force of reckoning for different aspects of contemporary living. But there is still disagreement as to the scope, organization, and knowledge-power dimensions of market rationality. Neoliberalism as social phenomenon has been studied mainly by reframing Marxist concepts of class ideology and structural change at the national and global levels. A New Left critique views neoliberalism as a class-based ideology that attacks the welfare state in advanced liberal countries such as Great Britain.[31] At a broader level, neoliberalism is conceptualized as the latest stage of capitalist global structural and hegemonic domination. For instance, Stephen Gill argues that neoliberalism is an epoch-marking order that relies on the quasi-legal restructuring of relationships between nation-states and transnational agencies. He claims that this global disciplinary regime is accompanied by a hegemonic notion of inevitable progress and social hierarchy associated with "market civilization."[32]

These modalities, which construct the framework of a neoliberal North versus a South under siege, appear to have spawned two schools of thought in anthropology. The first identifies a Northern "culture of neoliberalism" that engenders Southern responses including occult economies, messianic movements, and other social upheavals.[33] The second view seeks to identify "neoliberal states" that centralize capital and monopoly power "at the global level." David Harvey invokes "the neoliberal state" as an ideal-type and thereby unwittingly presents the state as an entity of singularity. This approach encounters conceptual problems when confronted with East Asia, the world's most economically dynamic region. Harvey refers to "the *strange* case of China," apparently because of analytical difficulty in reconciling the coexistence of Chinese socialist formation with feverish capitalist activity.[34] As we will see, the dynamic and novel combinations of neoliberal interventions and Asian political cultures challenge typological approaches based on a simple geographical North-South axis, or a typology of nation-states. Rather than taking neoliberalism as a tidal wave of market-driven phenomena that sweeps from dominant countries to smaller ones, we could more fruitfully break neoliberalism down into various technologies: the kind of political exceptions that permit sovereign practices and subjectifying techniques that deviate from the established norm. Neoliberal forms articulating East Asian milieus are often in tension with local cultural sensibilities and national identity. While technocrats embrace business agendas and legitimize ideals of human talent and self-enterprise, many ordinary people remain ambivalent and skeptical about market criteria and its assault on collective values and community interest. The challenge for ethnographic research is not to find an "appropriate" scale of action—national, global, or local—but to identify an analytical angle that allows us to examine the shifting lines of mutation that the neoliberal exception generates.

Neoliberalism as a Technology of Governing

As anthropologists, we are skeptical of grand theories. We pose big questions through the prism of situated ethnographic research on disparate situations of contemporary living. Years ago, Clifford Geertz noted that in an interpretive approach, there is "the need of theory to stay rather close to the ground. . . . Only short flights of ratiocination tend to be effective in anthropology; the longer ones tend to drift off into logical dreams, academic bemusements with formal symmetry." Today, our inquiry goes beyond "the conceptual world in which our subjects live,"[35] but our approach may still be characterized as low-flying, an analytical angle that stays close to discursive and nondiscursive practices. Our goal is to engage in midrange theorizing about observable contemporary human phenomena in a variety of mutating human situations. We seek to capture the shifting lines that disarticulate and rearticulate elements in constellations that constitute the site or object of investigation. It therefore seems appropriate to study neoliberalism not as a "culture" or a "structure" but as mobile calculative techniques of governing that can be decontextualized from their original sources and recontextualized in constellations of mutually constitutive and contingent relationships. This milieu is a space of betwixt and between that is the site of the problem and of its resolution.[36]

Neoliberal governmentality can be traced to Foucault's notion of "biopower," a modern mode of governing that brought "life and its mechanisms into the realm of explicit calculations and made knowledge/power an agent of the transformation of human life." This political technology centered on the management of life oscillates between two poles of development. One pole centers on "the body as a machine: its disciplining, the optimization of its capabilities, and the extortion of its forces." The other pole focuses on the species body as biological machinery and a basis of collective well-being and reproduction.[37] *Biopolitics* thus refers to a series of regulatory controls exerted on the population and on individuals in order to harness and extract life forces. Neoliberalism is merely the most recent development of such techniques that govern human life, that is, a governmentality that relies on market knowledge and calculations for a politics of subjection and subject-making that continually places in question the political existence of modern human beings.

The British governmentality school proposes a theory of neoliberalism as an art of governing whose logic is the condition of individual active freedom.[38] From their perspective, neoliberalism is dealt with not as a general economic doctrine but as a technology that grounds the imperatives of modern government "upon the self-activating capacities of free human beings, citizens, subjects."[39] Thus, in our empirical project, we want to investigate how neoliberalism — Hayek's prescription of the *Homo economicus* as the basis of a free political order[40] — becomes translated, technologized, and operationalized in diverse, contemporary situations.

Nikolas Rose maintains that neoliberalism as a mode of "governing through freedom" has become a dominant style of government in Great Britain and other advanced liberal democracies. Neoliberal policies of "shrinking" the state are accompanied by a proliferation of techniques to remake the social and citizen-subjects. Thus, neoliberal logic requires populations to be free, self-managing, and self-enterprising individuals in different spheres of everyday life — health, education, bureaucracy, the professions, and so on.[41] The neoliberal subject is therefore not a citizen with claims on the state but a self-enterprising citizen-subject who is obligated to become an "entrepreneur of himself or herself."[42] For instance, under the "Third Way" initiative, there is a new stress on responsibility at the community level, and new requirements that individual subjects be responsible for themselves.[43] Neoliberal technology reorganizes connections among the governing, the self-governed, and political spaces, optimizing conditions for responding technically and ethically to globalized uncertainty and threat.

It is obvious that neoliberalism as political rationality is not confined to the milieus of advanced liberal democracies, but it has barely been investigated outside North Atlantic situations. Indeed, one can say that "economic globalization" indexes this disembedding and reembedding of neoliberal rationalities across multiple global sites.

Neoliberalism as exception is deployed in political settings as varied as postcolonialism, authoritarianism, and postsocialism.[44] The spread of neoliberal calculations and choices has been abetted by international agencies such as the World Bank, in the form of prescriptions such as "political entrepreneurialism" in emerging countries, where discourses of life-long learning and expertise encourage citizens to self-manage and compete in global knowledge markets.[45] As an array of techniques centered on the optimization of life, neoliberalism migrates from site to site, interacting with various assemblages that cannot be analytically reduced to cases of a uniform global condition of "Neoliberalism" writ large. What then are the conceptual implications of neoliberal modes of governing — as exceptions and as exceptions to — for our thinking on the changing form and ethics of citizenship?

(Dis)Articulations of Citizenship

An angle of analysis that hovers above daily life espies the ceaseless adjustments and readjustments of ethics in relationship to ongoing social forces. Specifically, market-driven intrusions have realigned citizenship elements in different ways, thus challenging unified models of citizenship, on the one hand, and the national framework of its claims, on the other. It is becoming increasingly clear that the temporal dimension of citizenship is less fixed than we had previously presumed, as flows of people and ideas attenuate citizenship protections, and new articulations of claims emerge in novel political spaces.

Heretofore, influential concepts of citizenship have been based on a binary opposition between the rights of citizenship rooted in a national territory and a stateless condition outside the nation-state. This politico-legal concept is based on the practical reality that only the nation-state can implement citizenship entitlements and protections claimed through recognized political membership.[46] Indeed, citizenship as political status continues to be exceedingly important for asylum seekers and refugees, for whom gaining citizenship in a host country is the most basic step toward being recognized as modern human beings.[47] Nevertheless, contemporary flows of capital and of migrants have interacted with sovereignty and rights discourses in complex ways to disentangle citizenship claims once knotted together in a single, territorialized mass.

As many have noted, formal citizenship by itself seldom guarantees that one will be able to vote and participate in political life (political rights), or receive equal treatment under the law (civil rights). Consequently, T. H. Marshall coined the term *social rights* to describe the need of social protections for women, the poor, minorities, and others vulnerable to gender, class, and racial discrimination that undercuts their standing as equal citizens.[48] This early-twentieth-century conception of citizenship—as imagined political identity, as the right to equal rights—is rooted in the assumption that the nation-state controls a citizenry that is relatively stable and fixed to the national territory.

More recently, the discourse of rights has introduced a strategy that opens up the space of shared citizenship beyond the terrain of the nation-state, incorporating the disruptions and flows of globalization. This opening allows for debates over the variety of citizenship claims at the local and regional levels within the European Union (EU). Prorights movements talk about "disaggregating" citizenship into different bundles of rights and benefits, so that European states can differently incorporate diverse non-European migrants and noncitizens.[49] It has been claimed that limited benefits and civil rights constitute a form of partial citizenship, or "postnational" political membership for migrant workers.[50] Such claims of postnational citizenship may have exaggerated the gains made by migrants without formal citizenship.[51] One may also add that a negative process of disaggregation is also under way, despite the dominant discourse of rights. Marshallian social rights are being dismantled as the welfare state shrinks (especially in Germany) in response to global markets. The process of disaggregating rights and benefits in favor of migrants, and against the interest of workers, is under way in Europe.

I conceive of the disarticulation and rearticulation of citizenship differently. The new alignments of citizenship elements, I argue, are fundamentally linked to dynamic and varied conditions engendered by mobile neoliberal technologies of governing and self-governing. There are spatial and temporal dimensions to the disconnection and reconnection among citizenship elements and techniques of unfettered capitalism. First, components formerly tied to citizenship — rights, entitlements, as well as nation and territoriality — are becoming disarticulated from one another and rearticulated with governing strategies that promote an economic logic in defining, evaluating, and protecting certain categories of subjects and not others. In some milieus, the neoliberal exception gives value to calculative practices and to self-governing subjects as preferred citizens. Meanwhile, other segments of the population are excepted from neoliberal criteria and thus rendered excludable as citizens and subjects. Variations in individual capacities or in performance of market skills intensify existing social and moral inequalities while blurring political distinctions between national and foreign populations.

In global circuits, educated and self-propulsive individuals claim citizenship-like entitlements and benefits, even at the expense of territorialized citizens. Expatriate talents constitute a form of movable entitlement without formal citizenship. Citizens who are deemed too complacent or lacking in neoliberal potential may be treated as less-worthy subjects. Low-skill citizens and migrants become exceptions to neoliberal mechanisms and are constructed as excludable populations in transit, shuttled in and out of zones of growth. We are beginning to see a detachment of entitlements from political membership and national territory, as certain rights and benefits are distributed to bearers of marketable talents and denied to those who are judged to lack such capacity or potential. The neoliberal exception is allied to a moralized system of distributive justice that is detachable from legal citizenship status. Articulations between citizenship elements, entrepreneurial traits, and global circuits fragment what we long assumed to be a homogeneous collectivity and a unified space of citizenship. A conceptual focus on dis- and rearticulations of citizenship elements with technologies of neoliberalism and of exceptions to neoliberalism identifies the problem-space for the investigation of mutations in citizenship and its value-giving criteria.

Second, articulations also refer to discursive practices as ongoing negotiations of citizenship in conditions of displacement. Articulation as a conceptual temporality permits the exploration of claims as a contingent emergence within particular assemblages of market rationalities, politics, and ethics. The stress on discursive negotiation or translation of contradictory elements within the space of conjuncture sidesteps a predetermined opposition or adversary position among elements but maintains a conceptual openness to unexpected possibilities and resolutions. Homi Bhabha has also noted the "contradictory and ambivalent space of enunciation" that keeps cultural meanings unstable as they are appropriated and reinterpreted anew in the crosscurrents of power.[52] A context-specific inquiry allows us to capture how opposing interpretations and claims can and do interrupt, slow down, deflect, and negotiate neoliberal logics and initiatives. The temporality of transmission, translation, and negotiation in this fluctuating space is fraught with political complication, contingency, and ambiguity.

The temporality of enunciations at the intersection of disparate events and forces is reason to be wary of sweeping claims about cosmopolitan citizenship. For instance, Jürgen Habermas has bemoaned the onslaught of deregulated markets and its creation of a "democratic deficit" in public life.[53] He has called for the creation of a Europe-wide public sphere and constitution that can defend cherished ideals: social security, public social services, gender and class norms, rejection of the death penalty, and so on. Such claims of a European civilization and shared political democratic culture reflect growing cosmopolitan thinking and feelings, and an emergent discourse of cosmopolitan citizenship. European commentators have pointed to a new global public sphere in the activities of multilateral agencies such as the United Nations and human rights organizations.[54] But feelings of solidarity and greater inclusiveness cannot be conflated with the construction of actual institutions of Cosmopolitanism. Indeed, some observers have argued that the pluralized world communities invoked by Kantian Cosmopolitanism are still more ideal than reality.[55] The United Nations lacks the power to enforce its many instruments on human rights, and it is highly susceptible to the influence of leading nations to initiate humanitarian interventions — or launch military invasions. Indeed, the American preemptive invasion of Iraq was a serious blow to the ideal of cosmopolitan right, and it is unclear how the United Nations will recover its lost mandate to speak on behalf of all of humanity. Furthermore, the

values of Cosmopolitanism—individualism, universality, and generality—
have historically also been associated with the conquest and transformation
of non-European societies.[56] Discourses of Cosmopolitanism have been a
vital part of the civilizing mission of imperialism, and they have thus been
treated with skepticism by populations in formerly colonized countries.[57]
Thus, it is important that our analysis of citizenship specify the situated
nature of enunciations in a field of space-time interrelationships without
relying on a telos of predetermined inevitability. The situated entanglements
of geopolitics, market logic, exceptions, and ethical discourses require a conceptual openness to contingency, ambivalence, and uncertain outcomes.

Sovereignty and Exception

In recent years, the spatialities of sovereignty have become a key issue in in-
quiries into the nature of modern power. One position is staked out by "the
new international relations" school. John Ruggie maintains that despite
claims that globalization weakens state power, sovereignty is an attribute of
"territorially defined, fixed and mutually exclusive enclaves of legitimate do-
minion."[58] In contrast to this uniform spatiality, postcolonial views insist that
the colonial legacy of "the bifurcated state," based on the urban-rural divide,
continues to structure sovereign rule in Africa.[59] More nuanced views of African sovereignty include descriptions of the state apparatus marooned in the
capital-city, of garrison-entrepots, corporate enclaves, and NGO-administered
spaces.[60] My concerns overlap with these, but my conceptualization is different in not seeking spatial dynamics in colonial antecedents of divide-and-
rule, in roving brigands of militarized accumulation, or in an invasion of
"global capital" and NGOs.

Rather, my focus is on the selective deployment of the neoliberal exception, on the one hand, and exceptions to neoliberalism, on the other, that are
instrumentalized in the spatializing practices of sovereignty. This spatializing
dynamic articulated by neoliberalism and its exceptions is distinctive in East
Asian environments, where the state tends to be robust and centralized, compared to the weak and dispersed political formations in Africa. As mentioned
above, Schmitt's view of state sovereignty is based on the strategic and situational exercise of power that responds to crises and challenges by invoking
exceptions to political normativity. "All law," he argues, "is 'situational law.'"[61]
The contingent exploitation of the exception—as neoliberal technologies, or
as exclusions from neoliberalism—is skillfully applied in some Asian contexts.

For instance, the reemergence of China onto the world scene was marked by the creation of "Special Economic Zones" (SEZs) and "Special Administration Regions" (SARs). These new spaces were brought into being by techniques of calculative choice institutionalized in mechanisms and procedures that mark out special spaces of labor markets, investment opportunities, and relative administrative freedom. Calculative mechanisms that code these spaces as zones include special taxation and investment schemes, urban budgets, infrastructural development, and some degree of autonomous rule. The logic of the exception in this case was to meet the crisis of centralized socialist production and to launch market reforms that produced spaces and conditions radically at odds with those in the rest of the country (chap. 4).

In Asian milieus, the option of exception has allowed states to carve up their own territory so they can better engage and compete in global markets. Neoliberal calculations are applied to practices of human territoriality, or to the control of populations through the reinscription of geographical space.[62] As the case of China illustrates, zoning technologies encode alternative territorialities for experiments in economic freedom and entrepreneurial activity. The logic of the exception fragments human territoriality in the interests of forging specific, variable, and contingent connections to global circuits. The resulting pattern of graduated or variegated sovereignty ensures that the state can both face global challenges and secure order and growth. It is also crucial to note that these strategies produced through the logic of the exception are free of the "Enlightenment" package of free-market ideology, modern political liberalism, and participatory citizen-subjects. While the state retains formal sovereignty, corporations and multilateral agencies frequently exert de facto control over the conditions of living, laboring, and migration of populations in special zones. As the administrative controls, citizenship, and territoriality once fused in a sovereign state are teased apart, we see what are in fact overlapping sovereignties. The neoliberal exception thus pries open the seam between sovereignty and citizenship, generating successive degrees of insecurity for low-skilled citizens and migrants who will have to look beyond the state for the safeguarding of their rights.[63]

The exception thus allows the institutionalization of innovative spatial administration that goes beyond what can be suggested by the view that distinctive economic action folds in a multiscalar formation. Some view the appropriate scale for examining the spaces of economic globalization as preexisting administrative units such as locality, city, province, country, and "regional economy."[64] Another view holds that the effects of global forces are staggered according to personal, urban, national, and regional scales.[65] There is the danger, however, that the language of scales projects a conceptual architecture that is at risk of taking itself too literally.[66] The images of scales suggest that market calculations are interested in an economistic structuring of political landscapes, when we should view space "as constantly shifting" and seek to "re-describe materiality as a constantly emergent process."[67] The logic of spaces of exception is that they are not always defined by prior political boundaries but brought into existence by neoliberal calculations that demarcate human territoriality in relation to opportunities presented by the deliberate mobilization of flows and resources.

The sovereign exception, for instance, has become more flexible in relation to "external" spaces and populations as well. In some Asian contexts, there is a technopolitical reconceptualization of the elastic possibilities of the external environment in terms of a fluid "ecosystem." Freed from the notion that the nation-state is a fixed territoriality, entrepreneurial governmentality corrals experts, knowledge, and skills from far-flung sources. There is an interesting convergence between the logic of optimization and ecological principles of symbiotic interdependence and synergy that comes from a density of interactions. As technocrats redesign the Asian city and its external environment, the national terrain is both fragmented into specialized nodes and extended as the homeland (oikos) is embedded in an "effervescent ecosystem" of global capitalism. For instance, Singaporean technocrats are assembling knowledge capital, research institutions, and sciences to develop a vibrant frontier in biotechnological research. Ecological principles of nursery, niche formation, symbiosis, and synergy among a critical mass of life-forms inform political strategies for repositioning the home-nation in a transnational space of dis- and rearticulated biopolitical interrelationships (chap. 8).

Contingent spatializations reveal that the logic of the exception allows innovative combinations of disciplinary and regulatory regimes in transnational production networks. On the one hand, the cartography of economic globalization is not a hierarchical scheme of global, national, metropolitan, and local levels, or divided into Western societies of regulation versus Asian societies of discipline. On the other, Hardt and Negri, invoking Gilles Deleuze, make an epochal claim that we are in a transition from a disciplinary society to the society of control in which "mechanisms" of control become more "democratic" and are "distributed throughout the brains and bodies of the citizens" rather than through the operation of specific disciplinary technologies. The systems of control are "free-floating" and regulatory in nature, producing "a smooth space of uncoded and deterritorialized flows." This assumed globalized uniformity in labor regimes prompts Hardt and Negri to claim that the "delocalization" of productive forces has decontextualized labor exploitation, making it "non-place"-able.[68] Despite the quick embrace of this formulation, it is a mistake to associate flexible transnational networks with nondisciplinary labor, for ethnographic research reveals that transnational production systems continue to exploit incarceral modes of labor control.

The logic of exception in global capitalism allows the combination of managerial and labor regimes in transnational networks that carve striated spaces — or "latitudes" — shaped by the coordination of systems of governmentality and regimes of labor incarceration. Again, research shows that labor tactics and rebellions tend to be highly context-specific, and they do not easily coalesce into a global mass movement or multitude, with its promise of global citizenship. In short, while business management practices are highly mobile, their transmission, translation, and implementation in diverse zones are always situated, relying on an array of institutionalized labor practices that are contingent and varied in their political possibilities (chap. 5).

The oscillation between neoliberalism as exception and exception to neoliberalism has also engendered ethical geographies, emergent spaces of would-be NGO administration. For instance, the intersection of politics of inclusion and of exclusion creates situations in which talented expatriates are incorporated as prototypical ideal citizens, while low-skill migrants brought in for labor extraction are politically excluded. Such noncitizens frequently appeal not to the state, but to nonstate agencies to protect their rights as migrant workers and outsiders. Here, NGO articulation of claims for migrant workers, trafficked individuals, and asylum seekers increasingly depend on normative mechanisms that can map spaces that are exceptions to neoliberalism. These spaces are suggested by the circulations of migrant labor and the distribution of their exploitation. By mapping a biocartography of the politically excluded, NGOs negotiate with various governments and cultural authorities for a transnational sense of moral responsibility to migrant workers and trafficked individuals. In short, emergent geographies of claims are mapped by novel political systems that are neither state nor market, but that articulate with both (chap. 9). Questions of citizenship and ethics are thus entangled in the intersections of diverse institutions that administer spaces, labor, and life.

Sheer Life: Exceptions to Ethics?

Techniques of economic globalization are invested with a moral calculus about more or less worthy subjects, practices, lifestyles, and visions of the good. *Ethics* is used here in the ancient Greco-Roman sense of a practice of the self, or normative techniques in self-care for attaining a particular mode of being.[69] An ethical regime can therefore be construed as a style of living guided by given values for constituting oneself in line with a particular ethical goal. Religions — and, I would argue, feminism, humanitarianism, and other schemes of virtue — are ethical regimes fostering particular forms of self-conduct and visions of the good life. Ethical notions of citizenship include the expression of national spirit, a style of being subjects who express the key values of a particular nation. In the formation of nation-states, national culture, humanism, and religions have interacted in shaping an "imagined community," a shared vision of the common good.[70]

Some larger conceptions of citizenship can be traced back to Enlightenment ideals of shared humanity. At the end of the Second World War, Hannah Arendt posed the question of our "human condition" in the midst of a Europe awash with refugees and stateless peoples. Our human condition, she argued, is given to us in the three kinds of fundamental human activities in which we engage: as biological life-forms, as laboring beings, and as political actors.[71] This conception of a unified human condition became the basis of global claims by the stateless for the right to citizenship. Once again, in a Europe flooded with migrants, Giorgio Agamben has recast Arendt's idea of the human condition. Because of their exclusion from national citizenship, undocumented workers, asylum seekers, and war refugees, he argues, are reduced to the inhuman condition of "bare life." Thus, the sovereign state is the producer both of modern humanity, by giving protection to citizens, and of bare life, by denying it to noncitizens. Only the erasure of the division between People (political body) and people (excluded bodies), he maintains, can restore humanity to the globally excluded who have been denied citizenship.[72] There is thus a shift from discussing citizenship as simply rights endowed by the nation-state, to a broader solidarity with noncitizens whose claims for inclusion in the human family are part of our own ethical questions of how one should live in a globalized world.

Agamben thus poses a universal norm of humanity as the only analytical and ethical measure of living situations. There is also the perception that the logic of exception is only invoked against the politically excluded. There are two conceptual problems with this exclusive focus on the legal and the simple bifurcation of the population into two halves: political beings and bare life. First, this axis discounts the validity of other universalizing moral discourses — the great religions, in particular — that pose alternative ethical norms of humanity.[73] For instance, Islam has its own vision of transnational virtue, with its own internal struggles over ethics that are not exclusively couched in terms of human rights. In chapter 1, I discuss how the Islamic community — *umma* — is also a universalizing scheme for ethical subject-formation and articulation of spiritual belonging. Globalized sites of hypergrowth also articulate situated ethical regimes that may or may not interact with human rights discourse. A strict adherence to Agamben's universal division of humanity into those with rights and those without would miss the rich complexity and the possibilities of multiple ethical systems at play.

Besides human rights, other visions of the good life also provide normative guides and ethical claims for the performance of virtue within a given domain of living. The interactions of biopolitics and technological reason crystallize ethical problems of contemporary living, and various resolutions to questions of human life are posed within this shifting matrix. Stephen Collier and Andrew Lakoff have coined the term "regime of living" and defined it as a "situated form of moral reasoning . . . [that] is invoked and reworked in a problematic situation to provide a possible guide to action."[74] If contemporary regimes of living are increasingly brought into interaction with neoliberal logic, then ethical subject formation is forged in a particular constellation of elements, rather than indexed to a universalized notion of the human.

Agamben's fundamental reference of bare life in a state of permanent exception thus ignores the possibility of complex negotiations of claims for those without territorialized citizenship. He argues that outside citizenship, all noncitizens are reduced to "a zone of indistinction between outside and inside, exception and rule, licit and illicit, in which the very concepts of subjective right and juridical protection no longer [make] any sense . . . power confronts nothing but pure life, without any mediation."[75] But in this rigid binary opposition, Agamben seems to preclude the possibility of non-rights mediation or complex distinctions that can buttress claims for moral protection and legitimacy. It is politically and ethnographically incorrect and even dangerous to present the concentration camp as the norm of modern sovereignty. The shifting legal and moral terrain of humanity has become infinitely more complex.

Economic globalization is associated with staggering numbers of the globally excluded. Despite legal citizenship in some country, millions of migrant workers, refugees, and trafficked peoples who have the most minimal hold on survival have become even more imperiled and elusive. It is clear that legal citizenship is merely one form of human protection. Marginalized peoples are excluded from an environment of rights because they are often hidden from view, or they live in "failed states," or as displaced peoples they are effectively stripped of rights once on the move. In these situations of humanitarian crisis, legal citizenship is merely one of multiple schemes for (re)ordering and (re)evaluating humanity.

Increasingly, a diversity of multilateral systems — multinational companies, religious organizations, UN agencies, and other NGOs — intervene to deal with specific, situated, and practical problems of abused, naked, and flawed bodies. The nonstate administration of excluded humanity is an emergent transnational phenomenon, despite its discontinuous, disjointed, and contingent nature. Collier and Lakoff describe such situations as the "counter-politics of sheer life" — a form of situated moral reasoning that variously assembles bare life to make claims "in terms of their needs as living beings."[76] Indeed, bare life itself has its own moral legitimacy, and its relationship to ethics and to labor is always open to neoliberalism as exception. The resolutions of human plight are always messy, unsatisfactory, and power-laden, but the problem of the politically excluded is on our global conscience, and in practice it has been aligned with logics of the state, moral economies, and market institutions.[77]

For instance, in regions of Africa, poor citizens have become even more politically excluded because of disease, starvation, and war. But health has become a prerequisite for human status, articulated in a discourse of "therapeutic citizenship" that makes claims not on the state, but on drug companies.[78] Another example of group claims on the basis of biological survival is emerging in Southeast Asia, where a vast female migrant population unprotected by labor laws is exposed to rampant abuse overseas. In such cases, biopolitical otherness rooted in race and alien status may be reversible by claims of biological welfare addressed not to the state but to the moral economies of the host society (chap. 9).

In short, bare life does not dwell in a zone of indistinction, but it becomes, through the interventions of local communities, NGOs, and even corporations, shifted and reorganized as various categories of morally deserving humanity. Such technoethical situations are an index of the growing power of humanitarian-corporate complexes to grade humanity in relation to particular needs, prioritized interests, and potential affiliations with powers-that-be. Articulations of moral claims (therapeutic citizenship, biological welfare, and the moral economy), perhaps more frequently than the invoking of human rights, frame ad hoc or temporary resolutions to daunting human problems.

Situated NGO interventions are often determined by the nexus of political and ethical forces they encounter on the ground. In short, the counterpolitics of survival are crystallized through the interrelationships of biopolitics, labor markets, and systems of virtue. Such ethical problematizations may circumvent human rights or citizenship, coming to rest on resolutions that reflect contingent and ambiguous ethical horizons of the human.

The dynamic tension between neoliberalism as exception and exceptions to neoliberalism, and their complex articulations of citizenship and sovereignty are set out in the following chapters, which are grouped into four parts. Each section assembles a set of arguments around how neoliberalism as reason and technique articulate regimes of citizenship and novel forms of spatialized administration in diverse Asia-Pacific milieus.

Part I explores the logic of exceptions as applied to women and minorities in Southeast Asia and the technoethical interventions of transnational humanitarian or ethnic movements. Chapter 1 discusses the politics of the Islamic exception that supports Muslim women in their quest for political and gender equality. The tensions among neoliberal values, religious patriarchy, and local and transnational feminisms constitute the public sphere where women's claims are both politically enabled and morally constrained. Chapter 2 focuses on the political space configured by cybercapitalism, elite overseas Chinese, and the violent fallout from the Asian financial crisis in Indonesia. Transnational interventions on behalf of Indonesian Chinese threaten to undermine the latter's claims on the state to safeguard their citizenship. In Asian sites of globalization, articulations among market-driven forces, ethnic governmentality, and gender ethics are shifting conditions for renegotiating citizenship and for tying entitlements to multiple state and nonstate institutions.

Part II traces how neoliberal strategies open up new possibilities for reconfiguring political spaces and spurring innovative systems of political rule. Chapters 3 and 4 demonstrate that the neoliberal exception is invoked in authoritarian sovereignties that apply calculative choices and mechanisms in their administration of special zones and centers. In Southeast Asia, the articulation of spaces of exception and ethnic schemes produces a patterning of graduated sovereignty for reordering and governing populations. In China, zoning technologies are an instrumentalization of market logic in creating spaces for experimentation with market reforms and linking with overseas sites.

Chapter 5 challenges the concept of Empire as the globalized space of capital and of resistance by a multitude. The research shows transnational production systems that inscribe latitudinal spaces structured by regulatory as well as coercive labor regimes. The particular articulation of latitudinal spaces with situated labor institutions and labor politics should warn us against easy claims of a counter-Empire.

Part III traces the neoliberal logic in the spatial dynamics of global capitalism. Circulations between sites of education and zones of knowledge employment have a deterritorializing effect on citizenship claims by residents and by migratory subjects. Chapter 6 considers the globalization of American universities in relation to the itineraries of Asian students seeking education abroad. The intersection of humanities, the university-as-business, and market-driven expertise raises questions about the ethical goals of higher education as it goes global. Chapter 7 describes a reverse trans-Pacific flow as well-paid American jobs are moving to low-wage Asian sites. Labor arbitrage as a neoliberal exception threatens to strip middle-class American men of their sense of entitlement to good jobs and the American Dream. Territorialized citizenship is being fragmented by transnational logics of exchange, accumulation, and disenfranchisement.

Part IV presents three Asian metropolitan milieus at the edge of emergence. The logic of neoliberal exception has created new citizenship criteria, new sites of hypergrowth, and new lifestyles of calculative choices. These emergent forms of autonomous action and competition are hinged to new gradations of excludable subjects. Chapter 8 focuses on the premium placed on skilled expatriates as Singapore positions itself as the hub of an "effervescent ecosystem." Chapter 9 discusses the parasitic articulation of a neoliberal Asian lifestyle that reduces a multitude of foreign domestic maids to slave-like labor. The juxtapositioning of go-getter citizens and neoslaves creates a humanitarian crisis of regional scope, attracting NGO resolutions attuned to situated moral economies. The final chapter presents Shanghai as a new assemblage of global business knowledge, self-propulsive urbanites, and self-ironic commercial culture in a "socialism with Chinese characteristics." A new planet is set into motion by the strategic deployments of neoliberal exceptions: a combination of calculative choices, blatant careerism, unbowed triumphalism, and ambiguous ethical outcomes.

This volume does not pretend to cover all aspects of citizenship mutating in relation to neoliberalism as exception and exceptions to neoliberalism. The Asia-Pacific is undergoing dramatic changes, and the fast-changing environments provide sites for exploring how things that used to be fused together — identity, entitlement, territoriality, and nationality — are being taken apart and realigned in innovative relationships and spaces by neoliberal technologies and sovereign exceptions. Emerging articulations of neoliberal forms, sovereign experiments, and regimes of citizenship have radically changed the political and spatial possibilities of being actualized and of being human. Specific technologies of governing and of self-governing produce a variety of meanings and room for maneuver, negotiation, and ethical doubt. What does seem clear is that neoliberalism as exception, whether as commando-style raid on emerging economies, as stealthy encroachment on governing reason, or as techniques of self reengineering and self-enterprise, is challenging conventional thinking about governance and about citizenship. Rights, entitlements, and claims are now malleable, subject to the crosscurrents and force fields configured by market-driven modes of governing, knowledge flows, and NGO interventions. Myriad disarticulations and rearticulations occasioned by the logic of the exception transform the elements we used to associate with a unified concept of citizenship into values placed on humanity that are increasingly varied, fragmented, contingent, and ambiguous, but permanently subject to ethicopolitical critique.

PART I

ETHICS IN

CONTENTION

In the aftermath of the 1995 Fourth World Conference on Women in Beijing, many internationalist feminists felt triumphant as they headed for home. Bina Agarwal, an Indian economist, declared, "Many Northern women today are finding common ground with Southern women. . . . This is not to argue that the North-South gap has disappeared. But among women's groups there is growing recognition of the importance of forging strategic links. One could say 'romantic sisterhood' is giving way to 'strategic sisterhood' for confronting the global crisis of economy and polity."[1]

Strategic Sisterhood

Strategic sisterhood is a new mechanism to confront the entangled issues of globalization and women's rights. The term implies a contingent North-South feminist partnership for intervention in countries where the gender gap is huge. Because of their participation in a transnational feminist public, feminists can draw on their international alliances to hold their own government to account.[2]

Yet a lacuna remains in this strategic sisterhood intervention.[3] Cosmopolitan feminism focuses on the unequal distribution of gender rights across the world, but its focus on feminist individualism comes into direct conflict with alternative ethics that are rooted in collectivist norms and goals. Strategic sisterhood is a concept that seeks to disseminate democratic principles of gender equality throughout the world. Drawing on Kantian democratic liberalism, the strategic sisters' notion of gender citizenship is conceptualized in absolute, universalistic terms of individual freedom and equality, regardless of the geopolitical inequalities and diverse ethical systems. Mantras from the North like "women's rights are human rights" propose global human standards without regard to other moral systems and visions of ethical living.

While feminists may think their challenge is to find a universal solution to the plight of women across the world, we need to ask how these messages will be received in places that have emerged from Western colonial domination and are just now forging their own postcolonial identities and ethico-political future. Northern feminists[4] and many of their elite Southern counterparts often skirt the issue of how to improve women's conditions without being seen as the new imperialists. Besides being more sensitive to an imperialist logic in promoting their transnational system of civic virtue, internationalist feminists may also recognize that their own self-image as autonomous individuals depends on their "liberation" of oppressed sisters in the Third World.[5]

In internationalist feminist discourses, women in postcolonial situations are framed as the dual victims of age-old cultural traditions and postcolonial nationalism. This formulation is supported by the view that the women's question is inseparable from national emancipation in emerging countries.[6] In countries like India, women and the home represent "the original site on which the hegemonic project of nationalism was launched." Because colonial and postcolonial struggles have been based on national ideologies of community, any discussion of the women's issue is always framed in terms of the national project and collective interests. Postcolonial scholars maintain that outsiders talking about women's rights are tampering with "the inner spaces of community" and thus "the life of the nation." We need to understand, therefore, how a national discourse of community is able to negotiate with subaltern ones on its "own terms for the purposes of producing consent."[7] Narratives of nation and community position women within special conditions for expressing their moral agency. For instance, a patriarchal dimension in the rise of Asian tiger countries mobilized young women as a cheap labor force for multinational corporations.[8] For postcolonial leaders and their citizens, women's emancipation, far from just being a question of individual rights, is fundamentally about the national project and the nationalist prestige of cultural difference. These issues are especially potent at the historical juncture when many postcolonial countries are finally emerging as economic competitors to the West, and they are especially sensitive to having women's rights ideology imposed from the West.

But postcolonial situations are dynamic sites of change, and over time the local and transnational variables have shifted in relation to each other. Because postcolonial milieus are constantly unfolding, the question of women's emancipation is becoming less of a stark choice between universal feminist values or domestic political agendas. Instead of a dichotomy between feminist internationalism and female-dominated nationalism, the postcolonial milieu in Southeast Asia is shaped by the intersection of nationalism, capitalist development, and religious institutions. The women-state patriarchal link is itself undergoing change, thus creating an opening for feminist claims against religious patriarchy. In the Malaysian case to which we will now turn, the state exception of "moderate Islam" promotes public conditions of possibility for women's status to be problematized in relation to Islamic patriarchy. This triangulated nexus between nationalism, women, and religion shapes the ground for feminist articulation of claims and their transformation into rights.

Women Wrestling with Ethics

Across the Islamic world, Muslim feminists are struggling against both Islamic patriarchy and authoritarian governments that have been unwilling or unable to support women's quest for gender equality. Malaysia, a developing country dominated by a Malay-Muslim majority, seems to be an exception. Malaysia is considered the most affluent and progressive Islamic (but resolutely multicultural) nation, one that has positioned itself as a bastion of enlightened Islam. This exception of "moderate Islam" has multiple political implications — a kind of soft nationalism that reins in the excesses of Islamic radicals, grooms its population for global labor markets, and supports a rigorous female public presence. The mix of Islamic nation and capitalist culture is reflected by the self-representations of Malay-Muslim women — many in body-conscious dresses and jeans, and some in full *pardah* (veil) — in the streets, workplaces, and leisure centers. The state-capitalist partnership also creates a public space that allows Muslim feminists to challenge *ulamas* (Islamic scholars and officials) and to wrestle with Islamic ethics in order to express a situated form of gendered Muslim citizenship.

In postcolonial Muslim nations, male reason enshrined in political institutions is not the only mode of systematic exclusion. Because indigenous Muslim leaders adhered tightly to a juridical-legal view of Islam as a defense against colonial rule, male power entrenched in religious authorities has endured in postcolonial formalization of Muslim practice. The anticolonial nature of juridical Islam has thus eroded more contingent and flexible religious notions of gender relationships throughout Southeast Asia.[9] Thus, after decolonization, religious authorities, as the defenders of the cultural community, continue to challenge state projects that could undermine their domination in the realm of ethics. Thus, despite capitalist development and democratic elections, male religious authorities dominate the postcolonial public sphere as a site of religious ethics.

Access to the modern economy allows women to challenge the reigning rationality and ethics of the public sphere. In her study of the French Revolution, Joan Landes argues that male reason, as the basis of civil rights, was counterposed conventionally to "femininity" — a cluster of attributes that included domesticity, frivolity, and eroticism — and was the basis for women's exclusion from the political realm. The gendering of the public sphere was premised on the exclusion of women from civil rights and the silencing of their voices in public.[10] But the private-public divide that is the basis of national politics also includes the exclusion of women by "public" religions that continue to subordinate women through ethical practices.

Male reason is thus aligned not only with civil citizenship in the public domain but also with religious reason, that is, with determining the ethical norms of gendered self-conduct and public behavior. Women's entry into the public sphere thus entails not only a challenge to male rationality and control of politics, it also plunges women into debates about the ethics of female self-management and their role in society. I borrow Jürgen Habermas's ideal-type formulation of the public sphere as a realm of debate and negotiation, without his strict normative criteria of rationality and communicative competence.[11] Indeed, Homi Bhabha has highlighted the crucial temporal dimension of public rhetoric and claims, the "to-and-fro" nature of the symbolic process that "reveals the discursive ambivalence that makes 'the political' possible." The "ambivalent juxtaposition[ing]" of the factual and rhetorical creates an interstitial relationship of alternative possibilities in political interpretation and negotiation.[12] I can only allude here to a fraction of the highly complex ongoing interplay between ulama claims and feminist counterclaims as to what constitutes appropriate gender ethics. The interstitial ambivalence in this public swordplay produces contradictory instances in which feminists gain some ethical points against die-hard patriarchs but also compromise on some aspects of embodied freedom.

Malaysia's emergence as an industrializing country presents an interesting case study of the qualified success of Muslim feminists in wresting control of Islamic ethics regarding female behavior. Within two decades, state development policies have filled industrial zones, campuses, and cities with young Muslim women drawn mainly from villages dominated by Islamic clerics and teachers. But for Islamic authorities the mass presence of women in the public domain poses a number of problems. Malay-Muslim men confront a historically unprecedented number of unmarried Muslim women in the public domain. Muslim women's entry into the modern economy is seen as a challenge to male authority and economic dominance, the basis of their virility. There are feverish visions of unregulated female sexuality freed from the ethical order maintained by fathers, brothers, and husbands.[13] As elsewhere in the Muslim world and beyond, some men perceive women's participation in modern public life as a form of "erotic aggression."[14] Furthermore, educated and working women have begun to challenge the male monopoly in deciding ethical precepts and practices for all Muslims.

In an immediate backlash, resurgent Muslim movements demand that women in public should adhere to even stricter norms of ethical conduct than were in force before. But women — as students, teachers, professionals, government officials, and entrepreneurs — cannot so easily be retraditionalized and forced to submit to regimes of control. The deployment of "male reason versus female passion," however, poses the biggest challenge to feminists. While Muslim feminists are not afraid to claim gender equality as supported by Islam, they wrestle with the ethics of proper female conduct permissible within the strictures of Islamic teaching and image of community, or *umma*. I argue that only when the state reins in the power of clerics and ulamas can feminists make public claims for a female citizenship that reinterprets both Islamic tenets and universalist ideals of gender equality. But while official moderate Islam firmly connects Muslim women's laboring bodies and the body politic, feminists, in their ethical negotiations, can only claim a kind of contingent Muslim feminist body that is always open to alternative interpretations in the umma.

Moderate Islam and the Ulamas' Backlash

Malaysia, a former British colony, has over the past two decades emerged as a booming "Asian tiger" economy.[15] The country has a majority population of Malay-Muslims who are generally happy to be governed by technocrats dedicated to capitalism and expanding a consumer culture. Rapid development and social change has increased class differentiation among the Muslim-Malay majority (also called *bumiputera*), giving rise to a growing professional Malay middle class (the *Melayu Baru* [new Malays]) and a small corporate and ruling elite.

Although the official religion of the country is Islam, there is a clear separation of state and religion.[16] The country is governed according to civil law, but Islamic courts based in individual states control marriage, divorce, family, gender, and sexual matters pertaining to all Muslims. These Islamic courts are run by religious judges (*kadis*), who both interpret and implement Islamic laws. They are advised by religious counsels (*muftis*) who have the power to issue religious rulings (*fatwas*) covering Muslim behavior. There is thus a division of labor when it comes to the social citizenship of Muslims, with Islamic authorities insisting on an Islamic definition of social rights and behavior within the family and the state protecting the social rights according to universalistic criteria of equality.

By soft-peddling nationalism, the country continues to attract foreign investors, who are not frightened away by masses of women in black robes or hot-headed Muslim radicals. "Moderate Islam" became the slogan for Malaysia, a country that has maintained its firm attachment to capitalist markets and to Western democracies by resolutely controlling backward-looking Islamic radicals, both local and foreign.[17] The ethos of moderate Islam has helped foreign companies develop a vibrant high-tech manufacturing sector and has encouraged young Muslim women to work alongside non-Muslims and under the supervision of foreign men. But increasingly, as moderate Islam continues to promote female participation in all levels of society, its policies are challenged by radical interpretations of Islamic laws, especially in the area of women's conduct in public.

Because the ruling party[18] derives its legitimacy from the Muslim-Malay majority, it has to be careful in its handling of tensions between the modern state bureaucracy and the religious authorities represented by the Islamic courts. Instead of launching a frontal assault on Islamic judges and theologians, the state has supported feminist groups like Sisters in Islam, a small but active group of professional women who publicly challenge many of the courts' interpretations and decisions concerning Islamic law, or *shari'a*. While the Sisters' rigorous responses to the religious authorities have created the space for a genuine debate — one that is filled with religious, legal, and sexual language — in many ways they act as surrogates for the government, and its vision of a corporate Islamic culture that promotes self-discipline, capital accumulation, and loyalty to the state.

In everyday life, Malaysian Islam has always been infused with a kind of customary (*adat*) liberalism and tolerance of gender difference and cultural diversity;[19] what has been striking in recent cultural changes is not so much the rise of a new Muslim feminism but rather the radicalism of the social claims made in the name of Islam by religious leaders. The spread of higher education for Malays has increased the number of lower kadis who adminis-ter a network of family courts throughout the country. By using their inter-pretation of the sharia'a as the absolute criteria for issuing religious ruling and punishments in the area of family and gender relations, the kadis and muftis play a role in defining what is "authentic" Malay-Muslim culture. They have become the official articulators of Islamic truths, used to shape public opin-ion on a wide range of issues pertaining to Malay-Muslim modernity.

As Malay society becomes further transformed by capitalism and con-sumer culture, kadis and ulamas — many of whom work as teachers, civil servants, and public activists — have vociferously articulated an Islamic mas-culine ethos that counters women's widespread participation in the public life and increase in social power. Ironically, this religious radicalism is born at once of the ulamas' new bureaucratic power and of their simultaneous decline in social authority. The emerging urban educated and professional classes, the "New Malays," exposed to a range of knowledge and to diverse sources of authority, have become less susceptible to ulama injunctions about how they should conduct their everyday lives. Increasingly "othered" as a cul-turally backward, premodern moral authority by the technocratic leaders of a market-driven society, Islamic authorities seek to recuperate their moral power over "their" women by imposing a regime of renewed religious moral-ity. Brackette Williams has argued that subordinated male agency seeks re-demption through the "retraditionalization of wayward women" by calling for the revival of domestic feminine virtues and for women's protection from outside dangers.[20] In Malaysia, Muslim clerics' call for the retraditionaliza-tion of women in the home even includes demands that they submit to an expanded polygamy. Such religious radicalism seeks to recuperate declining ulama power and to fend off the state's attempts to limit the traditional power of Islamic authorities in everyday life. The ulamas' reassertion of ethical con-trol thus involves a strategy of relocalization,[21] whereby spatial practices rein-stall a rigid public-private divide already broken by the mass influx of women into the secular public domain.

Relocalizing Women, Revitalizing Polygamy

Until the mid-1990s, the truth-claims of religious clerics have rarely been challenged, and never by women in Malaysian history. Ordinarily, Muslims identify *ulama* (masculine) speech with religious truth, objectivity, and reason. Ulamas' power resides in their control of sharia'a and their power to punish by invoking certain categories as eternal, God-given truths. As commanders of this ethical regime, religious clerics shape everyday practice, regulating techniques of self-care and interpersonal interactions that normalize relations of difference and inequality — especially Muslim men versus Muslim women, and Muslim versus non-Muslims. As the authorized interpreters of Islam, Muslim clerics wield enormous power in articulating a particularistic view of the Malay moral order that is based on gender inequality. But increasingly, the solidity and reach of their moral power is undermined by the state sponsorship of global Islamic conferences where Muslim scholars discuss more progressive interpretations that make Muslim ethics central to an alternative modernity — alternative to both Western cultural ethics and to archaic Islamic practices.

In these forums, scholars challenge the use of the historical sharia'a — or Muslim law as implemented in the Prophet's time — as the model for modern Muslim society. Under historical sharia'a, legal theory recognizes tiers of citizenship distinguished on the basis of faith. They are the Muslim umma who have full citizenship and exclusive political power; the "people of the book," who are protected as second-class citizens; and unbelievers, who merit no protection by the Islamic state. Dissenting Islamic scholars have pointed out that historical sharia'a is a problematic guide for managing contemporary societies, where multiethnic populations exist as equal citizens within the polity. Abdullahi Ahmed An-Na'im observes, "Not only is equality not envisaged by the sharia'a, but women's access to public office and public life are generally precluded."[22] A feminist points out that in historical sharia'a, Muslim women were regarded as simply "appendages" of fathers, brothers, and husbands, "and men exercise[d] domination over women and enjoy[ed] a monopoly of political power and force."[23]

And yet, in contemporary Malaysia (and elsewhere), radical ulamas frequently invoke the historical sharia'a in order to reinstate a religious order based on controlling and localizing women. Thus radicalized ethics depends on the localization of disciplinable subjects — that is, women who can be locatable or transferred to a confinable space defined functionally by these ethical leaders: the home and marriage.

In addition to their status as the legitimate interpreters of Islam, much of the power of ulamas' words rests on the popular Islamic belief that men tend to be ruled by reason and women by passion in their everyday lives. It is widely believed in Malay-Muslim culture that men are inherently rational or reasonable and women inherently more passionate and out of control.[24] Tapping into these beliefs, ulamas use masculine speech, representing rationality, to typecast female thinking and practice as unruly, unreliable, and irrational, thus unsuitable for both understanding Islamic texts and for claiming gender rights. In the ulamas' view, because men are more rational, they have certain God-given rights over women and represent the normative citizens of the public sphere, or umma. Women by definition are less rational and have fundamental obligations in the domestic domain linked to their ascribed roles as wives and mothers.[25] Morally, women are second-class citizens who derive their status from men and who are dependent on the male intellect. In particular, Muslim clerics have claimed Islam-endorsed rights for men to regulate women in their domestic and public lives. Invoking *sunnah* (practice of the Prophet) and verses in the Quran, ulamas take as God-given men's superiority over women and husbands' power over their wives — religious rules that they want reinstituted in all areas of Malaysian life.

The ulama stronghold from which antiwomen Islamic fatwas are issued is the Malaysian state of Kelantan, the home of the Islamic Party of Malaysia (it abuts Patani, an equally neglected and insurrectionist majority Muslim province in Thailand). Historically a seat of Islamic culture, Kelantan is a rice-growing province that has in recent decades been marginalized by the headlong economic development transforming the rest of the country. As Clive Kessler has noted, the impoverishment of the Kelantan peasantry accounts for much of the support given to the fiery ulamas, who speak directly to the peasants' needs and aspirations.[26]

In many ways, radical Islam operates as a political opposition to the economic transformation of the country presided over by ruling elites in Kuala Lumpur, who pay insufficient attention to the social costs of such change. The ulamas' pronouncements contain a subtext of protest against the renting of the social fabric of Malay society by development, and against the threats to their Islam-vested masculine order. As such, while the inspiration and substance of their message are historical, their reactions are very much part of contemporary social struggles over the ethical contours of Malaysian modernity.

In 1991, the chief minister of Kelantan maintained that "Islam grants men greater ability to lead than women." He extrapolated from his reading of religious texts that men were physically and intellectually superior to women. Accordingly, women were better suited to stay at home and care for children, and women should not have outside employment, as it created opportunities for undermining their morality.[27] Their chief mechanism appears to be the expansion of polygamous practices. Although Islam permits polygamy, only two percent of Muslim marriages in Malaysia are polygamous.[28] A man's right to many wives is again justified in terms of men's rationality in contrast to women's irrationality and immorality. But when it serves their purposes, some men will claim that men are "adulterous by nature" and that Islam has sought to accommodate their sexual drive by sanctioning polygamy. Others suggest that the Quran says that a wife who agrees to her husband's taking a second wife will go to heaven.

Ulamas have used an ingenious argument that ties men's polygamous desires to the changing demographics of employment and marriage. Industrialization and development have increased the number of never-married Malay women over thirty years old to more than sixty thousand.[29] Ulamas urge women to allow their husbands to take a second wife or more as a way of preventing extramarital affairs and alleviating the problem of unmarried women. They point to the rising numbers of professional Malay women whose chances of marriage are slim, except and unless they become second wives. By thus posing polygamy as a double solution to men's allegedly unruly passions and to single women's unwed state and supposed sexual drought, they are recasting polygamy as a regime of localization, whereby free single women are brought into matrimony, and men's domestic supervision. This call seems to be a solution to the fear that single professional women, no longer supervised by their fathers and brothers, have become uncontrolled and uncontrollable under Islamic family law. The ulamas even suggest that widespread polygamous practice will end men's pursuit of extramarital affairs and prostitution. Thus, polygamy, presented as a solution to unruly passions, is a scheme to cast a wider net of Islamic law over those who would otherwise be outside its jurisdiction. Perhaps on a more elevated level, the ulamas see in widespread polygamy not only the satisfaction of male lust, and the moral regulation and protection of single professional women, but also the end of the "need" for commoditized sex, the latter two phenomena being associated with the modernization of society.

Such a proposal, if implemented, would threaten the government's economic policy, which aims to increase women's participation in all levels of the economy. Indeed, calls for polygamy are embarrassing to the Malaysian government's vision of itself as an enlightened regime. Moderate Islam represents prosperity and well-being, with its ideal of two-career families the foundation of a technocratic future. Without wishing to appear to be anti-Islam, government officials have deflected the polygamy proposal by suggesting a less "hasty solution" to the admittedly rising number of unmarried Malay women.[30] Policy makers use the occasion to push the government's own view of gender roles in marriage and in the economy. They note that the Quran encourages both men and women to work, balancing marriage and family with their jobs, all three contributions to the Muslim nation. This focus on complementary gender's contribution to the private and the public sectors is contrasted to the ulamas' proposal to relocalize women within marriage and polygamous male control. Nevertheless, Islamic judges, whose power derives from their control of a network of sharia'a courts in different Malaysian states, maintain a religious normativity for those who wish to take more than one wife. In this sense, perhaps, conservative kadis serve the interests of an emerging Malay bourgeois male order that is ambivalent about women's domesticity and about public women.

Reasoning Sisters: Partners in the Interpretive Tradition

Ironically, the very emergence of a bourgeois public sphere — where the only public persons who count are male — has also led to the rise of the new Muslim feminists. The very language of the ulamas in defining a Malay-Muslim masculine public provides the symbolic terms whereby women, like men, engage in the invention of a modern political identity. But where concepts of Islamic reason, law, and nature are invoked to sanction normative gender inequality and to construct separate private and public spheres,[31] Muslim feminists justify their demands for equality not in terms of their civil rights but on the basis of their alternative readings of the Quran and hadith (reports of the sayings of prophet Muhammad and his companions). In this role, they must define themselves as worthy participants in the great Islamic tradition of moral argumentation and moral advice proffered in the public arena. They use secular arguments for equality in citizenship only as secondary justifications. Talal Asad has discussed, in the Saudi Arabian context, the Islamic tradition of offering moral advice — *nasiha* — to political elites. In noting the vitality of this tradition of moral reasoning, Asad challenges scholars who maintain that such religious or "ideological politics" are the mark of premodern societies that will be succeeded by secular, rational politics in modern societies, as though modern politics are devoid of moral assumptions.[32] The difference in Muslim societies today is that women want to be copartners in debating and forming such ethical regimes.

To combat the ulamas' monopoly of control over Islamic ethics, feminists like the Sisters in Islam must first legitimize their claims as rational and therefore equal moral partners (sisters) in the interpretation of Islamic texts. The first of feminists' struggles with ulamas is over women's intellectual and moral capacity to interpret Islam for themselves, instead of relying solely on ulamas' interpretations. This assertion of women's intellectual role in Islam is part of Muslim feminists' worldwide strategy to increase higher education for girls. A feminist remarks that "no Muslim society can adequately survive without its women contributing to all aspects of society. Men have gone too far in their aggression and incitement of conflict. Muslim women must work alongside their male Muslim brethren and even lead them to establish links of brotherhood and sisterhood across the ummah."[33]

At a meeting of Muslim feminists held in New York, Boutheina Cheriet of Algiers observed that "at Beijing, for the first time, the right to religious higher education became a demand. That would then give us credibility in interpreting the texts."[34] Indeed, Muslim feminists from around the world have formed links to compare experiences and strategies for combating patriarchal rule in the name of Islam. They all agree on the critical importance of education, in religion, Arabic, and even English, in order to raise their social and religious status vis-à-vis men, who because of their privileged access to higher education have historically monopolized the interpretation of Islamic law and the governance of Islamic practice. American professor Amina Wadud has become a Malaysian public figure by calling for a female voice in Quranic interpretation. She has stated that "the Muslim woman has only to read the text [the Quran] — unconstrained by exclusive and restrictive interpretation — to gain an undeniable liberation."[35] Higher education will provide women with the skills and authority to become partners with men in constituting the umma.

In acquiring a role as respected interpreters of Islam, it is equally important for Muslim feminists to conduct themselves chastely, as reasoning sisters rather than as passionate mothers, wives, or lovers. In Malay adat, sibling relationships are generally of equal standing, and birth order rather than gender confers authority and privilege over junior members of either gender. By casting themselves as sisters in Islam, Muslim feminists assert the authority of the *kakak* (elder sister), whose reasoning and guidance are often sought and respected by male siblings. Besides the English term *Sisters*, the feminists are also referred to in Malay as *Puteri Islam* (princesses of Islam). The construction of women's public role in terms of traditional Malay sibling relationships and aristocracy compels respect for the feminists' opinions.[36] The sisterly persona of religious austerity is as important as the acquisition of religious training by Muslim feminists. Such carefully managed identities allow the Sisters to act as authoritative figures who, in the words of their leading theoretician, Noraini Othman, provide "religiously and culturally authentic ways of participating in [Islamic] modernity."[37] By cultivating an image as knowledgeable and patient reasoners, Sisters suggest that they are even more respectable and morally disciplined than the ulamas, their rivals in ethics.

Second, the Sisters seek to enlarge the public space for debates over Islamic truths beyond the control of ulamas' forums. By invoking the Islamic tradition of *ijtihad* (independent judgment), feminists call for the recognition of a wider sphere whereby an educated Muslim public, not limited to Islamic theologians and judges, can engage in interpretive reasoning and debate about Islamization in their own countries. By arguing that ulamas' claims are not divine revelations but man-made interpretations (however authoritative), feminists have opened a space for women's voices in debates about religious truths. This interpretive Islamic community (*ummahi ijtihad*), according to Othman, enlarges the grounds on which Islamic law "must now be renovated and refashioned."[38] In their brochures, the Sisters express their desire to provide a "public forum on the modern nation, state, and Islam . . . , with special focus on minorities and women (as a Muslim minority)."[39] The Sisters see themselves as builders of a Muslim civil society (*Umma Madani*), a term which has recently been picked up by government officials in their attempts to counter the widespread appeal of ulamas' assertion of a masculine public sphere in Malaysia.

Establishing Gender Equality in Islam

In their battle against ulama denigration of women and strategies to relegate women to the private domain, the Sisters have invented themselves as public intellectuals who lead debate and counter ulama proposals in the nation's media and academic forums. For instance, the Sisters have rejected as "fallacious" the view that women are inherently inferior and men inherently superior.[40] In a letter to the press,[41] they have argued that there was no basis for such claims in the Quran or in the hadith, both of which contain examples of women leaders. Here the influence of Muslim feminists from other countries has been crucial. Fatima Mernissi, a Moroccan feminist, was among the first to make such discriminations among the Islamic texts.[42] Thus the Sisters in Islam hold that the Quran endorses gender equality, whereas the hadith has been the source of much of the idea that Islam condones gender inequality. They call on the new resurgent Islam to meet challenges of contemporary society "in a principled and intelligent fashion," and they ask why it was "so difficult for many of us to accept the universal truth, wisdom and beauty of the Quran that insistently enjoins justice and equality between women and men?"[43] The Sisters argue that an Arabocentric, narrow, and anachronistic reading of Islamic laws informs contemporary male chauvinist interpretations. While the ulamas' rigorous ethics are ostensibly to protect women (and men) from the evil temptations of modern society, they reveal men's desire to dominate women by deploying religious truths.[44]

A proposal of the ulamas — to make the *hijab* (veiling) universally compulsory for women — drew the following response from the Sisters: "Men have dominated women politically in many Muslim societies and this control has been falsely equated with legitimate authority. Institutions were established to support and reinforce men's prejudices, enabling them to evade their responsibility towards Allah and other human beings." Citing relevant verses, the Sisters argue that "coercion is contrary to the spirit of the Quran which states that there is no compulsion in Islam." The way to protect women, according to Islam, is through decent and respectful treatment of women. The Sisters note that by reading the appropriate Quranic verses, women would be able to make their own choices based on their faith in Allah. Coercive dress policy "in fact runs counter to Islam's emancipatory emphasis on reason and freedom as the basis of human morality."[45] Here, the Sisters, by using appropriate Islamic phrases, produce an alternative religious language for female emancipation and independent decision making, thereby representing women as modern public figures alongside men. Their discourse has drawn a strong reaction from the public, including a letter to the *New Straits Times* of Kuala Lumpur bemoaning the "coercive" effects of the dress code and its unsuitability for "an urbanized sophisticated Malay society."[46] Another letter to the same newspaper praised the Sisters' "courage, clarity, and faithfulness not only to the spirit but also to the letter of Islam."[47] By facing up to the challenge of the Muslim clerics, the Sisters have invented public speech for Muslim women, thus strengthening their resistance to the ulamas' invented Islamic bourgeois patriarchy.

The Sisters have also responded vigorously to the claims that men's rights to beat their wives and to marry several are given to them by Allah. This was most brazenly expressed by a letter writer to the *New Straits Times* named

Zahar, who argued that "because men are adulterous by nature," Islam in its great wisdom sought to accommodate that need by sanctioning polygamy. In reply, the Sisters maintained that the Quran does not give men a "blanket right" to practice polygamy, which is only encouraged under extenuating circumstances like war. Again, citing appropriate verses, they reject the popular misconception that the Quran and the hadith will receive in heaven women who allow their husbands to practice polygamy: "This is a destructive tactic to manipulate women into feeling that they would be bad Muslim wives if they object to their husbands' polygamy. . . . There is no basis in the Quran to say that polygamy is Islam's solution for men's alleged[ly] unbridled lust."[48]

Furthermore, the Sisters argued, "The solution, as found in the Quran and the hadith, or teachings and practices of the Prophet Mohammad, is a change of attitude from indulging in promiscuity to one of self-discipline and respect for the opposite sex."[49] This call for a change of mind, not of wife, reflects the Sisters' strategy of calling for reason's mastery of passion (an Islamic ideal), thus reminding Muslim men that their purported monopoly on reason is tenuous at best, both in their interpretation of religious texts and in their conduct of family relations. What men need, the Sisters patiently reminded, is more self-discipline, something that Muslim men have always claimed women lack.

More recently, ulamas' call for the imposition of *hudud* laws governing illicit sex, infidelity, and rape represents a tightening control over sex outside marriage. In 1993, Islamic clerics helped push through a hudud bill in Kelantan whereby people convicted of illicit sex (*zina*) can be given one hundred lashes (in the case of the unmarried) or stoned to death (for married offenders). Although the bill would have jurisdiction only within the state of Kelantan, it stirred a lively feminist debate in the rest of the country. A female lawyer pointed out that under the hudud law, any unmarried woman who is pregnant or has given birth can be convicted of zina unless she can prove zina by the male party. The stringent rules for proving rape require a victim to provide four righteous men who can testify to having witnessed "the act of penetration of the sex organ of the male into that of the female partner" — a difficult burden of proof, to say the least. A rape victim who fails to produce such witnesses can be charged with fornication, as well as false accusation, punishable by eighty lashes. A male law lecturer countered that hudud law also discriminates against men, as they cannot claim female sexual consent when they are accused of rape: "So long as his 'instrument' is in, he goes [convicted] as long as there are four just male witnesses."[50]

Such explicit talk about sexuality and (illicit) pleasures, and the questioning of restrictions on women have become everyday public fare. There is a proliferation of women's groups and forums dealing with women's rights and advancement in Malaysia that criticize zealous ulamas' "anti-women subtext" and patriarchal impulses. Besides women's groups associated with major political parties, like the UMNO Women's Wing; there are women's religious groups, academic groups devoted to gender studies, employees' organizations, and activist groups against sexual violence. In meetings, women's leaders have criticized "chauvinist and macho religious officials" and "narrow-minded ulamas" for causing women untold misery by supporting polygamy.[51]

Women's groups, with male supporters, have become a force in claiming Muslim women's social citizenship cast in terms of reinterpreted Islamic principles. They seek not only to express a female voice in Islam but also to renegotiate a wide range of issues pertaining to Islamic kinship codes and male-female relations. Some Malay men have written to the press in support of the feminists, deriding the call for increased polygamy as a mark of ulamas' "ignorance of reality." A male writer to the *New Straits Times* compared proponents of polygamy to "heedless tyrants, hypocritical Quran reciters, and ignorant sufis."[52] Women's leaders have protested that Islamic kinship rules enable Muslim men to pass on their citizenship to foreign wives but do not similarly recognize Muslim women with foreign husbands.[53] As professional women become more cosmopolitan, they demand the right to pass their citizenship to foreign spouses. Clearly, such calls for ethical and legal symmetry between men and women reflect the transnational quality of Malaysian modernization and the desire to be free of some aspects of Islamic norms on descent and marriage.

Must Feminists Be Virtuous to
Challenge Islamic Patriarchy?

Ironically, the ethical claim for gender equality under Islam, accompanied as it was by the explosion of sexual discourse, has produced its own disciplinary constraints on feminists, and on Muslim women in general. In their anti-ulama struggles, the Sisters oppose not only gender equality to masculine privilege but also moral righteousness to sensuality. To legitimize their own role as respectable Muslims worthy of interpreting the texts, the Sisters cultivate an ascetic self-representation. This female chastity has been indirectly conditioned by ulamas' branding of women as more passionate, irrational, and immoral than men, which according to the ulamas justifies religious control over women. The ulama strategy thus compels feminists to appear cool, reasonable, and morally above reproach in order to be effective in issuing rebuttals and in negotiating for (morally acceptable) gender rights. The Sisters must display more self-discipline than their male accusers. They must make the case that women are morally deserving and rational subjects with equal standing before Allah. In this construction of gendered citizenship — in which personal ethics underwrite claims of gender equality — women's desires must be channeled away from pleasures that men can brand and damn as passionate and disruptive.

Although Malaysian feminists have gained an international reputation as among the most progressive Muslim women, they have not yet articulated women's most basic right, that is, their right to control their own bodies. While male lust has been naturalized in male discourse, female passion is still taboo, and the feminists appear to agree with the implicit expectation that female sexuality is controlled by kinsmen or Islamic injunctions. While men's sexual freedom under Islam is taken for granted, there has been no mention of women's right to sexual autonomy, even the right of women to premarital sex. Thus even state nationalist ideology does not allow for women's absolute equality with men, as autonomous subjects. A focus on sensuality and sexual freedom is by no means a foreign concept to Malay culture. The Sisters have been so busy battling chauvinist ulamas and proving their own moral worthiness as equal Islamic citizens that they have not formulated a wider vision of women's rights that can incorporate adat celebration of sensual pleasures and women's sexual assertiveness.[54] There are no public debates or publications about women's sexual experiences, desires, or passions; indeed, the public construction of Muslim sexuality is defined mainly from male perspectives. Thus, while the female voice is now widely heard in public debates about Islamic ethics in modern Malay culture, this public discourse has been tolerated and abetted by government officials who also seek to weaken the ulamas' power to define what Islam means in Malaysian political culture.

Feminism in the Shelter of Moderate Islam

For now the Sisters and other women's groups are concentrating on shaping an Islamic modernity that sutures the laceration between the political and the domestic, and that combines secular and Islamic elements. In this role as public intellectuals, Muslim feminists are the most dynamic interpreters of a modern Islam today, in Malaysia and elsewhere. Such feminist movements suggest a more complex picture than the usual one of postcolonial society riven by irreconcilable or contradictory forces of nationalism and modernity.[55] Indeed, the very nature of feminist struggles to shape the public sphere, as represented by the Sisters in Malaysia, suggests the interweaving of impulses of religious nationalism and modernity.

These gender conflicts in the public sphere are modern in two senses. First, these feminist movements suggest ways of combining secular and Islamic elements in an "authentic Muslim culture of modernity."[56] By recasting Islamic beliefs and norms in contemporary terms, Muslim feminists are articulating a nationalist vision of Islamic modernity compatible with the state vision, which is different from, say, the modernity of other Muslim countries (like Kuwait or Iran), or from that of Western democracies like, say, France. These movements are also modern in the sense that they are shaping the civil society so that different groups, mediated by the state and by private interests, can engage in debates to contest and transform ethical regimes, whether of the state or public institutions like Islamic courts and their clerics. In the process, they renew and extend the umma — as a divinely sanctioned, religio-political space of rational discussion, debate, and criticism — for the modern era.

Islam in Malaysia is a patchwork of the most liberal as well as the most radical strands of Islam. The interweaving of these apparently opposed elements is represented in cities by Muslim women in full pardah mingling with others in close-fitting dresses and jeans. Observers attribute the strength of Muslim feminists in Malaysia to the higher degree of development there than in other Muslim countries. Noraini Othman, the leading spokesperson for the Sisters, seems to agree: "I do feel that here in Malaysia we have slightly more space to do this because we have a less patriarchal system. We are the most developed Muslim economy right now, and so we see ourselves by accident as historically placed to play this role."[57]

But there is nothing accidental about the growth of Muslim feminist ethics in the context of a state strategy to rein in radicalized forces in Islam. Official moves to defeudalize Islam in Malaysia have been increasing over the past decades, as the state seeks to standardize the interpretation and implementation of Islamic laws by setting up an Islamic university, an Islamic bank, and an Islamic center within the prime minister's office to align Malaysian Islam with the modern knowledges, skills, and procedures of the non-Muslim world.[58] Official Islamization in Malaysia is cast as fundamentally friendly to and at home with global capitalism, and at ease with the multicultural contexts and modern forms and skills of the modern era. For decades, this Islam-ization policy has stressed that self-discipline, thriftiness, and capital accumu-lation are Islamic values, and that Islam requires Muslim countries to be rich, independent, and progressive.[59] TV programs calling Muslims to prayer also urge them to "follow the path of progress." The capital, Kuala Lumpur, is to-day a center for enlightened Islamic capitalism, where corporate towers over-shadow mosques, and international hotel rooms are equipped with Qurans and symbols indicating the direction of Mecca. Compared to other emerging Muslim countries, Malaysia is very aggressive in seeking global capital and in promoting itself as a new center for high-tech industries, most of this development being dependent on American capital and its associated "deca-dent" cultural liberalism — consumption of alcohol and pork, "indecent" clothing, "immoral" sexual behavior, etc. — that enlightened Muslims can coexist with though not participate in.

The regime of corporatist Islam is reflected in bureaucratic discourses on the material and spiritual riches of "moderate Islam" and by relentless criti-cism of radical Islamic authorities. A former government official, himself a former leader of a university *dakwa* (missionary) movement, had emerged as a strong critic of gender bias in the kadis' implementation of shari'a: "Islam is built on the foundations of justice for all. When the implementation of these laws is associated with men's prejudice against women, then we are in for a lot of trouble."[60] Men are favored over women in matters like spouse abuse, marriage, divorce, inheritance, and polygamy, so that when women approach religious officers to obtain justice they "run smack into male prejudices and are not treated well."[61] These criticisms are part of an ongoing state campaign to support women's movements and to protect the women (and their chil-dren) from domestic violence. But because of the unresolved issue of male power within the Muslim household, a new "anti–domestic violence law" merely enforces the cease-and-desist order without making wife-beating itself a crime.

Kadis claim that the anti–domestic law does not apply to Muslims, for whom "family matters" are dealt with in Muslim courts. Thus, in response to women's protests over marital rape, religious clerics insist that under Islam, a man has the right to marital sex under any circumstances.[62] Even Muslim lawyers trained in the Western tradition reject adopting the notion of marital rape by questioning its cultural appropriateness for Malaysia. The president of the Bar Council maintains that since marital rape is a "Western concept" it is not suited to Asian cultures: "We should not blindly import concepts unsuitable for our cultural background and values." He resists in particular the "individual rights" idea behind the right of a woman to refuse sex to her husband. Other lawyers claim that even if a law against marital sex was on the books, there is the problem of evidence, difficulty in getting witnesses, which may result in "just the word of one person against the other." Furthermore, they fear that such a law may enable women to use sex as a bargaining tool and to take revenge on their husbands.[63] Widespread belief that a Muslim wife must obey her husband's lawful commands has restrained state power in dealing with gender inequality within the home.

A furor over "baby dumping" by suspected factory women also allowed the kadis to retain control over family issues, despite government attempts to provide a secular solution. The government proposal of incubators in public places produced a debate about loose morals, the tarnished image of Muslim women, the responsibility of men, and the need for compassion toward un-wed mothers. Ulamas argued against baby banks, saying that baby dumping is "not a Malaysian practice," and that it goes against "the cherished values and traditions of Malaysian society on sex, marriage, and the family system; the integrity of the family institution as perceived by the Malaysian public must not be compromised."[64] Ulamas fear that the anonymous services pro-vided by public incubators may encourage extramarital sex, which is a "sin." A mosque official (*iman*) comments that "adultery is not an individual act. It involves the whole society when there are loose morals and children are born out of wedlock. Without the stigma [against unwed mothers], people would not hesitate to have children out of wedlock."[65] After a fatwa was issued against the idea of a baby bank, the government shelved the baby-bank pro-posal. Control over the interpretation of normative family relations remains the bedrock of ulama power. Wisely, for now, governmental support for Muslim feminists has been focused on regulating gender relations in the public sphere, where civil law can more safely override religious law.

The activities of the Sisters have countered the traditional belief that eloquent women are never chaste, for as public speakers they conduct them-selves with more self-discipline and appear more respectable than the fiery ulamas.[66] But state support is vital to ensure that the new role of Muslim women in ethical debates is not silenced by the ulamas' warnings of a weaken-ing Muslim ethics. State efforts to standardize religious laws have begun by tackling gender discrimination in clothing and public comportment. The recent arrest of three Muslim women by clerics who charged them with taking part in a beauty contest has increased public support for the govern-ment's reigning in coercive and arbitrary implementation of sharia'a. Officials protested that the religious offense for which the women were charged—

exposing the *aurat* (nakedness) — should also apply to Muslim men who expose their legs, whether in work, sports, or in bodybuilding contests.[67] Such gender discrimination by religious authorities suggested that they were not serious and were picking on women. A media report notes that the state should amend sharia'a so that "people should not be subjected to different standards of the same law. The mode of enforcement [of religious laws] should also not shock the people or raise doubts on fair play."[68] Because the government can step in as a "disinterested" actor concerned about presenting itself as a moderate Islamic nation, the Sisters' efforts to reframe the ethics of Muslim gender citizenship are highly promising.

Muslim feminists show that it is not impossible to use religion in order to win gender rights in a Muslim society. A recent feminist victory in Morocco vindicates similar attempts to transform gender citizenship within the ethical framework of Islam. Asserting the "egalitarian" nature of Islam, feminists led by Nouzha Skalli, a member of Morocco's parliament, were a major force behind new legislation that is the most far-ranging in improving women's rights in the Muslim world. Since January 2004, women have gained the right to divorce their husbands and collect alimony, and they have received new property rights. The age of marriage is increased from fifteen to eighteen. Polygamy has been all but abolished, since only in rare cases can the Prophet's requirement of equal treatment of wives be achieved.[69] This new law protecting women's rights has stirred strong interest among feminists in neighboring Muslim countries. But the success of such experiments depends on a particular alignment of political factors.

The Malaysian case shows that, ironically perhaps, the exception of moderate Islam creates the space for feminists to challenge entrenched ulama power by participating in public ethical debates. But one cannot assume that the matter is closed, since the conditions of possibility have depended on a particular articulation of neoliberal logic, politics, and ethics. Indeed, such feminist entitlements remain open to challenge by other translations and claims, including by radical Islam,[70] that are emerging within the fluctuating space of the assemblage.

Transnational Sisterly Solidarity?

The work of the courageous and astute Sisters in Islam deserves respect from Western feminists and feminist theorists and should not be dismissed or marginalized for accommodating Islamic ethics and paternalistic nationalism in forging gendered citizenship. After all, questions of gender relationships, womanly norms, and self-conduct are the stuff of ethical regimes, and, in order to change them, people in a given situation continually reinterpret what is good and worthwhile in their lives. Without respecting and engaging situated ethics, transnational sisterhood would have a hard time forging a "common strategy." Instead, internationalist feminism will be viewed as an imperialist venture that seeks to hold the postcolonial state hostage and to undermine ethical regimes and public morality.

As I see it, the kind of unlocatable sisterly solidarity represented by internationalist feminists such as Agarwal is still "romantic" and reluctant to deal with the pragmatic implications of what is at stake for dominated women everywhere. "Strategic sisterhood" as formulated is not strategic enough, given the complex geopolitical inequalities, global markets, and situated ethical worlds that feminists seek to intervene in. Truly effective sisterly solidarity articulates with situated constellations of power where feminists contest, negotiate, and even collaborate with diverse actors and institutions that share their view of the good life. To be truly strategic, internationalist feminists must recognize and deal pragmatically with alternative ethical imaginations of female citizenship forged within different milieus. An open-minded transnational sisterly solidarity should recognize its own limits and take the first step of acknowledging the validity of diverse ethical regimes (of which feminist humanism is but one) and the diverse situations within which questions of gender equality can be posed, negotiated, and resolved. While the ethical critique of inequalities should never cease, cosmopolitan feminists should recognize the nexus of heterogeneity, contingency, and ambiguity that haunts all forms of political agency, everywhere.

CHAPTER two

Cyberpublics and

the Pitfalls of Diasporic

Chinese Politics

In 1998, a global Chinese (Huaren) website mobilized worldwide protests against the attacks on Chinese in Indonesia that had been triggered by the Asian financial crisis. This set of events provides the occasion for a discussion of the necessary conceptual distinction between diaspora and transnationalism. I maintain that diaspora as permanent political exile is often conflated with contemporary forms of fairly unrestricted mobility. *Diaspora* however, is increasingly invoked by elite migrants in transnational contexts to articulate an inclusive ethnicity that includes disparate populations across the world who may be able to claim a common racial or cultural ancestry. Such spurious ambitions have gained momentum through the communicative possibilities of the Internet, so that the formation of networks and "translocal publics" is merely a mouse-click away. Indeed, the rise of diasporic politics may inspire in website members an unjustified sense that cyber-driven humanitarianism will foster, not endanger, citizenship embedded in nation-states. The interplay between diaspora discourses and Internet-based interventions has produced a disembedded form of racialized citizenship that poses the question of who is accountable to whom in a transnationalized world.

The Triggering Event

In August 1997 a financial firestorm swept through Southeast Asia, bringing chaos and suffering to millions in Suharto's Indonesia. Following the precipitous decline of the rupiah in late 1997, millions of Indonesian workers laid off from their jobs returned to poverty-stricken neighborhoods and villages. A picture of Suharto signing away his power, with the stern IMF chief standing over him, his arms crossed, had been a widely publicized image of national humiliation.[1] A handful of army generals, indigenous business competitors, and Muslim intellectuals deflected anger against the ruling elite by stirring racist nationalist feelings against ethnic Chinese. Indonesian Chinese were called "new-style colonialists . . . who plunder the people's wealth" and traitors who keep their wealth in U.S. dollars and send their money overseas. Rumors flew about Chinese shopkeepers hoarding food, raising food prices, and about Chinese "traitors" fleeing the country with ill-gotten capital. Such metaphors of evil, combined with the invisibility and unpredictability of market forces, turned fears into rage.

In May 1998 and the following weeks, ordinary people looted and burned Chinese stores and homes, while soldiers stood by, observing a destruction that mimicked the devastation visited on the lives of the poor. In the chaos of the destruction, soldiers disguised as hooligans were reported to have attacked dozens of girls and women, many of whom were ethnic Chinese. Human rights activists claimed that the rapes were organized rampage by military men out of uniform. A related process of witch hunting was set off by rumors about anonymous men in black called ninjas who killed Muslim leaders and dumped their mutilated bodies in mosques. In some neighborhoods, local vigilante groups hunted for ninjas, who were killed on sight, their heads paraded on pikes. Such grisly attacks, and the demands by the masses for some kind of redistribution of "Chinese" wealth in favor of the *pribumi* (indigenous) population, again made the scapegoat community stand for the ravages of the global markets.

It is important to note that while ethnic and religious differences have long existed in Indonesia, under Suharto's New Order regime (1969–98) a few Chinese tycoons (*cukong*) enjoyed special political access, which enabled them to amass huge fortunes and dominate sectors of the economy. The majority of ethnic Chinese (numbering some four million) are small business operators, professionals, and working people who bear the brunt of a historical legacy of anti-Chinese sentiment and suffer from a legal status as racialized citizens.[2] The Suharto government, through inaction, had practically "legalized" attacks on Chinese property and persons, allowing the army to manipulate events to displace anger against the Suharto regime onto the ethnic Chinese.[3] The seeming global indifference sparked an international response among ethnic Chinese communities around the world, linked through the Internet.[4]

Huaren Cyberpublic

On August 7, 1998, and the days following, coordinated rallies protested the anti-Chinese violence in front of Indonesian embassies and consulates in the United States, Canada, Australia, and Asia. These rallies were held mainly in cities in North America — Atlanta, Boston, Calgary, Chicago, Dallas, Houston, Los Angeles, New York, San Francisco, Toronto, Vancouver, and Washington. In Asia, demonstrations took place only in Hong Kong, Manila, and Beijing. China issued a rare warning to Indonesia that redress should be provided for the victims of the riots and mass rapes.

The global protests were organized through a new website called Global Huaren ("Global Chinese People"), set up by a Malaysian Chinese emigrant in New Zealand called Joe Tan. Enraged by the seeming indifference of New Zealanders and the world to the anti-Chinese attacks, Tan contacted ethnic Chinese engineers and professionals based in Canada, Australia, and the United States. They saw parallels between the plight of Chinese in Indonesia and European Jews. They established the World Huaren Federation (WHF) in order "to foster a stronger sense of identity among Chinese people everywhere, not to promote Chinese chauvinism but rather racial harmony."[5] Huaren chapters have been formed mainly in Southeast Asian cities, but they are beginning to appear on every continent, and the federation anticipates a membership of ten million in a few years.

This spiritual "revolution" in Chinese political activism is attributed to the fact that "at least four million of us around the world are computer users, computer geeks and techies," according to an American Chinese attorney, Edward Liu, who heads the San Francisco chapter of Huaren. As reported on its website, this construction of a global Chinese public identifies race as the unifying feature. Tan maintains that the WHF is not intended to encourage Chinese chauvinism but "to eradicate the intimidation which some governments are subjecting Chinese and other ethnic minorities to. We want to ensure that such atrocities will never happen again to anyone of any race and color." He adds: "Like any other race, the Chinese are expected to be responsible citizens in their country of birth or adoption."

The ethics of this interventionist citizenship are resolutely web-based, since ethical expressions of global Chinese citizenship are limited to Internet practices that send diaspora narratives and images to zip across borders and link up with a multiplicity of websites. This diaspora public is formed by overseas Chinese professionals based in New Zealand, Australia, Canada, and the United States, many of whom have no prior experience with or links to Indonesia. Global Huaren seeks to act as a kind of placeless political watchdog on behalf of the Chinese race.

Edward Liu, who spoke at a San Francisco rally, criticized President Habibie (President Suharto's successor) for being complicit in a de facto "ethnic cleansing" of Chinese influence in the cultural, economic, and social fabric of Indonesia.[6] He thanked ethnic Indonesians such as Father Sandiawan Sumardi and other pribumi human rights advocates who risked their own safety and lives in support of the victims. He condemned the "Chinese Indonesians" who were at one time cronies of Suharto but "now have ingratiated themselves with Habibe [sic] in the same rotten system of corruption, cronyism and nepotism." He went on to lecture the Indonesians: "Chinese Indonesians have a right to be good Indonesians. They have a right to be Chinese culturally too. They have a right, as I do, as a Chinese American of Filipino background to be proud of my ties. I am proud to be a Chinese. I am also proud to be a Filipino. I am also proud to be a San Franciscan and an American."[7]

This speech demonstrates extreme insensitivity to the situation in Indonesia. Liu makes distinctions in racial terms, and seems to give primacy to Chineseness, when most ethnic Chinese prefer to refer to themselves as Indonesian Chinese, and not the reverse. Liu seems to essentialize the Chinese race and to conflate race with culture. He criticizes Habibie, who though politically weak had worked to improve the citizenship protections of ethnic minorities.

The diaspora politics protesting anti-Chinese activities around the world is cast in the language of moral redemption for the Huaren race, posing the need to balance racial protection against economic advantage. For instance, the World Huaren Federation was lauded by the *Straits Times* in Singapore, which claimed: "Previously, Chinese communities were more concerned with commercial and economic matters. The ethnic Chinese in Indonesia had been pummeled by rioting in the past decades — but they had always absorbed the punishment meekly to preserve their commercial interests. This time around, a landmark shift occurred with modern communications technology becoming the unifying force."[8]

In online discussions on the Huaren website, the attacks on Indonesian Chinese have stimulated a moral resurgence around the concept of a Chinese race. New American Chinese have logged on to confess their "shame" for having failed "to help Huaren refugee[s] in Vietnam and in Cambodia." A subscriber urges his coethnics: "Don't sell our pride and value for short-term personal and materialist gain. Wealth without pride and compassion is not success or achievement." He bemoans the fact that wherever any Chinese was mentally or physically discriminated against, the majority of the "so called 'successful' business Huaren" were nowhere to be seen.[9] A respondent notes that for the past two decades many Chinese emigrants were ashamed of China and Vietnam for being communist and poor countries, and their lack of sympathy to the Chinese boat people was influenced by the "Western propaganda machine." Now his own view has changed:

> How and when I realized that I was not just an internationalist (I was a parasite) but a human first and foremost, I can't pinpoint. . . . Being racial is not necessarily negative. Racial discrimination and persecution is obnoxious but it is necessary to contribute towards one's race. One is as whole as [what] one's ancestors [have] built in the past, and each man in the present must maintain and build for the descendants. . . . [The] Chinese must begin to let loose their embrace on self-gain. . . . the stronger must fend for the weaker, the more able to contribute more. This is something new to [us] Chinese and we must set the example.[10]

This new ethical consciousness of what it means to be a transnational Chinese is an immediate response to the plight of Indonesian Chinese as excepted citizens. Unfortunately, the political intervention relies almost entirely on cyber-driven practices of confession, criticism, and jingoism.

The Uses of Diaspora

In the fields of colonial history and anthropology, diaspora in the modern period was applied to successful but often persecuted mobile minorities. The term *trading diaspora* was applied to migrant Indian entrepreneurs in Africa and *trading minorities* to ethnic Chinese traders in Southeast Asia.[11] This concept of diaspora as a comparative historical form derives from the historical role of Jewish merchants in Western Europe. Historians seeking to understand the formation of ethnic and nationalist identities have stressed the Jewish diaspora in terms of its role in international trade, manufacturing, and modernization. For instance, in a book that compares the migrant Jews and Chinese as "Essential Outsiders," scholars note parallels in the activities of ethnic entrepreneurs that made them agents of capitalism as well as targets of political violence during the rise of nationalism in Europe and in Southeast Asia.[12] In early modern Southeast Asia, overseas Chinese were first referred to as "the Jews of the East," a phrase that denoted greed, exploitative relations with native populations, and disloyalty.[13] In the immediate postcolonial era, immigrant Chinese and in some cases Indians — both as economic minorities and as participants in the nationalist struggles of their respective homelands — presented major political problems for the host country. In newly independent Indonesia, ethnic Chinese constituted an internally excluded minority positioned outside normal political protections. Chinese subjects were forced to choose between mainland Chinese citizenship and Indonesian citizenship, thus putting to rest their legal if not political ambiguity.[14] In other Southeast Asian nations where ethnic Chinese are also an economically dominant minority — Burma, Thailand, Vietnam, Malaysia, and the Philippines — *diaspora* remains a term fraught with meanings of excepted and contingent citizenship.

In recent decades, however, the study of "diaspora" has been disconnected from trading minorities and from nationalism. Expatriate intellectuals in Great Britain, North America, and Australia have appropriated diaspora to refer to a variety of contemporary cosmopolitan forms associated with anti-state sentiments, cultural hybridity, and progressive, transnational politics. Indian expatriates invoke diaspora to refer to the recreation of home culture in diverse locations and in tension to the nation-state.[15] In *The Black Atlantic*, Paul Gilroy views the African diaspora in terms of a shared history of political and cultural struggles against slavery and the racist policies of modern states.[16] The "double consciousness" of scattered black communities constitutes a transatlantic space of modernity, and its inventive dynamism cannot be framed by any single nation-state or set of ethnic traditions.[17]

This new meaning of diaspora, as an alternative political sensibility to nationalism in a transnational age, is now widely accepted in Cultural Studies. In the new journal *Diaspora*, Khachig Tölölyan argues for a concept of diaspora that goes beyond exile to include the experience of loss, dislocation, powerlessness, and suffering, as well as the feeling, articulation, and enactment of stateless power by a variety of dispersed communities.[18] James Clifford's concept of "discrepant cosmopolitanism" seeks to move beyond diaspora as a pure form (of desire for return and attachment to a homeland) to include cultures of displacement, colonization, adaptation, and resistance expressed in practices of "traveling-in-dwelling, dwelling-in-traveling."[19] More recently, Clifford has argued that diasporism is intertwined with indigenism in the "dispersed and connected populations" of the Pacific, whose lateral relations of exchange and alliance engage in "subaltern region-making" outside capitalist circulations.[20]

The particular histories of African, Indian, and Chinese diasporas have shown, however, that transnational forms, norms, and practices were conditioned, configured, and transformed within the overlapping spaces of modern capitalism, nation-states, and technology. Benedict Anderson has stressed the role of print capitalism in shaping modern imagined national communities.[21] Arjun Appadurai has asserted that contemporary media and travel are fostering diasporic communities in the fissures between nation-states and borderlands, giving rise to postnational identities.[22] But tensions between diasporic cosmopolitanism and nationalism remain vital, as in anticolonial struggles for national emancipation, in state attempts to regulate mobile ethnic populations,[23] and in the founding of new ethnonations within established nation-states. Indeed, Anderson warns that contemporary globalization promotes the transnational ethnicization process, resulting in a kind of "long-distance nationalism" that represents "a serious politics that is at the same time radically unaccountable."[24] The minority figure in the West who is tempted to play a national hero in his (imagined or real) homeland is a political problem inseparable from the theorization of diaspora today.

Diasporic Chinese intellectuals in the West have played a key role in the current invoking of a single diaspora that would gather in the constellation of dispersed Chinese communities in the world. Popular books such as *Sons of the Yellow Emperor* and *The Encyclopedia of the Chinese Overseas* seek to unite diverse flows of people in different parts of the world through their Chinese heritage and ancestral mainland origins.[25]

In recent decades, as new flows of well-educated, middle-class Chinese from Asia have flocked to North America, there has been an intensification of Asian American interest in a search for cultural roots.[26] The term *diaspora* is now invoked by activists and academics in order to claim an overarching framework for heterogeneous peoples who may be able to trace ancestral roots to China. On American campuses, ethnic studies, which originally framed the study of minorities within the American nation, began to be reoriented toward a study of "diaspora" and of roots in the homelands of immigrants. This is in part a recognition of the transnational connections sustained by new immigrant populations, but it is also a rearticulation of ethnic claims in a global space. Such *diasporic* discourses are deployed, however, mainly in political practices of newly empowered expatriate subjects who seek to define emergent social forms. Contemporary transnational flows and interactions of ethnic groups have engendered a yearning for a new kind of global ethnic identification. The proliferation of discourses of diaspora is part of a political project which aims to weave together diverse populations who can be ethnicized as a single worldwide entity.

Rey Chow is a dissident voice in cultural studies who has warned against "the lures of diaspora." By writing about coethnics at home or elsewhere in the world, expatriate intellectuals are implicated willy-nilly in the promotion of diasporic consciousness, but they must resist the self-serving pose of becoming spokesmen for "natives" in the Third World. She fears that a cultural studies tendency toward "gathering endangered authenticities . . . is also the possibility of dispensing with the authentic altogether." Such practices of othering—as a projection of cosmopolitan intellectual power and freedom to intervene at will—are frequently disconnected from the particular ground and history of anti-imperialist struggles linked to the liberation of their homeland.[27]

This complex and layered history is evident in the scholarship of overseas Chinese in Southeast Asia, which has analyzed internal fragmentation and cultural diversity within seemingly unified diaspora populations, but such works remain largely unfamiliar to contemporary diaspora studies.[28] More recently, *Ungrounded Empires* brought together interdisciplinary analyses of diverse ethnic Chinese flows and transnational subjectivity emerging within situations of "flexible" capitalism in the Asia-Pacific.[29]

There are now a number of studies that document the unexpected circuits and cultural complexity of diaspora Chinese, as well as their contemporary flows to cities across the world.[30] Nevertheless, despite such studies of multiple trajectories and ambiguity in identity, there is still a dearth of scholarly attention on these tensions between transnational networks and local ethnic situations in particular locations. Clearly, one needs to differentiate between *diaspora* as a set of differentiated phenomena and *the diasporic* as political rhetoric.

But *diaspora* is loose on the information highway and political byways, and elite diasporic subjects have picked up the term in order to mass customize global ethnic identities. The current assembly of coethnic groups under an electronic diaspora umbrella disembeds ethnic formation from particular milieus of social life. Indeed, as the above Indonesian incidents and Global Huaren have shown, information technologies play a big role in engendering feelings and channeling desires for a grand unifying project of global ethnicity, the diversity of peoples and experiences notwithstanding. As we shall see, "Chinese" peoples from around the world are one of the most diverse populations that has ever been lumped into a single category.

Contemporary Flows

There are approximately fifty million people of Chinese ancestry living outside China, and they are dispersed in 135 countries. Analysts and activists have often referred to this linguistically and culturally heterogeneous population as a single diaspora community, even though it has been built up over centuries of countless flows—first of exiles, then of migrants—out of the Chinese mainland. Most of the flows from China began in the late nineteenth century, when British incursions, the disruptions of agriculture and trade, and the resulting famines generated the great south Chinese exodus to Southeast Asia and North and South America. Previously, I have used the phrase "modern Chinese transnationalism" to describe the reemigration of overseas Chinese subjects who had settled in postcolonial Southeast Asian countries to North America and other continents.[31] The 1965 family unification law allowed the children of earlier waves of Chinese immigrants to join their parents in the United States. In the early 1980s, new waves of ethnic Chinese flocked into Canada, Australia, and the United States. In some cases, these were students seeking higher education; in others, they were families seeking resettlement abroad before the 1998 return of Hong Kong to Chinese rule. Economic affluence in Southeast Asian countries and in Taiwan also encouraged business migrants and professionals to pursue further opportunities of upward mobility in the West. At the same time, events in China produced political reasons for outmigration. These outflows from the mainland, Hong Kong, and Taiwan have been diverse, in some cases more remarkable for their differences than for their similarities.

Since the late 1980s, most ethnic Chinese immigrants to North America have been from mainland China (as opposed to ethnic Chinese from Taiwan and Hong Kong). China's opening to the global economy, the impending return of Hong Kong to rule by Beijing, and the Tiananmen Square crackdown were major causes for an outflow of students, business people, professionals, and ordinary workers seeking political refuge or economic opportunities in the West. Plunging into the market is referred to in China as diving into the ocean (*xiahai*), and many ambitious Chinese link expanded business and professional activities with seeking opportunities abroad. Legally, forty thousand leave for the United States, Canada, and Australia each year. Currently migrants from China are of a higher professional and economic status than earlier ones in the 1980s, and the perception is that the U.S. embassy is raising the bar for skilled immigrants from China, creating fierce competition among Chinese urban elites to enter the United States, either by making business investments, using family connections, applying to college, or contracting bogus marriages with American citizens. The other major category of mainland Chinese emigrants is that of illegal migrants, mainly from the southern province of Fujian, who seek entry into the United States and Canada. Many end up as exploited restaurant and sweatshop workers.[32]

Thus the people with Chinese ancestry in North America include citizens from China and overseas Chinese from a dozen other countries in which their ancestors had settled. Such immigrants do not see themselves as a unit since they have different national origins, cultures, languages, and political and economic agendas. They do not necessarily associate with, or view themselves as having any continuity with, earlier waves of immigrants from the mainland. Indeed, the range of nationality, ethnicity, language, and class origins among Chinese immigrants is vast and unstable, splitting and recombining in new ways. For instance, in Vancouver, affluent Hong Kong emigrants are very insistent in setting themselves apart as "high-quality people" from poor Chinese illegals smuggled in shipping containers. In the United States, even among the recent waves of immigrants from China and Taiwan, great distinctions in terms of class, dialect, and regional culture are brought by the newcomers to the new country. Such divisions are only a few of the reasons why one cannot assume a unified diaspora community constituted by people who may be construed as belonging to the same ethnic grouping or hailing from the same homeland. There is great diversity among peoples who may be able to claim Chinese ancestry, and they may or may not use diaspora-like notions in shaping their public interests or political goals. I therefore suggest that instead of talking about given identities, it may be more fruitful to attend to the variety of publics where specific interests intersect and are given particular formulations.

Translocal Publics among New Chinese Immigrants

Given its currency in the age of transnationalism and multiculturalism, *diaspora* should be considered not an objective category but, rather, an ethnographic term of self-description by different immigrant groups or publics. More and more, diaspora becomes an emotional and ideologically loaded term that is invoked by disparate transnational groups as a way to construct broad ethnic coalitions that cut across national spaces. Previously, I have used the term "translocal publics" to describe the new kinds of borderless ethnic identifications enabled by technologies and forums of opinion making. These publics play a strategic role in shaping new ethnicizing and cultural discourses for audiences scattered around the world.[33] Here, I identify three kinds of milieus that have different potential to shape transnational ethnic Chinese fields of political action.

Diaspora as an Extension of the Motherland : The "global Chinese" Internet public sees itself as an extension of the homeland. On its web pages, members articulate a spurious connection between the digital-driven diaspora and earlier waves of Chinese patriots who possessed the conviction that the experience and status of Chinese abroad was directly proportional to the status of China in the international system. In the early twentieth century, overseas Chinese patriots struggled to shape an identity that was continuous with the rise of nationalism at home: "If Chinese people were bullied locally, that was because China received no respect internationally. To be Chinese, anywhere in the world, was to be a representative of the motherland, to have a stake in the future of China, and to recognize the claims of China and Chinese culture over their loyalty."[34]

Today's Chinese diaspora intellectuals and elites appear to be speaking out of sync with this particular nationalist struggle. Those who view themselves as an extension of territorial nationalism are primarily new migrants from the Chinese mainland whom the Chinese government calls *haiwai huaren* ("Chinese abroad"). They may be living and working in the United States, but their hearts and politics are tied to the interests of the Chinese nation.[35] One can say that there is one transnational public that takes mainland China as its frame of reference, a second transnational public which is an extension of Taiwanese nationalism, and a third network of emigrants from Hong Kong. These different publics may overlap at the margins, but their orientations are toward politics and social relations with the home country. Their very status as minorities in the West allows them to assert a kind of discursive power that makes them national heroes on the other side of the world.[36]

Translational Identities of Southeast Asian Immigrants : Southeast Asian immigrants with some kind of Chinese ancestry do not fall naturally under the category of *haiwai huaren* (or the older term of *huaqiao*), although in their remigration to North America some conditions exist for re-Sinicization, as I discuss below. Ethnic Chinese whose departures from Southeast Asia have been historically shaped by earlier migrations out of China (since the early sixteenth century), European colonialism, postcolonial nationalist ideologies, and globalization tend to stress their nationality rather than their ethnic status. Under colonialism, creolized and mixed-race communities—called Straits Chinese in Malaya, mestizos in the Philippines, and Peranakans in the Dutch East Indies—flourished. But in almost all of postcolonial Southeast Asia, a series of native, colonial, and/or postcolonial government actions have integrated different kinds of Chinese immigrant communities as ethnic minorities (Malaysia), as an ethnically marked shopkeeping class (Thailand), or as a stigmatized ethnic group that passes into the dominant native community only by "erasing" the stigma through intermarriage and the adoption of dominant languages and cultural practices (Vietnam, Cambodia, Myanmar, the Philippines, Thailand, and Indonesia, with varying degrees of severity). Thus people refer to themselves as Malaysian Chinese, not Chinese Malaysians. Among ethnic Chinese in the Philippines, Thailand, or Indonesia, Chinese ancestry is often eclipsed or uninscribed by name, language, and cultural practices as part of forcible state integration. In countries where religion has not played a major role in assimilation, people with Chinese ancestry have become part of the ruling class. In all countries but Singapore, where a majority of the population is of Chinese ancestry, Chinese ethnicity is politically underplayed because of the state emphasis on majority rule. Thus such differences in group identity and relationships to nationalism make for extremely complex assemblages of ethnic, cultural, and national identity among overseas Chinese. After a few centuries of migration and settlement, Southeast Asian peoples who can trace Chinese ancestry think of their identities as produced out of a cultural syncretism which is associated with Westernized middle-class attributes and cosmopolitanism, although there has been a revitalization of ethnic Chinese connections to China since the 1980s. But in Southeast Asian countries, any political suggestion of diaspora sentiments is avoided, for it implies disloyalty and lack of patriotism to the country of settlement.

When Southeast Asian Chinese subjects remigrate to North America (and elsewhere in the West), they tend to identify themselves in terms of their home nationalities and call themselves Thai, Cambodian, and Filipino American. Ethnic Chinese from these diasporas may be highly conscious of the fluidity of identity formation in the shifting field of modern geopolitics, and they are more likely to resist the hegemonic discourses of political nationalism among those immigrant Chinese who closely identify with China and Taiwan. Because they are relatively small in number and have come from different Southeast Asian countries, overseas Chinese from Southeast Asia, and especially

Indonesia, have not yet come together to self-consciously produce an all-inclusive ethnicity.[37] Indeed, many of them would fit Stuart Hall's notion of translated identity, seeing themselves as the product of a rich confluence of traditions, histories, and cultures.[38] For instance, Southeast Asian immigrants participate simultaneously in various media publics — from homeland print cultures to Chinese kung fu movies — in sharp contrast to people from the Chinese mainland, who rarely express interest in other Asian cultural spheres.

Ethnic Absolutism in the Cyber Age : For the disparate groups of immigrants who can claim Chinese ancestry, the issue of a broader, collective Chinese ethnicity emerges in multicultural America: Should they identify more strongly with their new nationality, their old one, or with a potentially resurgent ethnicity driven by ambitious Asian Americans?

I argue that the translocal publics constituted by professionals online are now directly engaged in the production of global ethnicities. Specifically, economic globalization has scattered a new kind of transnational Chinese professional (managers, entrepreneurs, engineers, programmers) throughout the world. Over the past two decades, alongside Chinese business migrants, tens of thousands of ethnic Chinese professionals from Southeast Asia and China have moved abroad to global cities while maintaining family, economic, and professional links with their home countries. These expatriate Chinese professionals have formed middle-class Asian neighborhoods in cities such as Sydney, Vancouver, San Francisco, New York, Washington, London, and Paris and are beginning to think of their Chinese identity in global terms. In North America, the concentration of ethnic Chinese professionals in particular cities (e.g., Sunnyvale, California), neighborhoods, and high-level corporate occupations has produced conditions for a diversity of people who claim ethnic Chinese ancestry to become re-Sinicized through the universalizing forces of cyberpower, and through discourses of human rights and citizenship.

Asian immigrants — professionals, managers, entrepreneurs, and venture capitalists — are powerful members of the American corporate world. In Silicon Valley, a majority of the foreign-born engineers are from Asia, mainly Taiwan and India. They maintain professional and business links with cities in Asia, fostering two-way flows of capital, skills, and information between California and Taipei. The very economic clout of such transnational Asian professional communities is, however, undercut by their invisibility in North American cultural and political life. Instead of sharing the histories of earlier waves of immigration from Asia, they constitute a globalized yet politically amorphous collection of ethnicized professionals, incompletely disembedded from their original homelands but playing a dominant role in international commerce and industry. They exist in a social vacuum, and the imbalance between professional power and political-cultural weakness creates conditions that seem ripe for the emergence of what Stuart Hall calls "ethnic absolutism." What can they turn to that will allow a kind of reterritorializing — a way of tracking back to those far-flung and myriad ethnic Chinese communities in Asia — which can help "restore coherence, 'closure,' and Tradition"[39] in the face of political displacement, cultural diversity, and existentialist uncertainty?

The Vicarious Politics of
Electronic Intervention

We can now return to the opening scenes of this chapter: Why did a group of high-tech ethnic Chinese from their Western outposts intervene in the 1998 anti-Chinese attacks in Indonesia? How has the Internet allowed for a simplification of identities, such as "Chinese people in diaspora"? What are the positive and negative effects of rapid Internet interventions on the political sovereignties and the situated realities of peoples in distant lands?

The distinctive practices of international business — space-annihilating technologies, digitalized information, and flexible recombination of different elements — provide a strategy for producing a unified ethnicity that is seemingly borderless. The Internet, Saskia Sassen has noted, is a powerful electronic technology that "is partly embedded in actual societal structures and power dynamics: its topography weaves in and out of nonelectronic space."[40] At the same time, the rise of digitalized publics means that people with limited access to the Internet are less powerful in affecting distant events than those connected to websites. Privileged émigrés who control the electronic network to shape diaspora politics seek to subvert and bypass the sovereign power of nation-states, but are they able to control the effects of their rapid-fire interventions? What are the consequences when diaspora is invoked to assert an ethnic solidity and to deploy human rights discourses, thus framing particular conflicts and problems in terms of global racial identity? As we shall see, such rapid and remote electronic responses to localized conflicts can backfire against the very people, situated outside electronic space, who they intended to help.

Following the international uproar over the anti-Chinese attacks, and appeals by various NGOs in Indonesia, President Habibie quickly tried to reassert state control and to revise legal discriminations against ethnic Chinese minorities. In early October 1998, he decreed that all government bodies provide equal treatment and service to all Indonesians. A new law also seeks to revise all policies and laws that are discriminatory "in all forms, character and ranks based on ethnicity, religion, race, or family records."[41] The terms *pribumi* and *nonpribumi* were to be discontinued in all government offices and activities. This news was greeted by Huaren spokesman Edward Liu with an invective about official "doublespeak" and an urging that global Huarens react with "a great deal of skepticism and sarcasm." "If true," Liu wrote on his group's website,[42] "this is indeed a small stride in the right direction. . . . if this is merely a political placebo — empty rhetoric camouflaging a sinister, bad-faith . . . public relations attempt to stem the flight of Chinese Indonesian human and capital . . . and sanitize the bad image of Indonesia as a lawless, racist society — then we are afraid the downward spiraling of Indonesia will continue."

Liu goes on to warn that in "an increasingly globalized and digit[al]ized world, Indonesia can least afford to expunge and erase ten million of its most productive and resourceful citizens of Chinese descent. . . . The eyes of the Global Huaren are fixed on Indonesia." This language of the multinational diaspora subject is shunned by people who consider themselves fundamentally — culturally, socially, legally, and politically — Indonesian. By creating invidious essential difference between races, the diaspora discourse reinforces the alien status of Indonesian Chinese who had long suffered under the dual citizenship policy of Suharto.

What happens when electronic messages from a cyber community are received in sites of political struggle on the ground? On the one hand, we can applaud Global Huaren for its timely mobilization of protests around the world, which has cast a spotlight on the Indonesian atrocities, compelling Habibie to take action protecting minorities. On the other hand, some of the tactics of Global Huaren have misfired and jeopardized efforts to rebuild trust between Indonesian Chinese and the pribumis after the crisis.

The Huaren website has carried repeated stories and pictures, including bogus ones, of ongoing rapes. For instance, in mid-1998 the Huaren website circulated a picture, later found to be false, that depicted an Asian-looking rape victim in a shower-stall. This stirred anger in Indonesia. Another Internet account reported that a woman claimed her rapists invoked Islam. The story went on to note that since the coming of Islam "the act of raping women has been assumed to be the most effective way to conquer races." Despite controversy surrounding the truth of this story and these claims, rumors were produced about a Serbian-style master plan to drive the Chinese out of Indonesia through ethnic cleansing. Furthermore, by deploying inaccurate narratives and fake images of victims' bodies, the diaspora website enacted a second process of victimization on a larger scale, casting the violent events in resolutely gendered and racial terms of assault on Chinese people everywhere.[43]

Indeed, to Indonesian Chinese who fled the country and to many overseas Chinese in Southeast Asia, the attacks might have seemed like the result of a policy of ethnic cleansing.[44] But we have to be wary about making such strong charges, since, after all, a government-sponsored team traced the rapes of minority women to a special branch of the Indonesian army (Kopassus) headed by Suharto's son-in-law, then lieutenant-general Prabowo Subianto. In other words, the attacks on minority women were limited to a renegade faction of Suharto's army and were not the result of official government policy.[45] There is no evidence that the Indonesian public had been engaged in a campaign to oust Indonesian Chinese. Overseas accusations of ethnic cleansing have been adamantly rejected by Indonesian leaders such as President Habibie and General Wiranto. Furthermore, Abdulrahman Wahid, of Indonesia's largest Muslim organization, the 35-million-strong Nahdlatul Ulama, and another leader, Amien Rais, went on record to condemn whatever rapes had occurred and to express their fear that such Internet-fueled rumors could deepen racial and religious divisions.[46] Furthermore, the actual number of rapes was controversial.[47] The public, including many pribumi-operated NGOs, seem more likely to believe that the army was directly involved in all kinds of abuses, partly to displace the rage in the streets against the government onto Chinese and other minorities. While these questions will probably never be fully resolved, the Indonesian Chinese who have not fled the country reject the tendency of overseas Chinese to blame *all* of Indonesia for the violence and to reject their talk of ethnic cleansing. Attempts to consider Chinese people in the world as a diaspora race distinct from their citizenship in particular countries may jeopardize the postcrisis efforts of Indonesian Chinese to rebuild their society within a broad-based coalition fighting for human rights in Indonesia.

Embedded Citizenship or Cyber-Based Race?

The horrendous events of 1998 have convinced more Indonesian Chinese to participate in human rights activities that serve a variety of marginalized groups. Three national commissions — one on human rights, one on women, and one on children — are building a coalition around issues of antimilitarism and citizenship based in international law. Feminist NGOs formed a national commission, Violence Against Women, following the army-instigated rapes of minority women in Java and throughout the archipelago.[48] The Urban Poor Consortium has been fighting for the rights of the unemployed and the homeless. The Commission for Missing Persons and Victims of Violence (Kontras) is urging support for an international tribunal to investigate reports of military collusion in the killing of East Timorese, despite the strong objections of the Indonesian state. Other groups include the Committee against Racism in Indonesia (CARI), which is combating racism and pressuring the Indonesian government to stop the systematic killing in parts of Indonesia (Aceh, Ambon, West Timor, and Irian).

In contrast to Global Huaren, Indonesian Chinese using the Internet to mobilize global support have stressed their sense of embedded citizenship in Indonesia. We can say that such counterwebs seek global support for Indonesians in general, and not exclusively for ethnic Chinese, as is the case with Global Huaren. There are multiple websites set up by Indonesian groups, and their messages focus on the suffering of a range of victims. A website called "Indo-Chaos" operates in both Bahasa Indonesia and in English and is directly connected with the United Front for Human Rights in Indonesia.[49] It commemorates the Indonesian Chinese victims of sexual violence but also deplores the Indonesian army-instigated violence against other ethnic groups in Aceh and East Timor. An NGO called Volunteers for Humanitarian Causes notes that, altogether, 1,190 people were killed in Jakarta alone in the 1998 riots.[50] Yet another website set up by Indonesians stresses the status of the victims not as Chinese but as Indonesian citizens and appeals for help in its campaign "against human rights violations, injustice, and racism."[51] A leader of CARI, the antiracism group, emailed me the following message:

> The responses of the Chinese communities in Australia and the West to the May Tragedy were obviously overwhelming and to large degree welcomed by the Chinese in Indonesia. It is always good to know that the International communities, including governments, defended the Indonesian Chinese rights and condemned Indonesian government for their failure to protect their citizens. The problem with these protests was associated with the way some of the demonstrators expressed their anger. Some of them used anti-Indonesia expressions and burnt Indonesian flags. Some even ridiculed Islam religion. Such attitudes . . . prompt reactions which further jeopardize the positions of the Indonesian Chinese in Indonesia. We need to urge the International communities to

direct their protests to the Indonesian government and military forces, not the people in general. We should avoid actions which induce racial or religious conflicts at all costs.

This statement is not only an expression of the importance of a nonracial approach to humanitarian intervention; it is also a plea for the international community to recognize and respect the embedded citizenship of the majority of Indonesian Chinese who have chosen to remain. Indonesian Chinese have much work to do to reimagine Indonesian citizenship by repairing their damaged image and reassessing their own relations with the government and with their fellow Indonesians. Besides forming a political party and many associations to fight racism and discrimination, they have lobbied the government to erase all forms of official discrimination. As mentioned above, the government recently banned all forms of discrimination on the basis of distinctions between pribumi and nonpribumi. Indonesian Chinese are now working to induce the government to recategorize ethnic Chinese from the excluding label "Indonesian citizens of alien Chinese descent" (*warga negara asing/keturunan Cina*) into the category of "ethnic groups" (*suku bangsa*), which they would occupy alongside hundreds of other ethnic groups in the country.[52] Ethnic Chinese groups have reached out to pribumis in a process of "native" empowerment through the construction of a people's economy (*perekonomian rakyat*). Some have given their support to an affirmative action program to channel economic and social resources toward the uplift of the indigenous majority. Thus what Indonesian Chinese do not need is to be made part of an ethnicizing transnational public.

Cyberpublics: Promise and Risk

Global Huaren is only one Internet example of a phenomenon that relies on digital practices to shape a kind of virtual ethical citizenship. To what extent do cyberpublics represent genuine humanitarian interventions? Do they count as elements in an emerging "global civil society?" "We live in a world of 'overlapping communities of fate,'" David Held and his coauthors wrote in *Global Transformations*, "where the trajectories of each and every country are more tightly intertwined than ever before. . . . In a world where [powerful states make decisions not just for their own people but for others as well, and] transnational actors and forces cut across the boundaries of national communities in diverse ways, the questions of who should be accountable to whom, and on what basis, do not easily resolve themselves."[53]

Translocal publics can indeed challenge the sovereignty of nations and can have humanitarian effects, bringing international opinion to bear on the mistreatment of a nation's citizens. International interventions, for instance, have stopped bloodletting in some conflicts (e.g., in East Timor). Cyberpublics based on nation or religion, such as the Falun Gong movement in China, shape a community of fate that evades state oppression, exposes injustice, and turns a global gaze on a state's shameful behavior. Digital networks thus can put pressure on governments to be accountable to their own citizens, as well as to the global community.

But a diasporic consciousness driven by the Internet may also inspire in its members an unjustified sense that an electronic-based humanitarian intervention will invariably produce positive effects. The actions of Global Huaren have demonstrated both the promise and the danger of romantic appeals to autonomy and citizenship beyond the reach of the state, illustrating the potential explosiveness of the vicarious politics of diaspora. A resurgent Chinese cyberidentity based on moral high ground may be welcomed in Beijing (though not always), but it is not necessarily welcomed by ethnic Chinese minorities elsewhere. The digital articulation of a disembedded global racial citizenship can create invidious essential differences between ethnic others and natives, thus deepening rather than reducing already existing political and social divisions within particular nations. The loyalty of local citizens becomes suspect when they are linked by race to global electronic patrons. Rapid-fire Internet interventions, unaccompanied by a sophisticated understanding of specific situations in different countries, may very well jeopardize localized struggles for national belonging and an embedded concept of citizenship. Furthermore, Internet discourses of a racialized diaspora cannot make up for the sheer anonymity of the members, clients, and other participants who can log in randomly from anywhere at any time.

Digital technologies thus endow elite expatriate subjects with a new kind of power that goes beyond providing the funds, information, and arms of traditional long-distance nationalism. By organizing web pages, member lists, and chat rooms, expatriate elites get to define the experience of coethnics anywhere in the world, to revive or shape cultural memories and incite the vicarious sharing of rage and suffering, thus calling into being a cyberpublic of communal belonging. The strategic deployment of decontextualized images in various media streams blurs distinctions between reality and fantasy, further thwarting our capacity to assess information and political action. The symbolic rather than referential truths of circulating images expand the power of expatriate activists to a reckless scale that overtakes what happened or is happening locally.[54] Websites allow a "false" amplification of the power of a few individuals who can proliferate at hurricane speed, making unsubstantiated claims about racial interest and fate. A video-game logic can create instantaneous simplifications of good global activists versus bad governments and racial oppressors versus victims, contributing to rumors that can fuel violent chains of events. Thus a virtual citizenship which can be activated by a keystroke has notoriously uncontrollable effects, putting into play disparate information and actors and exponentially confusing and conflating the stakes of particular conflicts and struggles.

Given the political hazards and the low threshold of accountability, some expatriate intellectuals have been critical of discourses that celebrate diasporic activism as expressions of antistate freedom. Being wary about the uses and abuses of diaspora consciousness is not to deny that complex accommodations, networks, and partial belongings can foster progressive politics among transnationalized peoples. Rather, our analytic task is to assess the political effects of particular diasporic claims, to consider what is at stake for people located and interlinked in unequal positions of economic, intellectual, and geopolitical power. Invited to endorse Global Huaren, Indonesia-born cultural theorist Ien Ang demurred, arguing that new kinds of solidarities have to be built not on "difference" but on overlapping grounds of "togetherness."[55] Similarly, other Asia-born scholars, including Rey Chow and Elaine Tay, are keenly aware of how diasporic strategies may reap academic gain and fame in the West but harm "native" populations on the other side of the planet. While digital technologies have given new life to diasporic yearnings, transforming them into cyberpolitics, progressive activists should beware of the unexpected repercussions on millions of people offline whose fates can be drawn together online.

PART II

SPACES OF

GOVERNING

CHAPTER tHREE

Graduated Sovereignty

Globalization has been taken to mean many things; our different concepts of globalization seem to color our understanding of the state and its relationship to citizens. By now, claims that "the survival of the state" is threatened by globalization have been met by powerful counterarguments.[1] One cannot deny that economic globalization — in the relentless pursuit of market free-dom — has brought about important changes in the state of "stateness." The fundamental question is what basic changes in the state, and in the analysis of the state, have been occasioned by global markets. For instance, it would be useful to understand how states manage a range of transnational networks that variously integrate them into the global market and political community. If we look at the responses of smaller states to the challenges of global forces, we discover that neoliberalism as exception and exceptions to neoliberalism constitute a two-pronged strategy for redefining state relationships with citi-zens and external institutions. Indeed, global markets have contributed to both the strengthening and the weakening of different activities of the state and thus have shaped its capacity to deal with global regulatory entities such as the IMF.

This chapter explores the dynamic relations between global forces and the actions of emerging Asian states in order to show how neoliberal logic reconfigures the territory of citizenship. The rise of the so-called new Asian tiger countries in Southeast Asia has been accomplished by their partially subordinating themselves to the demands of major corporations and global regulatory agencies. In the course of such interactions with global markets and regulatory institutions, the governments have created new economic possibilities, spaces, and political constellations for governing the (national) population. I make two conceptual claims about how interactions between neoliberalism and state action produce a variety of outcomes for unconven-tional spaces of government. First, the experiences of these small, relatively open Asia states present an instructive case of how postdevelopmental strategies influenced by neoliberal rationality treat populations in relation to global market forces, producing alternative spatialities of government and gradations in citizenship rights and benefits. Second, there is a clash of neoliberal calculations at different scales, as postdevelopmental geographies come into tension with international regulatory agencies that seek to open up national spaces to financial markets, thus exposing all citizens to market upheavals. Emerging countries, I argue, are compelled to be flexible in their conceptions of sovereignty and citizenship if they are to be relevant to global markets.

Postdevelopmental Government

Sovereignty is conventionally understood in a restricted sense: as state power that is centralized and concentrated in the military apparatus of the regime to ensure order and stability to safeguard the territorial integrity of the nation-state.[2] I believe this conception should be broadened. David Held has usefully distinguished between de jure sovereignty and de facto or practical sovereignty. He suggests that "the often weak and debt-ridden economies of many third world countries leave them vulnerable and dependent on economic forces and relations over which they have little, if any, control."[3] But even small or emerging states like the Asian tigers, while vulnerable to the pressures of global markets, still have the capacity to manipulate global relations and to adjust relations with their societies accordingly. Grasping how sovereignty functions in practice requires an understanding of the different mechanisms of governance beyond the military and the legal powers.

I consider government as the administration of populations, and the economy as an instrument of government that effects how population and space are variously constituted as political problems.[4] Michel Foucault has noted that modern power consists of interacting relationships among sovereignty (power over life and death), discipline, and government (regulation). This triangle of "sovereignty-discipline-government . . . brings about the emergence of population as a datum, as a field of intervention, and as an objective of governmental techniques." Such strategies of government isolate "the economy as the science and the technique of intervention of the government in that field of reality."[5] I use Foucault's insights on economic rationality in techniques for governing populations in a field of intervention, recasting them in the light of contemporary technologies of governing. Neoliberal reason, I argue, has taken economic rationality in a highly flexible direction that does not use the national territory as the overriding frame of reference for political decisions. Rather, the neoliberal stress on economic borderlessness has induced the creation of multiple political spaces and techniques for differentiated governing within the national terrain. Especially in emerging, postcolonial contexts, varied techniques of government rely on controlling and regulating populations in relationship to differentiated spaces of governance, with a graduating effect on sovereignty, and on citizenship.

Graduated Sovereignty : The countries of Southeast Asia have been called "developmental states" that base their legitimacy in their "ability to promote and sustain development, understanding by development the combination of steady high rates of economic growth and structural change in the productive system, both domestically and in its relationship to the international economy."[6] Others use the term *strong states* to stress the powerful bureaucracy, public enterprises, and state monopolies that have presided over capitalist development in Southeast Asia.[7] And indeed, in the 1980s and 1990s, Singapore, Malaysia, Thailand, and Indonesia—the "tiger economies"—have been strengthened by a great infusion of foreign direct investment, experiencing some of the highest rates of economic growth in history.

But there is a difference between developmentalism—which takes the national economy as the target of state action[8]—and what I call "postdevelopmentalism," or a more dispersed strategy that does not treat the national territory as a uniform political space. Market driven logic induces the coordination of political policies with the corporate interests, so that developmental decisions favor the fragmentation of the national space into various noncontiguous zones, and promote the differential regulation of populations who can be connected to or disconnected from global circuits of capital.

Since the 1980s, Southeast Asian states have not dealt with the economy as a whole entity but rather have fragmented the national territory and the population in the interest of economic development. Elements of postdevelopmentalism can be found in Latin America where, Guillermo O'Donnell has argued, the uneven reach of the state in newly democratized countries has created "brown" areas of neglect and marginalization.[9] But what is distinctive about Asian postdevelopmentalism is a checkered geography of governing resulting not from an anemic state apparatus but from a deliberative neoliberal calculation as to which areas and which populations are advantageous or not advantageous in appealing to global markets. The deployment of such postdevelopmental logic in effect produces a postdevelopmental geography

— the multiplication of differentiated zones of governing across the national territory — that has specific political effects.

Malaysia, Indonesia, Thailand, and the Philippines have labor, tourist, and timber zones, and postsocialist Vietnam and Burma have followed this logic of configuring the national territory into multiple zones of development. Newer kinds of spaces include science parks and knowledge centers in Singapore, Malaysia, and Taiwan. Indeed, China may have been most audacious in deploying zoning technologies, as evidenced by the three main planning strategies that have re-spatialized its capitalist development: special economic zones, special autonomous zones, and urban development zones (see chap. 4). Asian states have a tendency to deploy neoliberal logic for mapping spaces that are administered according to differentiated political conditions. Negatively defined, some zones are freed from national laws regarding taxation, labor rights, or ethnic representation. Spaces defined positively promote opportunities to upgrade skilled workers, to improve social and infrastructural facilities, to experiment with greater political rights, and so on.

This patterning of production and technological zones was designed to facilitate the operations of global capital; it thus entails de facto or practical adjustments and compromises in national sovereignty. The territorial concentration of political, economic, and social conditions mobilizes foreign investment, technology transfers, and international expertise to specific zones. I thus use the term *graduated sovereignty* to refer to the effects of a flexible management of sovereignty, as governments adjust political space to the dictates of global capital, giving corporations an indirect power over the political conditions of citizens in zones that are differently articulated to global production and financial circuits. By creating zones of graduated sovereignty, postdevelopmental strategies make these sites more "bankable" than other developing regions. In short, "graduated sovereignty" is an effect of states moving from being administrators of a watertight national entity to regulators of diverse spaces and populations that link with global markets.

Graduated Citizenship : But differentiated spaces of the political are often coordinated with diverse modes of government — disciplinary, regulatory, pastoral — that administer populations in terms of their relevance to global capital. Administrative strategies are informed by biopolitical considerations ("biopower") or "explicit calculations" about human life in terms of its growth and productivity.[10] The question is, what forms do biopolitical considerations take in Asian tiger countries, where reports of occasional political repression seem to overshadow our perception of different mechanisms of government?

Robert Castel observes the emergence, in advanced neoliberal states, of "differential modes of treatment of populations, which aim to maximize the returns on doing what is profitable and to marginalize the unprofitable."[11] Asian tiger states, which combine authoritarian and economic liberal features, are not neoliberal formations, but their insertion into the global economy has entailed the adoption of neoliberal calculations for managing populations to suit corporate requirements.[12] In postdevelopmental government, there is a mix of disciplinary, regulatory, and pastoral technologies aimed at instilling self-discipline, productivity, and capacity to work with global firms. In production zones, low-skilled and migrant populations are governed through disciplining techniques (e.g., extreme controls on labor rights) and surveillance at the workplace. Such disciplinary techniques over low-wage workers and migrants are intended to instill both productivity and political stability, thus creating conditions profitable for global manufacturing. In practice, low-skilled workers enjoy fewer civil rights and less welfare protection than higher-skilled workers in science parks and high-tech centers.

Citizens and foreigners in other zones are regulated with a lighter hand, especially members of dominant groups, who are given special treatment because of their race or ethnicity. Instead of being disciplined, they are treated to a pastoral mode of care that Foucault calls "individualizing power" directed at particular objects of government.[13] Pastoral techniques stress nurturing and special care that ensure the salvation of "the flock" while also attending to individual needs of survival and competition. In Asian states, preexisting ethnoracializing schemes (installed under colonial rule) are reinforced and crosscut by new ways of governing that differentially value populations according to market calculations. Thus, while low-skilled workers are disciplined, elite workers and members of dominant ethnic groups enjoy affirmative action and pastoral care. Such differential biopolitical investments in different subject populations privilege one ethnicity over another, male over female, and professional work over manual labor, within a transnationalized framework. The mix of market calculations and ethnic governmentality means that varied populations are subjected to different technologies of disciplining, regulation, and pastoral care, and in the process assigned different social fates. Let me examine the repatterning of postdevelopmental geographies and differentiated citizenship in Malaysia and Indonesia.

Malaysia: The Biopolitics of Postdevelopmentalism

There are good reasons for using Malaysia as an illustrative example of a state that is developing a system of graduated sovereignty. Since its political independence from Great Britain in 1957, the country has favored the political rights of Malays as an "indigenous" majority population that, in general, economically lagged behind the country's ethnic Chinese and Indians. But one can argue that from the early 1970s onward, a system of graduated sovereignty has come into effect as the government has put more investment in the biopolitical improvement of the Malays, or *bumiputera* ("princes of the soil," or original inhabitants), awarding them rights and benefits largely denied to the Chinese and Indian minorities. Special programs have given Malay subjects shares in state-held trusts, government contracts, business credit, scholarships, business licenses, university admission, and employment in the public or corporate sector. This, in effect, has created the world's first affirmative action system tied exclusively to ethnicity. The pastoral power that has been employed on behalf of the Malays has unevenly favored the middle and upper classes, and Malays as a community enjoy more rights, benefits, and claims than non-Malays. Ethnic Chinese, a majority of whom are business operators, professionals, and urban workers, are disciplined especially in the realms of cultural expression and economic activity, while most ethnic Indians have remained plantation proletarians. Thus this system of ethnicity-based governmentality has come to racialize class formation and naturalize racial differences in the country.

There are two aspects to Asian postdevelopmental strategy. On the one hand, there is the strengthening of nationalist concepts or ideologies about civilization, be it neo-Confucianism or the new Islam. On the other hand, there is the proliferation of state policies and practices through which different segments of the population relate or do not relate to global capitalism.

Globalization has induced new imagined communities that stress not merely continuity[14] but also a resurgence of ancient traditions that go beyond past achievements to meet new challenges of modernity. In Malaysia, a burgeoning sense of economic power and cosmopolitanism has inspired narratives of an Asian renaissance that harks back to precolonial centuries when Islam was the force that brought commerce and splendor to Southeast Asian trading empires.[15] The discourse claims that a new era of vitality and autonomy has dawned because of the vibrant economic transformation of the region. To political leaders, the revival of the term *civilization* by Samuel

Huntington[16] seems to validate such nationalist claims of "enduring" Asian civilizations that can engender a modern sense of regionalism. Alongside the discourse of the new Islam, the secular Malaysian state gained control of Islamic law as an instrument of and a rationale for national growth that weds a religious reflowering to an unswerving allegiance to the state. Islam should be used to turn Malaysia into a "model state," but what the politicians have in mind is not another Iran but rather a state in which a moderate and reasonable Islam helps to strengthen the state by working and meshing smoothly with global capitalism.

The new Islamic narrative is infused with messages of economic development and entrepreneurialism. The prime minister, Mahathir Mohamad, declared that "Islam wants its followers to be self-sufficient, independent, and progressive."[17] During the decades when the government wanted to create a large Malay middle class and a Malay corporate elite, Mahathir sought to demonstrate that

> there is no reason why the Islamic faith, properly interpreted, cannot achieve spiritual well-being as well as material success for the Malays. . . . The values listed in the Mid-Term Review of the Fourth Malaysia Plan were exactly the kinds of values to raise productivity at home, increase competitiveness abroad, and ensure political stability always. Among them were "better discipline, more self-reliance and striving for excellence" which together with "thriftiness" and "a more rational and scientific approach in overcoming problems" were "values which are progressive and consistent with the needs of a modernizing and industrializing plural society."[18]

State favoritism of middle-class and elite Malays seeks to make them competitive and enlightened Muslim professionals who can play the game of global capitalism. The Islamized norms of self-discipline in the production of the entrepreneurial and professional classes are buttressed by extensive affirmative action benefits in education, employment, and business activities. Young people are increasingly educated in Western universities through an economical twinning arrangement in which the first two years of a foreign curriculum are completed in Malaysia before students attend an American, Australian, or British university. A new class of superficially Westernized Malay professionals now runs the country according to American management principles, although efficiency and imagination could certainly be increased. As in the United States, public universities are being downsized and corporatized, while the social sciences — for example, anthropology — are being replaced by "social administration" studies. The outward symbols and forms of Malaysian urban elite culture are shaped more by Madison Avenue and Hollywood than by local culture. For instance, Kuala Lumpur (K.L.) has caught up with Singapore as a city of shopping malls. The American corporate presence in K.L. is so pervasive that the city seems like an economic and cultural extension of California.

But the truly privileged are the "preferred Malays" (as they are called by the public) — the lucky, but not always talented, few who have been favored by affirmative action policies and by an ethnic form of pastoral care. As the subjects of Islamic corporate power, their distance from the suddenly passé Malay culture seems mirrored in the contrast between the old Moorish mosques and the Petronas twin towers that pierce the tropical sky. On a palm-fringed hillock stands the Kuala Lumpur Hilton, where attendants in white suits and batik sarongs rush forward to greet well-groomed Malay executives wielding cellular phones as they step out of limousines. But with regional economic integration, the horizons of new professionals have stretched beyond Malaysia. These new professionals are joining a segregated stratosphere — one created by the corporate networks, political parties, professional groupings, clubs, golf courses, think tanks, and universities — that has increased cultural commonality among elite citizens of ASEAN countries, while the gulf between them and ordinary Malays who work in factories and on farms could not be bigger. In addition to being the main beneficiaries of pastoral care, a few preferred Malays also have special access to political power that grants some tax breaks and state bailouts for their failing companies.[19] The Malay elite thus enjoys both special state largesse and a corporate citizenship at a time of astonishing economic growth.

In contrast, most of the workers, who keep the economy flourishing, are strictly controlled and enjoy very limited rights. Two grades of cheap labor — factory and migrant workers employed in even lower-paid jobs — are subjected to legal and social discipline and Islamic forms of surveillance that induce self-control. In the free trade zones, low-paid workers, a majority of whom are young Malay women, are transported to distant workplaces where their bosses are often non-Muslim ethnic Chinese, Indian, or foreign managers. The state legally permits but in practice limits the activities of trade unions in these export-manufacturing zones, and policemen are quickly mobilized whenever workers go on strike. At the same time, state social policy benefiting the bumiputera ensures that the firms employ a majority of Malays in their workforce, and that minimal wages and cost of living allowances are granted to avoid charges of exploitation. The workers' freedom to pray during work hours also contributes to general norms that promote self-discipline and low levels of dissent.[20]

The immigrant labor market — which draws workers from Indonesia, Bangladesh, the Philippines, and Burma — has grown in response to labor shortages in the plantation and construction industries. Almost one third of the country's eight million workers are immigrants. Despite or because of this dependence on foreign labor even cheaper than homegrown female labor, the Malaysian state is especially strict in enforcing the time-limited contracts of employment and residence. Legal immigrants are employed in domestic service, construction, and on plantations. They enjoy limited rights of employment, but they cannot apply for citizenship. Illegals who slip into the country have no legal or social rights. While Muslim illegals may be more tolerated or better treated and can often pass as Malays, non-Muslim workers when exposed are deported, with no right of appeal. In the recent economic crisis, anti-immigrant sentiment has mounted, and ridding the country of illegal migrants is now considered a patriotic duty. The government selected female domestics from the Philippines as the first foreign workers to be expelled. But as the currency crisis worsened in Indonesia, tens of thousands of Indonesian workers have been sent home. Thailand has also expelled about one million Burmese and South Asian workers.

Another modality of governance is a mix of civilizing and disqualifying policies directed toward populations that are considered uncompetitive and that resist state efforts to make them more productive, in the eyes of the state. Official views of aboriginal peoples are highly ambivalent; they are a potential source for augmenting the Malay race and for attracting tourist dollars in theme parks. Administrators and developers also view aboriginal groups as backward and wasteful, frequently an obstacle to state projects and corporate development. Officials seek to lure the aborigines away from their nomadic life in the jungles and to persuade them to settle. Although aboriginal groups are also technically bumiputera and, like the Malays, entitled to special affirmative-action rights, in practice they have access to these rights only if they abandon the aboriginal way of life and integrate into the larger Malay population by becoming agricultural producers. Jungle dwellers who resist the civilizing mission of schools, sedentary agriculture, markets, and Islam are left to their own devices in the midst of destruction caused by the encroaching logging companies. Generally, aboriginal groups in practice enjoy very limited protection vis-à-vis their territory, their livelihood, and their cultural identity. The Penan foragers of Sarawak have developed two responses to territorial encroachment, each of which is shaped by a different sense of the Malaysian government's sovereignty. The Eastern Penan's blockade of logging activities has won them international attention; whereas the Western Penan have acquiesced to logging as part of their acceptance of Malaysian rule.[21] Either way, the risks to their survival as viable cultural, self-reproducing groups are enormous; in practice they are struggling mightily against encroachments that estrange them from their nomadic way of life, and reclassify them as would-be Malays and their lands as areas for development. Aboriginal groups in practice thus enjoy very limited protection vis-à-vis their territory, their livelihood, and their cultural identity. Frequently, the state seeks to evict rebel populations and open up their resource-rich areas to timber logging and the construction of golf courses and dams. Irredentist and outlaw groups also dwell in such "brown areas," and Southeast Asia is riddled with internal colonies of poverty and neglect. Again, these abandoned areas emerge not out of sheer neglect but out of a neoliberal calculation to invest in and insert groups differently into the processes of global capitalism. Such gradations of governing may be in a continuum, but they overlap with preformed racial, religious, and gender hierarchies and further fragment citizenship for people who are all citizens of the same country.

Indonesia: An Archipelagic Polity

While Malaysia has in times of crisis used the military against its own people, in Indonesia military coercion is a fact of everyday life for much of the working population and the marginalized. Again, the considerations of profitability, resource extraction, and productivity influence state policies toward different segments of the population. There is no official policy of affirmative action in Indonesia, and the national motto of "unity in diversity" stresses the multicultural range of this nominally Muslim nation. Under Suharto's New Order regime (1965–98), the state implemented a military-industrial complex that in the 1980s and 1990s transformed the nation into an industrializing, export-oriented economy. The New Order emerged out of the bloodbath of the mid-1960s, when over a million people were killed on suspicion of being communists. The new totalitarian state is based on two repressive apparatuses. First, a gulag prison system where thousands of political detainees have been held in primitive conditions. Second, the military—an armed bureaucracy of at one time almost half a million people—has a "dual function" of military and civilian control. Its centralized power is concentrated in Jakarta and in occupied places like Aceh, but army personnel and apparatus are distributed in small cities, villages, and industrial zones throughout the archipelago of over 200 million people.

In the industrial zones of Sumatra and Java, the army works hand in hand with factories to maintain social order among the labor force of seven million people, many of them young women who left rice fields to assemble watches, clothing, shoes, toys, plastic goods, and furniture. They earn less than a living wage in factories operated by ethnic Chinese and Korean subcontractors for brand-name companies such as Nike, Reebok, and Gap. Until 1994, women working twelve-hour days sewing Gap outfits, made less than two dollars a day, including overtime. That year, the Indonesian Prosperity Trade Union, calculating that the average worker needed to earn at least $2.50 a day, broke "the taboo on labor strikes" and called a national strike to protest low wages. After a long struggle, the government agreed to a minimum wage of two dollars a day, but this was unevenly enforced, coming into effect only in some urban factories. Indonesian factory women are still among the lowest paid in Asia, just slightly ahead of their counterparts in Vietnam and China. When I visited the area in mid-1996, workers claimed they needed at least five dollars a day to survive.

"Low-end" manufacturing work depends on gendered forms of labor control and harassment. Widespread surveillance and much of the daily control of female workers center on their bodies: in the provision of food, in the granting or withholding of permission for menstrual leave, in the pressure for family planning, and in the physical confinement imposed during work hours. Examples of sexual harassment include timing visits to the toilet and using the excuse of having to verify requests for menstrual leaves to conduct body searches. Workers are crammed into dormitories above or next to warehouses, thus creating firetraps. Managers punish the tardy by making them stand under the sun for hours and are quick to fire those who demand basic survival wages.[22]

Not only are workers rarely protected by labor rights, they are frequently harassed by the military. Whenever there is a strike, the army is deployed against the workers, no matter how peaceful they are. In my visit to the Tangerang zone, I noticed that military barracks are often adjacent to factory sites, and army personnel mingled freely with security guards outside the factory gates. I was told that the army could reach any factory within twenty minutes of an outbreak of worker insurrection. Indonesians think it is normal for the army to keep industrial cities secure for factories, and factory bosses routinely make "donations" to local commanders. While most workers are denied the minimum wage and the most basic social protection, they are constantly vulnerable to the state's repressive apparatus.

Despite the poor treatment of industrial workers, the state, in a policy that goes back to the colonial concept of Javacentrism, favors Javanese people over the more than thirty major ethnic groups in the archipelago, and the spread of Javanese from their overpopulated island has been a means for displacing local populations and consolidating the empire. Among these local groups are aboriginal peoples in jungle communities who fall in the official "tribal slot" of "isolated peoples" (*orang terasing*), or those who are "backward" (*terbelakang*) or "left behind" (*tertinggal*).[23] The state has not been content to define aboriginal peoples in simplified terms; it has sought progressively to erase, through different programs of arbitrary displacement, their very identity tied to ethnic territory. By introducing "efficient" extractive industries, state enterprises, the state has made inroads into aboriginal enclaves, opening them up for development. The ambiguous status of the tribal slot has allowed the state to resettle nomadic groups, or to encourage the resettlement of impoverished peasants from elsewhere under the transmigration project. For instance, tribal groups in Irian Jaya have lost their land to the American mining company Freeport-McMoRan Copper and Gold, which has since leveled two mountains and is planning to open more mines in the highlands. The displaced Amungme people have been neither compensated nor employed, and local authorities represented by the company import Javanese to staff their mining town.[24]

In West Kalimantan (Borneo), migrant Madurese have claimed land rights against the indigenous Dayaks by appealing to the nationalist concept of citizenship and the primacy of entrepreneurism extolled by the government.[25] The Dayaks are also fighting a larger battle against timber companies that are grabbing their lands. Security forces tied to timber concessions are routinely used to destroy Dayak crops and jungle resources, to enforce land theft, and to torture people into accepting "compensation" for land taken to develop plantations. The Dayaks, in defense of their territorially based identity in accordance with customary law (*adat*), have launched attacks on Madurese migrants and timber estate developers.[26] These clashes have produced killing fields in the jungles; the bloodshed has regained ferocity in the aftermath of the financial crisis in late 1998.

At the other end of the spectrum, state corporatism favors a tiny elite that controls corporations which monopolize the distribution of food and fuel and protect agricultural products from foreign interests. Such monopolies allowed the Suharto family to amass vast fortunes through their links with military officers and the wealthy Chinese who bankrolled them. Besides producing and reproducing a tiny political economic elite, state corporatism has helped to contain the centripetal forces — class, religion, ethnicity, island — that threaten to pull state and society apart.

State corporatism also involves awarding timber concessions in outlying areas to military generals, who practically run autonomous fiefdoms. Provincial governors, military officers, and business tycoons have begun to ignore the dictates of Jakarta and develop separate trading relations with foreign enterprises. In Irian Jaya, large areas of the Pancak Jaya-Grasberg mountain complex are under the control of Freeport Indonesia (a subsidiary of Freeport McMoRan), where the mining company controls authorities like the Tembagapura Community Development Project. In East Kalimantan, former Suharto crony Mohammed Bob Hasan controls huge concessions and has engaged in extensive clear-cutting in the name of "sustainable development" for plywood production. The nation's environment minister, who had been unable to get Jakarta to act to stop the destruction of the forest, called Kalimantan "part of a nation without government, like parts of America in the 19th century."[27]

Military dominance of the provinces has intensified separatist movements. Southeast Asia is riddled by "internal colonies": the East Timorese and Acehnese in Indonesia, Dayaks in Malaysia and Indonesia, the Moros in the Philippines, Shans and Karens in Burma, and the Patani Malays in Thailand. For decades, Indonesia amassed troops in Aceh and in East Timor (since the 1975 invasion). George Aditjondro notes that because "all ASEAN governments have their own 'East Timors' in their backyard," ASEAN has become "a conspiracy of repressive regimes, busy protecting each other's behinds."[28] Criticisms of human rights violations in these colonies by citizens and sympathetic outsiders are immediately suppressed by the state. Such outlaw groups are usually treated with overwhelming coercion (as in East Timor), but in other situations state support is simply withdrawn, so that a kind of low-grade struggle continues to fester amid poverty and neglect (as with the Patani in Thailand). State brutality against its outlawed citizens is highly influenced by market interests. Frequently, the state seeks to rid the territory of rebel populations and open the resource-rich areas they occupied to timber logging, petroleum pipelines, or dams.

Graduated sovereignty, as I have discussed it so far in Malaysia and Indonesia, refers to the differential treatment of populations in relation to ethno-racial differences, and the dictates of development programs. Segments of the population are differently disciplined and given differential privileges and protections in relation to their varying participation in globalized market activities. These gradations of governing — disciplinary, pastoral, civilizing/disqualifying policies, or military occupation and de facto autonomous domains — may be in a continuum, but their effects are to fragment citizenship for subjects who are all nominally speaking citizens of the same country. The elites are showered with economic, social, and political benefits, while others are abandoned and deprived of basic survival needs. As I have indicated, such variegated citizenship is of course greatly reinforced when the state reorganizes national space into new economic zones that promote international trade and investment.

Governing through Transnational Networks

The remaking of political spaces is not a technique confined within conventional national territory. Indeed, my larger argument is that the goal of graduated modes of ruling is to establish transnational linkage of sites. As Bruno Latour has noted, network relationships proliferate hybrid values and subjects, and postdevelopmental strategies, in governing through the mobilization and formation of networked spaces, create hybrid zones of government and citizenship.[29]

In the late 1980s, the liberalization of foreign trade regulations induced a massive influx of mainly East Asian investment, thus creating regionalized production networks in Southeast Asia. Building on preexisting corporate alliances, these interfirm networks are hierarchized, with Japanese firms providing the latest technological knowledge and skills, Taiwanese and Korean companies the management and goods, and local Southeast Asian firms the labor.[30] In recent years, a variety of Western companies and local firms have participated in these production networks as well. Such corporate patterning of investment, production, and trade flows among contiguous localities of three or more countries thus carve out "natural economic territories" called growth triangles (GTs) or subregional economic zones.[31]

Growth triangles are determined by an "economic geometry," in which location, the accessibility of cheap labor, the possibility of exploitation of complementary resources, and the proximity of a regional hub such as Singapore enhance the competitive advantage of the region in the global economy.

So far, three GTs have formed by linking contiguous parts of neighboring countries. The country configurations are Indonesia-Malaysia-Singapore (linked by the Singapore-Johore-Riau Growth Triangle, or Sijori); Indonesia-Malaysia-Thailand; and Brunei-Indonesia-Malaysia-Philippines. Sijori is a massive industrial park astride the Riau Archipelago that draws on the three countries' complementary labor and technical resources to enhance investment opportunities. From Singapore's perspective, this growth triangle allows Singapore to retain command/control functions at home while moving "low-end" jobs offshore. It takes advantage of cheap Indonesian labor, and it also ameliorates tensions over the presence of too many guest workers within the city-state. Sijori thus represents a zone of low-cost production in which Singaporean capital and expertise can be used to train and manage regional workers. It represents the low end of a system of zones in which the city-state is the site of continuously upgrading human capital.[32] The Southeast Asian state finds itself playing a subordinate role as facilitator of investments and provider of infrastructure and cheap labor to global capital. Such "extended metropolitan regions" are thus the result of refining the time-space coordinates of flexible production techniques[33] that have broad implications for the redesigning of national sovereignty.

What is the political architecture of such cross-border zones? We can try to tease out the legal and political compromises whereby the state temporarily cedes control of these zones, and the subjects within them, to quasi-state authorities. First, providing the location for growth triangles means that the participating state must be flexible in its relation with foreign capital, in a way that goes beyond giving the usual incentives of onsite infrastructure, tax breaks, and special export allowances. In Malaysia, participating firms negotiate on a case-by-case basis with the national industrial development authority. For instance, there is the implicit arrangement whereby union activities are suppressed, or corporate disciplining is allowed to curb worker activism.

What kinds of "conducive regulatory environments" and labor discipline prevail under corporate management? Both state and corporate authorities cooperate in determining the rules of inclusion and exclusion, and the rights and privileges of workers from different countries. The Sijori triangle, for instance, has a graded system of labor and material conditions in each of the triangle's nodes: In Singapore, one finds skilled labor and sophisticated business and control services; in Johore (Malaysia), skilled and semiskilled labor, recreation, and land; and in Batam and Riau (Indonesia), "low-cost, controlled" labor and some natural amenities (beaches).[34]

The GT logic has also reengineered gender relations across national lines. Different grades of workers are drawn from different countries. Tens of thousands of young Indonesian women are employed, alongside their semiskilled Malaysian counterparts, in industries set up by some eight thousand global companies. They are all supervised by male technicians and managers from Singapore. The integration of different tiers of labor markets can only limit the capacity of workers at the bottom, who are in an ambiguous, liminal order, to appeal to their own government for protection. The participating states are no longer interested in securing uniform regulatory authority over all their citizens outside or within these zones.

Second, the thinning of state power at these border zones is compensated for by the thickening of the regulatory functions of quasi-state authorities, which set the legal and social forms of control. Through the differential deployment of state power, populations in different zones are variously subjected to political control and to social regulation by state and nonstate agencies. More research needs to be done to discover what kinds of intergovernmental compromises are negotiated with corporate power. For instance, the Batam Authority (which controls the Indonesian part of the Sijori triangle) offers "fewer regulations" regarding land titles, various building permits, the number of expatriates to work at the enterprises, "and exemptions from the licensing requirements of the regional government authorities."[35] This means that the Batam Authority is autonomous of even the regional government and can enter into contractual relations with foreign capital. The chairman of the agency left no doubt as to its main function: "Social stability will be a key factor in attracting foreign investors."[36] The administration of the GT is so efficiently regulated that the May 1998 riots in Jakarta and subsequent disturbances in the rest of Indonesia caused no disruption among workers in Sijori. The Batam factories and ports operated like clockwork, and there were no street demonstrations calling for reforms (*reformasi*).

While the cross-border growth zones are the product of corporate networks, governments are also active in creating new sites that promote intraregional networks. The Malaysian state has established a technological center as a hub for second-tier information technology networks spanning sites in South and Southeast Asia. The grandly named Multimedia Super Corridor (MSC) is projected to become a "springboard to serve the regional and world markets for multimedia products and services."[37] The corridor, which links Kuala Lumpur to a new technological research center and a new international airport, dovetails with the policy of favoring corporate Malays, since they appear to be its main local beneficiaries. Malaysia already has a Silicon Valley in Penang, but it is dominated by ethnic Chinese technical and professional personnel employed in foreign electronic industries.

The MSC can be seen as a zone for experimenting with a daring variety of Islamic governmentality that draws on foreign expertise to train a new kind of Malay subject, one who will be fully at home in a multimedia world. Special cyber laws, policies, and practices attract foreign companies by promising not only tax breaks but a cheap pool of knowledge workers. Bill Gates of Microsoft and other high-technology industry executives from the United States and Japan have been persuaded to commit themselves to building enterprises in the zone.

In the drive to provide a new knowledge class, affirmative-action employment policies are suspended to free up the flow of capital, talent, and information that will ultimately favor the Malay corporate elite. Visas are readily issued to foreign experts to come and train locals, either in firms or in universities. Indeed, as I discuss elsewhere[38] the influx of Indian engineers, flown in by giant software companies such as Bangalore-based Infosys Technologies, is crucial in sustaining claims about an emerging digital knowledge labor force in Malaysia. There is also a multimedia university to train students. In order to attract Indian migrant workers, the infrastructural system is top quality, with residents given access to distance-learning technology, tele-medical services, and an electronic government. The MSC thus involves an enormous investment in a special political site, even before all the elements, especially expertise, are in place. By creating an infrastructural network, the MSC's planners hope to build a virtual hub that will breed a new kind of Malay computer-literate culture, hooked up to a second-tier information technology network. The official explanation for the MSC is that it is a "test-bed" to experiment safely with "modernization without undermining . . . traditional values";[39] in reality it will be a superprivileged zone where the Malay elite plugs into the world of high-technology industry. Singapore has orchestrated an even more ambitious set of technology flows in order to create a network of biotechnicity, with again, uneven citizenship conditions for locals and foreigners (see chap. 8).

Both the digital corridor in Malaysia and the biopolis-hub in Singapore are highly specialized sites that resulted from postdevelopmental strategies of reconfiguring space and reregulating populations and their flows. Stemming from neoliberal calculations for making advantageous connections with wealth and technology, such governing mechanisms create a galaxy of differentiated zones unevenly integrated into the structures of state power and global capital. Technology zones and growth triangles are plugged tightly into globalization processes, while aboriginal and ethnic-minority reserves are often disarticulated from national and regional centers of power. In short, the structural logic of globalization has not resulted in the solidification of differences among "civilizations" but rather in the proliferation of differentiated sovereignty within and across borders. While unifying images and forms of Asian values emphasize conformity, in practice, the biopolitical regulations of normalized and deviant subjects interact with ethnic rankings to create a graduation of citizenship rights, benefits, and moral claims across the political order and beyond. Such differential policies toward citizens and foreigners are reinforced when segments of the population are differently linked to global circuits of production, competitiveness, and exchange.

The Clash of Neoliberal Strategies

Above, I discussed a postdevelopmental strategy of emerging countries to maximize profitable connections with global capital through a checkerboard political process of graduated rule. Such neoliberal calculations, from the perspective of small or emerging countries seeking to be competitive, sometimes come into conflict with neoliberal logic at a higher scale, as when international financial imperatives of disciplinary neoliberalism force small and medium-sized countries to exercise spatial controls in a different way. This contradiction between neoliberal rationality, applied at the national and at the international levels, was well illustrated in the aftermath of the "Asian financial crisis."

A series of currency devaluations in late 1997 plunged Southeast Asian states into a crisis of de jure sovereignty. The very strategy of graduated sovereignty that embeds society in global production and financial markets can be their undoing, exposing them to disruptive economic forces. Asian states have responded in two interesting ways: Indonesia (like Thailand) submitted to the economic prescriptions of the IMF, while Malaysia resisted, instead reimposing its territorial state sovereignty.

The so-called Asian financial crisis was viewed by the international press as the outcome of reckless borrowing and lending, the building of megaprojects, and the lack of market controls in the tiger economies. Western observers tended to see the problem as one caused exclusively by crony capitalism or by a "lack of transparency" in economic practice. What was needed, they argued, was a heavy dose of neoliberal rules of global market efficiency imposed mainly through the IMF on Third World politicians. But Asian observers pointed out that global companies and bankers have been happy to work with these same problems for decades, and global institutions like the World Bank have lauded the capitalist takeoff in Asia.[40] Politicians like Malaysia's Mahathir, who was criticized for crony capitalism, preferred to blame international financiers like George Soros, whom he demonized as anti-Asia, and "anti–poor countries": "We are told that we must open up, that trade and commerce must be totally free. Free, for whom? For rogue speculators. For anarchists wishing to destroy weak countries in their crusade for open societies, to force us to submit to the dictatorship of international manipulators. We want to embrace borderlessness but we still need to protect ourselves from self-serving rogues and international brigandage."[41]

Indeed, while Asian economies were guilty of economic irrationality in their practices, very little attention has been paid to irrational financial markets that have made integration into the global economy a force that both strengthens and weakens the state. Gradually, as the financial crisis unfolded across a number of major countries, more observers admitted that the crisis was fueled by speculations in hot money and market panics that engendered massive outflows. Clearly worrisome were not only the effects of unstable markets on emerging states but also the moral hazards that might require the IMF and advanced states to bail out bad loans by profligate investors.[42] In any case, it is difficult if not impossible to distinguish between explosive growth and speculative bubbles, and debate continues about the causes of the crash.

The different responses of Malaysia and Indonesia to interventions by global monetary authorities reflected not only the relative strength of their respective economies, but also which parts of the state were losing control to or resisting control by global regulatory agencies. The IMF represents the strategic aspect of "disciplinary neoliberalism,"[43] whereby emerging states are subjected to rules that intensify their subordination to global market forces. As a result of the disastrous devaluation of the rupiah, Indonesia suffered a major reversal, with more than half its population living at or below the poverty level. The central bank is now more open to being inhabited by the global monetary agenda. The Indonesian response has been to submit to IMF prescriptions, after some initial resistance. Suharto was toppled, but the state led by a "family and friends cabinet" is essentially the same apparatus, with a much shrunken economic and military base and a diminished store of legitimacy. While the IMF prescriptions are necessary to improve banking practices and curtail corruption in high places, industrializing countries are now subjected to the same rules of benefiting global capitalist interests. For instance, fire sales have allowed foreign corporations to take over more local companies, especially in Indonesia and Thailand, thus further undermining national sovereignty.

In contrast to Indonesia, more healthy emerging countries responded to the financial crisis by strengthening the hand of the state against capital flows. The government of Hong Kong (a special autonomous region of China), in an unprecedented move, intervened to protect the property sector from foreign speculators. Chile added a penalty for the precipitous withdrawal of foreign investment. Malaysia imposed even more rigid controls on capital flows, challenging the truism that markets must have total freedom. In a partial recovery of national power vis-à-vis global capital, Mahathir had resisted the global agendas of financial traders, banks, and corporations, which he called "Anglo-Saxon capitalism." He put the government back in control of the interstate zone of financial dealings and currency trading. While Mahathir was demonized in the Western press, he was merely following a logical formula by the American economist Paul Krugman: in times of financial crisis, capital controls allow middle-range countries a temporary breathing space to stabilize their economies. These industrializing states have been found themselves on a tightrope, pursuing capital while seeking to protect society.[44] They (and in a different way, Russia) challenged the creditability of the IMF. Western economists now saw that the very irrationality attributed exclusively to crony capitalism has been magnified by an "online global oligarchy" driving much of the developing world into recession. Here we have the unfettered expression of neoliberal logic that takes the entire world as its game board and nations as checkers to be won. Fears of such extreme neoliberal rationality prompted the IMF and other global regulatory agencies to call for a new "architecture" of rules to control global financial markets. Unfortunately, Western observers often conflate subordination to the "dictatorship" of global markets[45] with the spread of democracy, so that any state that stands up to neoliberal disciplining at the international scale in order to protect its own neoliberal strategy of graduated sovereignty at the regional scale is framed as necessarily anti–human rights.

It is also unfortunate that the Mahathir regime played into this construction, combining Mahathir's anti-IMF stance with greater repression at home. Mahathir had his former deputy prime minister Anwar Ibrahim arrested for being an aficionado of the IMF (officially charging him for corruption and violating antibuggery laws, a British colonial detail now resurrected for political expediency). The government continued to prop up local companies that engage in risky investments, and it has not severed connections with favored developers.[46] Thus while Mahathir reasserted de jure state power vis-à-vis global markets, he continued the practice of preferential treatment for the corporate elite and its corporate partners, a mechanism that supports de facto graduated sovereignty.

But it was the arrest and sentencing of opposition leaders that stirred the middle classes from inaction in its privileged zones. Hundreds of young professionals took to the streets, like their Indonesian brethren, calling for the kind of *reformasi* that had removed Suharto from power. The evolving role of the middle classes may contain the seeds of a transformation in the logic of graduated sovereignty. They have been produced and nurtured according to a neoliberal logic of niche governmentality, and they have a weak and ambivalent role in relation to state power. In Western Europe, the bourgeois revolution gave birth to the liberal tradition, which, over the course of decades of struggle, set limits on state power and enshrined individual autonomy as a human right. In Southeast Asian countries, the middle classes are weak, most having been produced by the industrializing regimes in the space of two decades,[47] compared to the more than one hundred years of bourgeois development in the West. There is no homegrown tradition of political liberalism, and it is only under recent conditions of relative economic affluence that the new middle classes are beginning to fight for human rights against the state which enabled their own emergence. The financial crisis has ironically opened up space for the middle classes to fight even more vigorously for human rights reforms, because the state had suddenly increased repression of members of the middle classes and the elite circles, as well as of the marginalized segments of the population.

In emerging regions of the world, we find that the nature of state sovereignty must be rethought as a set of coexisting strategies of government within a single national space. The point is that the overall neoliberal-oriented agenda can mean lots of different rationalities and techniques, often working at odds with each other. There is discipline in the Foucauldian sense, there is labor discipline in the old sense; there are zones of corporatist power and zones of special production; there are "brown" spots of neglect; and there are heavily militarized sites of insurgency. In some cases, the national peripheries are reconstituted and governed by quasi-governmental-corporate authorities.

The model of graduated sovereignty shows that it is not so much a question of the market versus the state, but that market society at our particular moment in history entails the existence of some areas in which the state is very strong and its protections very significant, and other areas where it is near absent, because these zones must be flexible vis-à-vis markets, or they become structurally irrelevant. What we see, then, is a system of dispersed sovereignty, a model of galactic governance that may be traceable back to premodern roots in Southeast Asian trading empires,[48] but is now finely adjusted to the different "allocative mechanisms"[49] of global capitalism in relation to the assets of particular populations and sites.

The final question then is how these middle-range and emerging industrializing states have evolved vis-à-vis the constantly changing web of relations with international capital and affiliated agencies. As emerging economies become more vulnerable to neoliberal demands at the global level, to what extent are they being reconstituted and disciplined through the "structural adjustments" imposed by global agencies? It depends on how the game of neoliberal strategies at cross-purposes are played. China, the new workshop of the world, has sought to combine neoliberal policies in a series of zones at home while seeking membership in the World Trade Organization abroad (see chap. 4). This quest for regulation by global neoliberal rules has created tensions with extreme entrepreneurialism at home, as represented, for example, by the extensive and flourishing markets in pirated goods and intellectual capital. At the same time, there is a convergence between these two levels of neoliberal reason. The Chinese government is buying a high percentage of U.S. bonds (thus subsidizing America's gigantic debt) in order to be able to continue to flood U.S.-based Wal-Marts with cheap Chinese goods. In short, graduated sovereignty is the effect of market-driven strategies that are not congruent with the national space itself but that are biopolitically and spatially attuned to the workings of global markets. Ironically, then, emerging economies can be both threatened *and* sustained by the logics of neoliberalism.

CHAPTER four

Zoning Technologies

in East Asia

Concepts of regionalization and regionalism have dominated discussions of emerging global orders. With the rise of the European Union, scholars have begun to look for similar multilaterally negotiated regional organizations in the Asia-Pacific region. However, the search for regional forms in East Asia that may approximate the EU seems to set us up for the disappointing admission that regionalism and intergovernmental collaborations in East Asia are weak and fraught with political obstacles. Some have identified ASEAN + 3 (the members of the Association of South East Asian Nations plus China, Japan, and South Korea) as the major regional configuration in East Asia today, with the goal of "enmeshing" China in a "soft regime" of economic integration.[1] Such claims of a rising East Asian regional order seem dubious, more a vision shaped by politicians' rhetoric than an actually existing institutional structure. Indeed, the search for broad comparative ideal-types of regionalization in Europe, North America, and East Asia often uses Western modes of regionalization as the normative model, so that regional forms in East Asia are found to be lacking and defective. Alternately, one imagines that analysts in search of typologies may contrast the EU or the North American Free Trade Agreement (NAFTA) with Asian regional configurations, drawing up a set of oppositions such as multilateralism versus universalism, or the protection of civil rights versus compromises on them.

My analytical approach challenges such assumptions based on binary typologies. The EU is after all a unique experiment in transstatal rule that emerged out of specific historical experiences and institutions to meet contemporary global challenges. One would expect that significant regional alignments in East Asia would be rather different and distinctive, emerging out of the particular interactions between market calculations and diverse political entities. Regionalization in East Asia seems to take multiple forms, organized at different scales and based on limited groupings of sites or nations. Kenichi Ohmae first noted the rise of cross-border regional economies that link different sites and populations in the Asia-Pacific.[2] This perspective gives primacy to the role of economic systems and practices in shaping an emergent form of East Asian regionalization that overlaps nation-state structures. Others have pointed to Greater China — an alignment of China, Hong Kong, Macao, Taiwan, and Chinese communities in Southeast Asia — as a regional configuration emerging from cross-border trade.

My approach, in contrast to Ohmae's, gives primacy not to economic activities per se but to state strategies — informed by neoliberal logic — that produce conditions of possibility for such proliferating cross-border networks. Thus, unlike the EU, which was forged through multilateral negotiations, I argue that the regional space informally called Greater China is the outcome of the administrative strategies of a single state, China, in pursuit of greater cross-border trade. Flexible Chinese state practices, I argue, deploy zoning technologies for integrating distinct political entities such as Hong Kong and Macao, and even Taiwan and Singapore, into an economic axis. Furthermore, although zoning technologies are ostensibly about increasing foreign investments and market activities, they create the political spaces and conditions of variegated sovereignty aligned on an axis of trade, industrialization, and knowledge exchange. This China-dominated archipelago challenges widespread assumptions that economic and political forms of integration develop in different spheres. Greater China, I argue, is the spatial production of a state-driven scheme to integrate disarticulated political entities economically as a detour to eventual political integration.

This chapter begins with a rethinking of sovereignty not as a container concept but rather as a political order produced by an assemblage of administrative strategies. Contrary to claims that globalization engenders an "unbundling" of sovereign powers, I focus on specific state strategies that are designed to respond effectively to the challenges of global markets. Neoliberal logic, I argue, is influencing the way political reason relates to crises through the redemarcation of political space within and beyond the national territory. The political exception is increasingly deployed by many Asian states not to deny civil rights but to create regulation spaces of political economic experimentation. I also discuss the adoption of zoning technologies by the Chinese government for a creative respatialization of the national territory and for the realignment of mainland enclaves with various Chinese-dominated political entities overseas. China's Special Economic Zones (SEZs) and Special Administrative Regions (SARs) are the outcomes of a distinctive reterritorialization of the national space to develop sites of capitalist growth, but they also foster conditions of possibility for a potential political absorption of Taiwan. The zoning modality may have influence on the Korean peninsula as well.

Rethinking Sovereignty

Scholarship on sovereignty is still dominated by efforts to match specific nation-states to ideal-types of political orders: the Westphalian, liberal, or antiutopian models. Such views stem from adhering too closely to the Weberian model of the modern liberal state, that is, that these states rest on a bureaucratic administrative order which holds a legitimate and legal monopoly on the use of power.[3] This formulation has been recast in rigid terms by Anthony Giddens, who maintains that "the modern-nation state is a power-container whose administrative purview corresponds exactly to its territorial delimitation."[4] These views continue to be productive and relevant as particular expressions or problems of sovereignty. Indeed, the 2003 U.S. attack on Iraq is a useful reminder of the military power behind U.S. sovereignty. In East Asia, the container model of national sovereignty[5] has shaped the model of that Asian developmental state as epitomized by Japan and, until recently, South Korea, whereby government-business collaborations pursue structural change as a form of legitimation or as a national project.[6] Ironically, the original "developmental state" was the Soviet Union, which undertook the overall development of the country as an overriding national project. This socialist developmental model shaped China's modus operandi until the late 1970s. The developmental state is now synonymous with the new Asian capitalist powerhouses of Japan, South Korea, and Taiwan. This Northeast Asian state-directed capitalism is widely assumed to be the Asian model of state form, when in actuality the specific forms and articulations between state authorities and capitalist actors are rather diverse in terms of the institutions involved. For instance, there are striking differences in developmental state action between Northeast and Southeast Asian nations when it comes to state-business ties.[7]

It seems fruitful therefore to open up another line of inquiry, one that treats the state not as a political singularity but as an ever shifting assemblage of planning, operations, and tactics increasingly informed by neoliberal reason to combat neoliberal forces in the world at large. Thus while Asian states have been formally categorized by the Western media as "socialist," "authoritarian," and "social democratic," they can be highly variable and pragmatic in practice, responding swiftly and opportunistically to dynamic market conditions. In the previous chapter, I used the term "graduated sovereignty" to identify the rescaling of state power across the national landscape and the differential scales of regulation on diverse groups of citizens and foreigners.

This view of sovereignty—not as a uniform effect of state rule but as the contingent outcomes of various strategies—also informs my analysis of China. In the transition from a centrally planned economy to capitalist development, the Chinese state devised various strategies to address rather specific problems of capitalist development that will also contribute to the political imperative to reunite with breakaway territories. Strategies of reterritorialization become vital not only in stimulating markets in border zones but also in accommodating spaces of variegated governance. Obviously, the point is not to judge sovereign power by some formulaic or container view of sovereignty but to adjust our analytical tools to examine various instruments and procedures of governing.

Technologies of Ruling and of Exception

A view of government as practical rationality shows that the state of sovereignty or sociopolitical order is the contingent product of varied technologies that define, discipline, and regulate individual and collective life in a nation. This formulation suggests that, first, sovereign power depends on a network of regulatory entities that channel, correct, and scale human activities in order to produce effects of social order.[8] Narrowly defined "political" activities (e.g., elections, crackdowns, military actions) are merely one set of elements shaping conditions of ruling and political normativity. A more broadly based notion of politics includes the diverse and run-of-the-mill activities that exercise political power beyond the state. My focus is thus on technologies and procedures "that happen to be available, in which new ways of governing were invented in a rather ad hoc way, as practical attempts to think about and act upon specific problems in particular locales."[9] The exercise of power depends on a variety of technologies that target populations as well as territory in order to solve problems of wealth, growth, and security.

In the second half of the twentieth century, market calculations began to inform many areas of political rationality and action in emergent Asian countries. In the 1960s, at the behest of the World Bank, developing countries were encouraged to create suitable sociopolitical conditions and infrastructures for linking up with the world economy. By the 1970s and 1980s, export-industrialization programs shaped the political goals and justification of governments throughout Northeast and Southeast Asia. The marriage of market logic and authoritarian rule gave rise to the so-called Asian tigers—South Korea, Taiwan, Hong Kong, Singapore, and Malaysia. Neoliberal logic—which is abstractable, mobile, and dynamic—becomes embedded in Asian technocrats' vision of how to reorganize society, space, and individual attitudes in order to meet global competition. The economic boom went into a tailspin with the Asian financial crisis, but state planners and entrepreneurial citizen-subjects soon regirded themselves for conditions of freer access and greater risk. A study of shifting technologies of ruling captures this contingent and fluid nature of state sovereign practices that continually adjust and negotiate disruptions, upheavals, and crises. Changes in governing tactics are occasioned not only from the outside—by financial crisis, natural disaster, or insurrection—but also from within state sovereignty itself.

Carl Schmitt defines "sovereignty" as ultimately the power to call a state of exception to the normalized condition or the law. This bipolar formulation of sovereignty-exception seeks to capture the dynamic quality of sovereignty as the strategic and situational exercise of power in response to crises that threaten the integrity of the state.[10] Schmitt theorizes that a state capable of realistic response must be resolute in combating threats, and that sovereign exception even to suspend basic rights could be justified to preserve political unity and stability.[11] One need not agree with Schmitt's political stance to find his concept of the exception useful for analyzing contemporary state action that deviates from standard sovereign operations and legal normativity. The sovereign exception that I am interested in here is not the negative exception that suspends civil rights for some but rather positive kinds of exception that create opportunities, usually for a minority, who enjoy political accommodations and conditions not granted to the rest of the population. The positive exception is now invoked, especially in bureaucratically centralized societies, in order to allow privileged groups to face the challenges of globalization.

Indeed, the recent shift toward regional formations has come about through a series of political exceptions that allow governments to rethink the contours of sovereign power in relation to other sovereign entities. The construction of the EU is predicated on a series of positive exceptions enacted by individual governments to transfer aspects of sovereignty power to a higher centralized authority in Brussels. This form of regionalization opens up circulations of capital and labor, increasing opportunities for privileged Europeans to become more competitive in global markets. John Ruggie attributes the emerging architecture of the EU to a process of "unbundling" territory and sovereignty. Governments disaggregate different components of power —fiscal policies, security measures, etc.—and give up certain controls for the governance of overlapping national spaces.[12] Similarly, Stephen Krasner maintains that states in Eastern Europe have solved specific problems stemming from conflicting claims to authority by disaggregating sovereignty through the creation of various semiautonomous, semi-independent, and semilegal entities.[13] Saskia Sassen argues that globalization has led to "a partial denationalization of national territory and a partial shift of some components of state sovereignty to other institutions, from supranational entities to the global capital market."[14] Concepts of unbundling, disaggregation, and denationalization describe the administrative mechanisms that created EU regionalization, but these terms, with their assumptions of "giving up" parts of sovereign power, do not quite fit the rather different sovereign thinking and practices in East Asia, even though they are also responding to the challenges of neoliberalism.

The logic of exception deployed in the construction of the Chinese axis is marked more by a flexibility of state practices than by the unbundling or disaggregation of powers. In 1972, the Chinese state spectacularly invoked an exception to the normativity of socialist centralized planning. One may argue that the introduction of market reforms was a response to the political crisis of socialist backwardness, but a state of exception legitimized capitalist transformation without jeopardizing the political legitimacy and order of the socialist regime. China's opening (*kaifang*) and market reform policies have relied not on unbundling or denationalizing sovereignty but on the production of new spaces of exception and border-crossing powers. Post-Mao state strategies have displayed a flexibility and creativity in creating new capitalist spaces where none existed before on the socialist mainland. By examining the various technologies that zone land and mobilize economic resources at a distance while accommodating political entities, we capture a dynamic process of sovereignty often ignored in studies that assess sovereignty in terms of broad "liberal," "democratic," or "authoritarian" labels.

Zoning Technologies

A school of thought now reconceptualizing the relationship between politics and technology holds that the circulation of technical practices and standards create "technological zones," or overlapping political spaces of technological normativity.[15] One example is the EU, a region of multiple technological zones of uniform standardization, say, for the protection of intellectual property, or for the preparation of food for human consumption. My approach to zoning technologies, however, is about a slightly different phenomenon, or a more extreme form of zoning practice that creates spatially fixed and distinctive enclaves. "Zoning technologies" refers to political plans that rezone the national territory. The technologies of governing are the instrumentalization of a form of market-driven rationality that demarcates spaces, usually nonadjacent to each other, in order to capitalize on specific locational advantages of economic flows, activities, and linkages. By deploying zoning strategies, sovereign states can create or accommodate islands of distinct governing regimes within the broader landscape of normalized rule. The political outcome is an archipelago of enclaves, the sum of which is a form of variegated sovereignty.

Economic enclaves are not a new phenomenon, having their origins in Western colonial practices that created special treaty ports and customs areas in dominated lands, including China. In Asia, the first modern free trade zone (or EPZ, Export-Processing Zone) in Asia was established in Kaoshiung, Taiwan, in the mid-1960s. Under the promptings of the United Nations Industrial Development Organization and the World Bank, export-processing zones subsequently proliferated throughout Asia, as well as in Latin America and in the Middle East. The EPZ is a combination of old customs areas and export-oriented manufacturing. Thus EPZs combine tax-free holidays with other incentives for foreign investors to set up factories that produce export goods, train low-skill workers, and facilitate technology transfer.[16] The EPZ strategy succeeded export-substitution industrialization in developing countries, driven by the pursuit of foreign exchange earnings. In the initial decades of export-industrialization, EPZs were given a free hand to exploit abundant low-wage workers, most of whom were female. From South Korea to the Philippines to Malaysia, union organization among zone workers was routinely harassed by the police. These export zones were the sites of sustained labor struggles to combat industrial oppression and to raise wages; these zone-based struggles resulted in gradually improved living conditions for the new industrial workers in the Asian tiger economies.[17] Within two decades, the labor and technological gains in EPZs consolidated the industrial foundation of "authoritarian developmental states" such as South Korea, Taiwan, Singapore, and Malaysia. Larger transnational zones (so-called growth triangles) have been set up in Southeast Asia. In short, created by an act of exception, the free trade or export-processing zone "is like a country within a country,"[18] a technology that over time spreads its industrial, labor, and social gains throughout the nation.

Rezoning China

Learning from economic enclaves elsewhere in Asia, China has developed distinctive zoning technologies that create the forms for alignment of the mainland with overseas Chinese–dominated polities in an archipelago of variegated sovereignty. By invoking the exception, the Chinese state is creating far-flung economic and political zones that are marked off from the normativity established elsewhere in the planned socialist environment.

Economic Zones : The open policy called for the establishment of new "Hong Kongs" along the Chinese border to facilitate contact with foreign Chinese capitalist communities. Deng Xiaoping considered SEZs to be both an economic bridge and a political window on the outside world. Different kinds of zones were established in several steps throughout the 1980s and 1990s (see table 1).[19] The first decade saw the creation of major border SEZs, "open" coastal cities: Shenzhen adjacent to Hong Kong; Zhuhai across from Macao; Xiamen across the strait from Taiwan; and Shantou and Hainan, which have strong traditional connections to Chinese communities in Southeast Asia. Once market development in the coastal sites gained momentum, dozens of free trade zones, special economic and high-tech industrial enclaves, as well as tourist sites were located in interior cities to attract foreign exchange and accelerate inland development.

Four goals dictated political conditions in these zones: to attract and utilize foreign capital; to forge joint ventures and partnerships between mainlanders and foreigners; to produce wholly export-oriented goods; and to let market conditions (i.e., not politics) drive economic activity.[20] To realize the fourth goal, special managerial systems and labor service companies allow more flexible labor contracts and costs and impose less bureaucratic red tape than elsewhere in China. As some scholars have noted, SEZs have evolved into a unique system not only for export-oriented industrialization but also for spearheading the transformation of socialist China into a market economy.[21]

There are important aspects to SEZs that go beyond the conventional functions of EPZs elsewhere in East Asia. The location of SEZs in Guangdong and Fujian Provinces shows the government's interest in attracting investors from neighboring Chinese polities. Article 1 of the Regulations on Special

Table 1. Major Forms of Zoning in China

MAJOR BORDER ZONES

1980s Special Economic Zones (SEZs)
  — Shenzhen, Zhuhai, Shantou, Xiamen, and Hainan Island
1990s Open Coastal Cities (14)
  — Dalian, Shanghai, Wenzhou, Guangzhou, Beihai, and others

OPEN COASTAL BELTS
  — Yangtze River Delta; Pudong New Area (international investments)
  — Pearl River Delta (mainly Hong Kong–based investments)
  — Xiamen-Zhangzhou-Quanzhou Triangle (mainly Taiwan investments)
  — Shantung Peninsula, Liadong Pen., Hebei, Guangxi

SPECIAL ADMINISTRATIVE ZONES
  — 1997 Hong Kong SAR
  — 1999 Macao SAR

DOMESTIC INTERIOR ZONES, 1990S
  — hinterland provincial cities
  — 15 FTZs, 32 state-level economic and technology zones
  — 53 high-tech industrial development zones in large and medium cities
  — numerous tourist zones

Economic Zones in Guangdong Province, passed by the National People's Congress in 1980, proclaimed that "the special zones shall encourage foreign citizens, overseas Chinese and compatriots from Hongkong and Macao and their companies and enterprises (hereafter referred to as 'investors') to set up factories and establish enterprises and other undertakings, with their own investment or in joint ventures with our side, and shall, in accordance with the law, protect their assets, the profits due them and their other lawful rights and interests."[22] Besides gaining from overseas Chinese capital and expertise,[23] SEZs along the coast quickly lessened economic and income differences between the mainland and neighboring areas with which China seeks eventual political unification.

SEZs can also act as controlled spaces for dealing with social discontent and labor unrest that market reforms might provoke. The economic linkages, wealth, and capitalist experiments in SEZs also have served explicit political goals by managing the integration of Hong Kong, Macao, and Taiwan with mainland China. SEZs are also different from EPZs in that they enjoy a wider array of powers, including substantial autonomy for the local creation of business opportunities, as well as simplified administrative regulations for planning, banking, and insurance. These specialized areas report directly to the central authorities in Beijing on economic and administrative matters. Political order within the zones and open cities promote freewheeling entrepreneurial activities and labor exploitation to a degree not allowed in the rest of China. Unlike state enterprise workers, who are highly organized under the All China Federation of Trade Unions, zone workers are considered peasants unprotected by China's labor laws and are not entitled to social benefits due workers elsewhere in the country.[24] Under the SEZ law, the staff and workers employed by enterprises in these territories are to be managed by the enterprises according to their business requirements and, when necessary, may be dismissed, after going through the procedures provided in the labor contracts.[25]

Not only are migrant workers exposed to the full force of market conditions; they are discriminated against by zone authorities as if they were foreigners. Migrants must obtain a border pass, a work permit, and a temporary resident pass to work in the SEZs. In effect, zone workers, the majority of whom are rural women working under highly exploitative conditions, are systematically ignored by unionized workers in the rest of China. As rural migrants, they are not entitled to urban citizenship and the residential rights, education for their children, and access to various subsidies that such citizenship entails.[26] The massive influx of the "floating population," much of it young and female, supplies the SEZs with cheap labor for huge factories producing consumer goods for the global economy.

SEZs in China developed rapidly, especially after the Tiananmen crackdown in 1989, when a tidal wave of investment from overseas Chinese communities exceeded investments from Japan. By the early 1990s, SEZ-driven capitalist enterprises became synonymous with building connections with overseas Chinese. Under the banner of "Let Overseas Chinese Build Bridges, Let Them Create Prosperity!," newspaper articles reported that almost a half million Shanghainese had overseas connections, forming "a large invisible bridge" with Chinese capital from abroad.[27] In SEZs, local Chinese officials set up tens of thousands of township and village enterprises (TVEs) that bring together overseas Chinese capital and expertise with abundant cheap labor and land on the mainland. These hybrid enterprises are the nodes of cross-border production networks that strengthen Hong Kong's role as the gateway to China.

The pairing of the Shenzhen SEZ with Hong Kong is an especially apt example of how interactive zones across political borders act as both a hinge — linking socialist and capitalist spaces — and as a bridge — channeling actors, resources, and skills across zones.[28] Shenzhen, a village across the border of Hong Kong in the 1980s, has mushroomed into a Wild West frontier city with millions of inhabitants, becoming the mainland extension for Hong Kong business and industrial enterprises, as well as a center to screen out undesirable migrants for the metropolis. Tens of thousands of Hong Kong–based factories moved into Guangdong Province, and by the 1990s the Pearl River Delta had become an industrial extension of Hong Kong. Here Hong Kong managers train millions of poor rural women in manufacturing "the South China miracle."[29] Hong Kong's goal to become "the Manhattan of Asia" entails using Shenzhen to filter out poor working families from the rest of China, and as a place to dump the working poor who can no longer afford Hong Kong's stratospheric real estate prices. Meanwhile, Hong Kong's sophisticated and bilingual expertise in legal, financial, and business services is crucial to linkages between the mainland and global corporations and to translating foreign products and practices for mainland use.[30]

In coastal cities, expatriate Chinese are well-represented in all sectors vital to the mainland economy, especially business services, finance, manufacturing, transportation, and hotel management. The formation of the Xiamen-centered coastal belt to attract Taiwanese capital led to a frenzy of cross-strait economic activity. SEZ policies give local officials autonomy in forming joint ventures with foreigners, as well as in retaining revenues at the local levels. Taiwanese investors, capitalizing on ethnic and linguistic ties, forged interpersonal relations (*guanxi*) with local officials who further eased bureaucratic rules on tariffs.[31] With the formation of the Xiamen-Zhangzhou-Quanzhou Triangle, Taiwan has solidified its status as a major industrial power, as indexed by its thirty-odd intelligent industrial parks clustered around Hsinchu. These science parks maintain important technical, economic, and personal relationships with Silicon Valley firms, but Taiwanese industrialists have built thousands of factories in the greater Xiamen area. Most of the products manufactured in the Xiamen-Zhangzhou-Quanzhou Triangle are machinery, electrical goods, metals, and textiles.

Besides the Pearl River Delta complex and the Xiamen Triangle, the Yangtze River Delta as an open zone seeks to turn Shanghai, with its new financial center in Pudong, into the "dragonhead" of Chinese development. Shanghai is the leading center of Chinese capitalism, with a huge Western presence in commerce, manufacturing, and finance. In contrast to the other SEZs, where the emphasis is on low-tech processing firms and cheap labor, Shanghai and its surroundings are to become urban jewels in the Chinese capitalist crown, the sites of a stock market, high-technology, and business glamour. For instance, Western business schools and U.S. managers in Shanghai are seeking to transform white-collar Chinese workers into global corporate players. Meanwhile, Singaporean technocrats have been recruited to build Silicon Valley–style industrial parks in Suzhou and Wuxi. Singapore authorities act as both middlemen and guides in creating a new kind of industrial zone where conditions of doing business, living, and working adhere to certain technical standards. The goal is to transform Suzhou Township into a world-class industrial city with landscaped, tree-lined boulevards, an international school, and a strict balance between industrial and residential areas.[32] However, the implementation of Singapore's technocratic practices and norms — in building codes, water treatment, traffic controls, and so on — has been frustrated by the weakness of Chinese administrative and regulatory bodies overseeing the enclaves. Suzhou authorities learned the business benefits of zoning and started building competing industrial zones that lure foreign businesses with lower rents and free advertisements. Nevertheless, the autonomy given to business and administrative activities in these zones has engendered dense transnational business networks and more comfortable living conditions than can be found elsewhere in China.

Thanks to SEZs and open cities, sizable professional and business classes have emerged on the mainland, with growing connections to overseas Chinese locations. Free trade zones in Taiwan, Singapore, and Hong Kong exchange personnel, knowledge, and technology with SEZs in China. Singapore, and to a lesser extent Hong Kong, have been recruiting thousands of students, professors, and scientists from the mainland to work in universities and science parks in these cities (see chap. 8). Thousands of mainland Chinese travel to Southeast Asia to learn English, in the hope of eventually testing into universities in the West. The two-way flows of professional and business classes between China and overseas Chinese communities have created complex networks that amount to a de facto transborder integration of the socialist mainland with overseas Chinese capitalist citadels at the scientific, business, and personal levels. In short, the coastal zone authorities and open cities are spaces of exception to the centrally planned socialist economy. They enjoy autonomy in all economic and administrative matters in order to attract foreign investment and create jobs for millions of migrant workers and city

Table 2. Exceptions to the Centrally Planned Socialist System

---

I. ECONOMIC ZONES: Special Economic Zones, Open Coastal Cities, Open
Coastal Belts
  Powers and Privileges: Autonomy in all economic and administrative matters; exemptions from socialist central planning and regulation of investment and labor
  issues; market conditions determine wages and work conditions

II. ADMINISTRATIVE ZONES: Hong Kong SAR, Macao SAR
  Powers and Privileges: Mini-constitution or basic law for full-fledged capitalist
  activities; independent judiciary, executive and legislative Councils; democratic
  elections of all officials, except the chief executive; and freedom of speech
  (exemptions from mainland socialist laws governing national security are being
  politically contested)

Source: "Hong Kong Special Administrative Region," www.china.org.cn/english/feature/38096.htm

dwellers. Released from socialist practices governing labor, market conditions are allowed to determine wages and work conditions. Economic dynamism has greatly intensified social inequalities among the populations within
zones, as well as between the coastal areas and Chinese society at large. Zone
autonomy creates conditions of total market freedom but without the democratic rights that were demanded in Hong Kong on the eve of its return to
mainland rule (see table 2).

Administrative Zones : In the mid-1990s, the "one country, two systems"
policy created the Special Administrative Region for the reabsorption of formerly colonized or breakaway territorial possessions (Hong Kong, Macao,
Taiwan). Thus, while SEZs were intended to intensify cross-border networks
and economic integration, and the SARs are a formal accommodation of
different political entities, the synergy generated between the two zoning
systems is creating a kind of regionalization that makes political unification of
China and its breakaway parts inevitable.

Great Britain and the People's Republic of China, with minimal consultation of Hong Kong's people, negotiated the Basic Law of the Hong Kong
Special Administrative Region (HKSAR), a mini-constitution that allows "a
high degree of autonomy," so that the city's capitalist system and way of life
can continue for fifty years.[33] Thus, the SAR zoning system allows for Hong
Kong (and Macao) to return to Chinese sovereignty and yet maintain a legal

exception — specifically, a democratic way of life — to the rest of centrally planned socialist China. Under the Basic Law, Hong Kong leaders, not mainland officials, will serve in the government. HKSAR fully enjoys the power of decision over matters within its autonomous jurisdiction — executive and legislative councils, an independent judiciary, and final adjudication powers. The democratic structure of SAR governance is compromised by Beijing's appointment of the government's chief executive, Tung Chee Hwa (see table 2). Thus, Hong Kong returned to Chinese rule with a newly feisty Legislative Council intent on keeping democratic rights given to Hong Kong during the last decade of British rule (the first free elections in 150 years of British colonization were held in 1991). Many have seen the SARs model as a test case for the eventual reunification of Taiwan with China.

The SAR framework allows for experimentation with different degrees of civil rights in a vibrant capitalist setting, a milieu that acts as a laboratory for China's future. The strategic deployment of two zoning technologies — SEZs and open cities, on the one hand, and special administrative entities, on the other — has produced a system of variegated sovereignty or a mix of regional autonomy and centralized controls. As table 2 illustrates, SEZs enjoy more limited autonomous powers than do SARs. SEZs are technically an economic exception to socialist central planning and enjoy autonomy mainly in market and market-related activities in order to freely develop capitalism on the mainland, with the help of overseas Chinese and other foreign investors. Nevertheless, open economic areas contribute to political integration by strengthening legal procedures and practices that support transnational economic activities and relationships.

SARs are fundamentally in a state of political exception. These administrative zones possess their own mini-constitutions, independent political institutions, and judiciaries. Furthermore, a spectrum of democratic rights allows for free elections and freedom of expression, at least for the immediate future. In brief, then, SEZs represent particular orders of economic and administrative autonomy within centrally planned socialist China. SARs, in contrast, are unique orders of political autonomy within a flexible arrangement of one country, two systems. In practical terms, SEZs overlap substantially with the spaces of SARs, creating spaces of variegated sovereignty based on the synergy between untrammeled capitalist activities and electoral democracy within the body of socialist China. At the same time, these exceptional spaces are vital nodes in dense networks connecting the mainland to Taiwan and Singapore, allowing an axis of variegated sovereignty to come into being. As the Chinese leaders themselves have always indicated, "one China, two systems" is a temporary arrangement to facilitate reunification. The overlapping economic and administrative enclaves have created an institutional detour for incremental but eventual political integration, as well as sites for experimentation in civil society outside China proper.

A Detour on the Road to Political Integration?

In June 2003, six years after Hong Kong was returned to Chinese sovereign control, the city and the mainland signed the Closer Economic Partnership Arrangement as a step toward even greater economic integration. The agreement gives Hong Kong–based banks and companies market access to the mainland. Tariffs on hundreds of Hong Kong products have been removed, giving the city's economy an immediate boost following the outbreak of severe acute respiratory syndrome (SARS). The trade agreement is an economic gift to sweeten the simultaneous imposition of a new national security law to curb sedition and other crimes against the Chinese state. This state intervention into the SAR political environment triggered a demonstration on July 1 by a half million Hong Kong residents who wanted to uphold the policy of one country, two systems. To prodemocracy groups such as the Human Rights Monitor, the free trade pact is a kind of payback for business leaders in the Hong Kong government who have gone along with the steady erosion of civil rights, especially in journalism and the media.

The new security measure, Article 23 of the Basic Law, seeks to repress activities such as "subversion," "secession," and the leaking of state secrets, crimes similar to the "counterrevolutionary activities" banned on the mainland. The antisedition bill allows the police to search homes without a warrant, the government to ban groups already outlawed in the mainland, and the courts to impose heavy penalties for the "theft of state secrets."[34] Adopting the measure curbs the freedoms that permit diverse viewpoints, activities, and nonmainstream political groups to flourish in Hong Kong, thus bringing the SAR political order closer to that of the mainland.[35]

Although much of the Western press has viewed the street protests as a sign of democratic resistance, it is also important to situate the massive unrest in the context of steady economic decline since 1997. The Beijing-appointed chief executive was widely viewed by Hong Kong residents, rightly or wrongly, as an inept leader and a symbol of bad luck for the economy, and subsequently replaced. In addition to the financial crisis, property prices have plummeted, salaries and budgets have been cut, and unemployment is at an all-time high. The slow response to the SARS outbreak, which killed around three thousand people in the territory, further damaged the economy. Economic unease has been deepened by a pervasive sense that Shanghai is pulling ahead as China's economic engine, and that Singapore is displaying more efficiency in planning for and dealing with economic crises. Thus, street demonstrations reflected a massive discontent over the state of the Hong Kong economy and worries about a future further constrained by antisedition laws. Blaming prodemocracy groups, Beijing appeared to adopt a wait-and-see attitude and continue to uphold the "one country, two systems" policy, since the variegated sovereignty it accommodates seems a practical and coolheaded route to gradual political integration.

In short, special autonomous regions are testing sites for the controlled expression of civil rights in a Chinese market context. Its SAR framework has allowed Hong Kong to remain the freest economy in the world and to experiment with different degrees of political freedom that test socialist worries over national security. Hong Kong may never submit entirely to mainland forms of political control, but it must be noted that political practices in China proper are themselves undergoing transformation, as evidenced by the hands-off reaction to the massive dissent in Hong Kong, and by the limited response to worker demonstrations in SEZs. Thus, politically speaking, both kinds of economic and political spaces have instances of sovereign exception that contrast sharply with the political normativity in China. The Hong Kong demonstrations have proved not the weakness but the flexibility of the intertwined zoning systems, which can accommodate variations in degrees of civil liberty across sites.

Chinese sovereignty is basically legitimized by opening channels for cross-border trade, not by opening channels for civil rights. Problems of government are increasingly solved through the deployment of intellectual and practical techniques that foster economic success by opening up economies rather than political spaces. But market liberalism fostered through zoning practices can safely accommodate pockets of agitation for civil rights, allowing the kind of experimentation that is not easily tolerated in mainland China. New democratic forces in economic zones and in Hong Kong (and Taiwan) that have emerged with the growth of cosmopolitan classes coexist with the normative centralized regulation of populations in the name of national security. There is a new alignment between national security and economic freedom, but exuberant political freedom can only be permitted, and occasionally challenged, in special zones and regions. Zoning technologies seem the best technical mechanism for creating controlled spaces of economic and political experimentation that do not threaten collective and national security. The SAR mechanism thus becomes a detour—through the development of capitalist networks and the tolerance of civil rights demands—on the road to eventual political integration. The huge protests of Hong Kong citizens against the new internal security law did not fend off greater political integration, and Hong Kong is already firmly tethered in the business, technology, and personal networks that integrate it into the Chinese axis.

Finally, it is important to note that there are strong and weak links among the spaces of exception, open cities, and countries. The conditions secured by the economic and political spaces foster economic and communication links with mainland China. But even though Taiwan is not a SAR, the island has been drawn into mainland sites through Hong Kong and Macau. Beyond the zones themselves, the mobilization of resources and expertise from a large number of overseas sites supports a geometric increase in economic activities. With the entry of China into the World Trade Organization (WTO), the commercial, technological, service, and personal links among various ethnic Chinese places will only intensify across the region.

Sovereignty and Security: The Ethics of Exception

A dominant view of sovereignty and security maintains that governments operate along the lines of "organized hypocrisy," whereby states act in terms of their own specific interests even when they violate international rules.[36] This notion seems to be a rough translation of Carl Schmitt's concept of the exception that Stephen Krasner transposes to the international arena. One notes that the Chinese state often invokes the ethics of the exception (i.e., in the name of collective or national security) to legitimize crackdowns on dissidents, as in the Tiananmen Square incident and the banning of groups such as the Falun Gong. That practice is, of course, not exclusive to governments in Asia: we have witnessed the scaling back of civil rights in the United States as part of its government's response to the war on terrorism. But what seems interesting in China is that such exceptions to the law are increasingly made in settings of open economic borders and networks that heighten the tensions between economic freedom and political repression. The exceptions have become routine during orchestrated crises (e.g., the need for market reforms) and during unplanned ones (the outbreak of infectious diseases); technocrats

have become increasingly adept at keeping borders open to economic activities and networks while closing borders to political freedom, information,
and interconnection. This nexus between sovereignty and security in an open
economy therefore requires observers to go beyond a strictly military understanding of security to consider how questions of national security can be
handled not only by wielding military weapons but also by signing trade
pacts. Let us consider how my point about zoning technologies as a detour
on the road to political integration suggests alternative avenues for reconciliation in divided nations.

I suggest that one path for a Taiwan-China rapprochement runs through
ASEAN. Viewed from the lens of exception, one is surprised not so much by
the saber rattling across the strait as by the innumerable exceptions that have
allowed Taiwan to participate in zone developments and to develop networks
with sites throughout China. Politically Taiwan may be on the outs, but
economically it is a key player embedded in the economic and social fabric of
Chinese capitalist modernity. At the same time, Taiwan has sought to participate in China's markets by inveigling itself into multilateral organizations
that have relationships with the mainland. ASEAN is a ten-member group of
Southeast Asian nations that is increasingly repositioning itself in relation to
China and Japan. Since the 1990s, ASEAN has used a broad conceptualization
of regional security based on building regional economic networks that can
create greater opportunities for citizens in the region. Since the financial crisis
of 1997–98, there has been greater stress on making a broader coalition called
ASEAN + 3 (including China, Japan, and South Korea) or ASEAN + 4 (including them and Australia). What we see is a postimperial economic integration
of a region of more than a billion people, in thirteen or more countries, that
hopes to move in the direction of a common market and a common regional
currency within a decade. Taiwan is conspicuously absent in this lineup, but
not for want of trying. Indeed, the turn of the century was an especially tense
moment of saber rattling when outgoing Taiwanese president Lee Teng-hui
announced a "two states" theory to replace the "one China" policy. Subsequent claims by his successor Chen Shui-bian for "state-to-state" relations
with China intensified the dispute. Much attention has been given to the
triangular balancing of power between China, Japan, and the United States as
a way to contain Chinese aggression against Taiwan. Meanwhile, in addition
to the U.S. security umbrella, Taiwan wants the ASEAN Regional Forum to
provide a form of security against possible Chinese attacks.

But the ASEAN stress on the humanization of security and common regional destiny suggests another pathway for building political bridges. The new "security culture"[37] still operates according to the principles of consensus, consultation, and limited interference in member countries' domestic affairs. Norms associated with the "ASEAN Way" have allowed the organization to bridge political differences and to include formerly shunned states such as Cambodia and Myanmar. As far-flung places are drawn into ever widening networks of securitization, ASEAN and the Chinese axis of common economic interests help to deflect or to circumvent political conflicts, especially between China and Taiwan. Taiwan's formal membership in ASEAN is out of the question because of China's sensitivity, but by working from the backdoor Taiwan has already developed extensive informal economic relations with ASEAN members such as Singapore and the Philippines. Taiwan promotes itself as vital to peace and prosperity in East Asia and as a successful model of transition to political democracy, market economy, and civic society, unlike countries dominated by one-party rule. Despite its marginal position in relation to ASEAN + 3, Taiwan is already deeply interconnected with neighboring Asian countries. Furthermore, China's membership in the WTO has ended limits on direct travel and trade between China and Taiwan, allowing the island to play a bigger role in providing business-oriented research to the mainland. Conditions for a new kind of cultural rapprochement across the strait therefore will be in place even as China becomes more integrated into the global community.

The Chinese axis is also an imaginary line of cultural sovereignty that runs along an ideological plane of the graduated geopolitical field. As technological and commercial networks and economic zones increasingly articulate along a Chinese axis, we see an emerging political archipelago that suggests the wider possibilities of an "imagined community."[38] This loose alliance suggests a regional patterning anchored in China that is very different from Western discourses of regionalism such as the "Pacific Rim."[39] Instead, regional narratives increasingly invoke "East Asia," a rhetorical term that signals the growing connections between the Sinic parts of Southeast Asia (Singapore, Malaysia, Thailand, and the Philippines) with Taiwan, the Hong Kong SAR, and mainland China. For instance, overseas Chinese scholars have invoked a confluence of histories, languages, cultural, and kinship practices among widely dispersed sites to define an emerging field of Sino–Southeast Asian studies.[40] Despite ongoing political tensions and opposition to Beijing leaders, ethnic Chinese in the Asia-Pacific take great cultural pride in the emergence of China as a global actor. The imagined axis also creates an ideological space of exception within the Asia-Pacific, marking off a space of rising China-centric hegemony. The Sinocentric discourses, further enhanced by the mainland and Hong Kong popular media, are growing even as the People's Republic of China and the Republic of China remain in a standoff. Meanwhile, the economic integration between Taiwan and the mainland, especially in Fujian Province, Shanghai, and the Yangtze Valley, is so advanced that a de facto absorption has taken place even before a formal political integration has begun. Thus, the emergence of a Chinese axis is based on Beijing's very distinctive deployment of zoning technologies, which lay the groundwork for transnational market integration, making intelligible the political and cultural goals of variegated sovereignty in formation. As technologies of ruling, zoning mechanisms become an economic detour leading to broader political integration. It is therefore not unthinkable that the logic of the exception and zoning technologies have shown a path toward the reunification of divided nations.

A Modality for the Two Koreas?

North Korea is slowly emerging from its deep political freeze by building enclaves as stepping stones to further political collaboration and perhaps even reintegration with South Korea. During the 1980s and 1990s, North Korea sought to copy the Chinese zoning programs by setting up free trade zones in the northern cities near the border with Russia and China, but the Raijin-Songbong zone has not really taken off. Much more recently, under the cloud of a nuclear standoff with the United States, two new cross-border zones have been proposed. In June 2003, North Korean and South Korean officials and businessmen broke ground for a joint industrial park in Kaesong, just north of the Demilitarized Zone. About nine hundred South Korean businesses, many of them in textiles and garment manufacturing, have applied for spots in the zone, where they will enjoy cheap labor, tax cuts, and other benefits. The South Korean government and the giant conglomerate Hyundai will help prepare the site, including demining the land before building railway lines to connect the two countries. A more famous special administrative zone, modeled on Shenzhen in China, was also set up in Sinuiji on the Chinese border, where the Yalu River enters the Yellow Sea. The Chinese government is directly involved with business tycoons to oversee the enclave as an alternate space of governance. New business opportunities have drawn South Korean industrialists, who wish to see more zones in the North.

Thus viewed against the background of Chinese zoning practices, especially the dramatic case of Shenzhen–Hong Kong, it becomes clear that semiautonomous zones are not only initial attempts at implementing market-driven exceptions, they are also mechanisms for constructing the infrastructure, industries, and administrative units for possible reunification. The North Korean regime seems to represent a deviant sovereignty that is based on the power to take away life rather than the securitization of the health and well-being of the population. Biopolitical considerations only affect a tiny minority, whereas the majority seems condemned to bare life. The political elite in Pyongyang and privileged workers appear to be the only ones to enjoy a political existence of social benefits and pleasures, while the struggle for sheer survival is the norm for ordinary citizens. In this vast labor camp, the logic of exception creates a zone of living that secures minimal employment and living standards. Here, North Koreans can interact with South Koreans and other foreigners to develop access to external sources of capital, skills, and knowledge. These zones are places where notions of an eventual national reunification can be practically broached and tested, thus eventually creating an alternative imagining of biopolitical governing for the rest of North Korea, as well as suggesting a way to the eventual reunification of the two Koreas. Because these privileged zones are established outside the archipelago of labor camps, the North Korean use of the political exception is a reversal of the Agamben opposition between civilization as normativity, and the death camp as a zone of exception.[41] In theoretical discussions, the logic of the exception has been associated with the suspension of rights and the reduction to bare life, but in contemporary Asian situations, the sovereign exception has created conditions for giving life, freedom, and new political openings. The logic of the exception, for instance, has also allowed the Chinese state to release dissidents from prison camps under the criteria of need for medical treatment abroad.

Conclusion

Government is a problematizing activity that continually shifts the reasoning, techniques, and inventions needed to create the conditions of possibility for economic development, political stability, and regional organization. I have suggested that we go beyond a focus on state institutions to examine how a series of political exceptions in authoritarian and oppressive orders creates a diversity of spaces for experimentation with political freedom and transnational connections. "Market reforms" in mainland China have provided an opening for greater flexibility in sovereign rule, in the astute use of the exception to construct zones that spread economic networks and foster political integration.

Greater China is an axis that has its beginnings in a distinctive strategy of reterritorialization that creates zones of exception to normalized Chinese rule, and thus a detour leading to integration with Hong Kong, Macao, and perhaps eventually Taiwan. The axis of sovereignty and security is not delimited by national borders but increasingly relies on the production of a linked geography of technoindustrial nodes that can circumvent political obstacles and bridge politically divided entities. Elsewhere in mainland Southeast Asia, zoning strategies are building infrastructural-economic connections between former enemy states and economically divided regions. In the Asia-Pacific the innovative use of the logic of the exception to configure a series of political spaces is a dominant response to crises and a common strategy for forging connections of trade and politics.

Finally, it seems important to caution that even though the exceptions that facilitate Greater China have been innovative, one should not assume that the concatenation of zones and networks is a permanent formation. New contingencies or crises can very well bring about a different disarticulation or rearticulation of diverse elements that interact to define conditions of possibility for Chinese sovereign power and its spread of networks overseas. Other constellations of market logic, national security, and technologies may very well bring about other kinds of reterritorialization or remapping of sovereignty, security, and civil liberty in the Asia-Pacific.

PART III

CIRCUITS OF

EXPERTISE

CHAPTER five

Latitudes, or How Markets

Stretch the Bounds of

Governmentality

Mobilities has become a new code word for grasping the global. But the language of mobilities — *flows, deterritorializations, networks* — has inadvertently distracted attention from how the fluidity of markets shapes flexibility in modes of control. It is also surprising how little theorizations about globalization factor in specific networks of capital and labor, or draw insights from transpacific forms to rethink changing patterns of production, labor markets, and labor regimes.[1] Meanwhile, assertions about an empire claim that the mobile multitude of working people across the world can be subsumed under a united front to confront globalized capital.[2] But if the mobilities of capital presuppose the stretching of market power across multiple sites, can we assume a homogenization of labor control and worker politics? Or do transnational economies create striated spaces of production that combine different kinds of labor regimes? In addition, does economic globalization engender conditions for labor resistance on a global scale, as some have claimed, or situated modes of labor control and politics?

In this chapter I argue that capitalist systems are not in a simple transition from a disciplinary to regulatory modes of control. On the contrary, the logic of exception in transnational production permits the institutionalization of ethnic discipline and biopolitical technologies in the same lateral spaces, or *latitudes*. Latitudinal citizenship refers to both the spatialities of market rights and deterritorialized ethnic power to constitute labor relations across national borders. Focusing on capital flows in electronic manufacturing services, I trace the return of post-Fordist sweatshops to North America, as Asian-managed high-tech networks depend on ethnic enclaves where carceral labor practices shape a unified Asian-American ethnicity. While American worker rights have always been a contingent claim, the reemergence of high-tech sweatshops have made these rights even more uncertain, as American electronics workers compete directly with even lower-paid workers in South

China. The mobilities of global capital—in shifting high-tech sweatshops back and forth across the Pacific—define horizontal spaces of market rights that radically challenge territorially based principles of citizenship.

Spatialities and Politics

Nineteenth-century philosophers linked the globalization of commerce and production systems to the creation of a unified space of politics. Two views anticipated the rise of world citizenship. For Kant, international commerce had become the basis for the development of shared values about the unity of humanity, or cosmopolitanism.[3] For Marx and Engels, the internationalization of production systems would incite a worldwide proletarian revolution to establish a true global civil society ensuring universal social equality.[4] Here, we see a conflation of the global scale with a would-be universal citizenship based on values of shared humanity and human equality. But global capitalism at the dawn of the twenty-first century has not uniformly covered the planet, so the ideal of global civil society remains an uncertain project.

Nevertheless, Michael Hardt and Antonio Negri claim that with the "decline of the nation-state" and the "withering of civil society," the ideal of global citizenship is freed from its embedding in biopolitical technologies of national citizenship. In the "Empire" formed by globalized capitalism, the freeing of people from allegiances to particular nationalities creates "the mobile multitude," the antithesis of peoplehood produced by nations. This liberation of the working multitude from the chains of particular territorialized allegiances or carceral logics of sovereignty can constitute a new geography of confrontation with the repressive apparatus of capitalism's Empire.[5] Hardt and Negri make two claims about the changing techniques of labor control and politics of labor mobilization that make possible a counter-Empire of resistance.

First, they maintain that contemporary capitalism operates through "flexible and fluctuating networks" and that the global marketized landscape is becoming "a smooth space of uncoded and deterritorialized flows."[6] But while the geography of capitalism may no longer follow national borders, it is still striated by fluid but highly particularized and coded lateral spaces or latitudes. Consider, for instance, the carefully situated corridors of information technology (IT) that bypass "global cities" such as New York, London, and Tokyo[7]—as well as Silicon Valley (outside the San Francisco Bay Area), Route 128 (outside Boston), and the Research Triangle Park (outside

Raleigh-Durham, North Carolina). A "regional advantage" drawn from the synergy generated by a particular cluster of electronics firms, universities, venture capitalists, and city governments shapes rather specific networks in the information industry.[8] But, I would add, the variability and experimental approach to lateralized market power, while relatively free of sovereign control, is increasingly reliant on ethnicizing networks and practices that link sites and communities, rendering them elements of a highly particularized and symbolically coded latitude. I will argue that post-Fordist ethnicization is a contemporary lateralization of market power that is intertwined with deterritorialized ethnic forms that have come to replace state governmental technology.

Second, Hardt and Negri maintain that globalized capitalism has put into play a transition "from disciplinary society to the society of control," whereby the "carceral logics" of disciplinary institutions and technologies are being left behind as "mechanisms of command become ever more 'democratic,' ever more immanent in the social field, distributed throughout the brains and the bodies of the citizens."[9] But while state technologies may have become less central in labor disciplining, the passage from disciplinary to regulatory forms reflects lineal thinking rather than the actual technologies of governmentality deployed in key areas of globalized capitalism. For instance, global commodity chains for the production of consumer goods are highly dependent on subcontracted Asian factories scattered throughout developing countries that hire workers who are organized by ethnicity and gender. Korean managers run factories that employ Guatemalan women who sew clothing for American corporations like K-Mart, or Korean factories hire Indonesian women to produce Nike shoes. I will argue that latitudinal forms of market governmentality often deploy a mix of regulatory norms and ethnicized modes of labor incarceration. Indeed, Hardt and Negri's claims about the formation of a unified space of counter-Empire blithely neglects analysis of the actual, multiple, and segregated conditions of workers in the Empire's networks. Alternative concepts of the new spatialities of globalization and a situated analysis of labor dynamics are needed.

Latitudinal Citizenship and Ethnic Disciplining

Population flows and transnational market networks redistribute systems of power, creating transnational physical and social structures that stretch the bounds of governmentality, or the governing of conduct toward particular ends.[10] The latitudinal dispersal of managerial governing activities does not mean, however, that we are moving entirely to a society of control.

Gilles Deleuze defines control society as an environment of constant modulation shaped by latitudinal flows in which the human subject is in continuous training and monitored for persistent self-management.[11] Latitudinal citizenship, in other words, is shaped by this capacity to respond continually to the dynamism of the space of flows, to respond quickly and with agility to the ever changing conditions and requirements of market trajectories. Overseas Chinese business networks have long demonstrated border-crossing entrepreneurialism, having developed over time templates for doing business in the Asia-Pacific. Their bilingualism or multilingualism is merely part of their capacity to continually adjust with knowledge, speed, and skill to ever shifting conditions throughout their business networks.[12] David Stark has argued that the new entrepreneurial figure is an individual who possesses "asset ambiguity," by which Stark means the kind of talents that can exploit the blurring of borders between countries, races, skills, and cultural signs.[13] Today, ethnic Chinese merchants and managers are shifting from traditional trades to high-tech production systems that span the Asia-Pacific. They have come to embody the kind of citizenship associated with the society of control, performing the set of attributes that maneuver fluidly and opportunistically in a network of open flows. This regime of control is associated not with fixed personality attributes but with a set of flexible capacities, assets, and potentialities that can be plugged into parallel worlds of the market and technology. I call such calculated versatility in volatility, and flexible attitude and latitude to manipulate various codes and to exert lateral influence across political domains, "latitudinal citizenship." While latitudinal activity is continually monitored, not least by the fluctuating bottom line and unknowable market risks, it is also parasitic on older disciplinary forms.

Contrary to assertions that we have left disciplinary society back in the twentieth century, contemporary transnational production networks are underpinned by carceral modes of labor discipline. Ethnicized production networks depend on disciplinary institutions of ethnic enclaves, factories, and families to instill feminine values of loyalty, obedience, and patience, and to mold docile labor. Thus, disciplinary mechanisms render migrant workers governable in ethnicized ways, providing as well an ethnicizing connection to the agile and entrepreneurial managers who shape the horizontal space of markets. The combination of latitudinal citizenship and ethnicized disciplinary regimes can undermine territorialized rights of citizenship.

For instance, the architecture of electronics-production systems displays a striking interpenetration of high-tech systems with migrant or ethnicized techniques of labor incarceration. The geographical stretching of network economies is thus often accompanied by a temporal stretching, a regression to "older" forms of labor disciplining epitomized by the high-tech sweatshop. Electronics manufacturing operated by Asian managers is dependent on both free-floating market networks and zones of incarcerated labor, so that workers are disciplined both through space and in space. In other words, high-tech production depends not merely on the regulation of migrant flows of managers and professionals; it also requires the ethnicized mobilization of networks and workers in order to respond efficiently to changing market conditions, to monitor economic activity, and to shift among different systems of codes, all the time enforcing ethnic discipline and social cohesion in segregated labor sites. Contrary to expectations that global markets produce globalized conditions for labor solidarity, the deployments of latitudinal citizenship fragment and particularize labor pools.

Furthermore, high-tech production regimes are transpacific in scope, so that high-tech sweatshops in Silicon Valley are pitted against even lower-cost manufacturing sites in China. By coordinating labor discipline in multiple locales of production, Asian managers keep varied labor markets fluid and contingent on shifting labor costs. The temporal uncertainty of employment and the churning up of labor conditions in any particular site radically work against political coherence and worker organization.

Transpacific Ethnicized Networks

The Asia-Pacific is a region where techniques for converting value across various spheres are very challenging, especially for mainstream American managers. But it is also a region where ethnic Chinese entrepreneurs from different countries have a mix of assets built over time that allow them to solve problems of market exchange across long distances, exploiting different regimes of economic worth and profit by crossing borders between nations, economies, cultures, and languages. They can open doors to new places, translate instructions and values from low- to high-end labor markets, and build the institutional bridges necessary for circulating information, capital, goods, and people. For instance, Asian entrepreneurs are the creators and operators of many kinds of transnational networks needed to create regional hubs in Silicon Valley, Vancouver, and Los Angeles. Asian-American companies benefit in the high-tech field from cultural practices and rituals that link them with Taiwanese venture capitalists, thus generating ethnic-specific strands in the industrial-capital circuit. Through these connections, Dell Computer, the world's largest manufacturer of desktop monitors, relies on hundreds of component manufacturers in Taiwan and China. Thus intra-ethnic ideas and practices constitute transnational zones, making these spaces governable according to particular moralized regimes of doing business and labor practices.

Silicon Valley is thus rich in lateral networks of ethnicized power that connect far-flung worksites in Asia with high-tech citadels and migrant en-claves. The high ratio of mobile Asian managers in the electronics industry means that their practices now shape immigrant policies and labor techniques in California. Asian expatriates, many the graduates of American universities, represent one-third of the engineering workforce in leading companies such as Hewlett-Packard and Intel. Many U.S.-trained Asian engineers, program-mers, and venture capitalists contributed to the growth of the industry as a whole. By the turn of the century, almost a third of the chief executive officers were Asian born, and one-quarter of the Valley's businesses were run by Asian Americans. Many of them, formerly employed by the big corporations, have become crucial to the supply chain of the information industry. Immigrants mainly from Taiwan and Hong Kong operate small companies that constitute the local manufacturing base of the globally oriented corporations. In a simi-lar fashion, entrepreneurs from India form transpacific network economies that not only lead to mutual industrial upgrading but also become supply chains for high-tech professionals recruited by Silicon Valley firms through Indian universities and cybercities.[14]

American business opened the door for the influx of Asian engineers, in part in order to lower labor costs during the dot-com boom of the 1990s. The IT lobby (TechNet) pressured Congress to increase the number of temporary employment H-1B visas to over one hundred thousand per year. In 2000, a new law, the American Competitiveness in the Twenty-first Century Act, increased the cap to almost two hundred thousand per year for three years.[15] These regulatory measures thus play an important role in selecting skilled migrants from Asian countries who came to dominate the manufacturing and software portions of the computer industry. Under the H-1B visa program, elite skilled workers were admitted to the country for six years, but they were now free to pursue permanent residency, or "the green card," while working for an American company. The demand for temporary software expertise from India prompted Indian entrepreneurs to set up consulting firms for importing short-term software engineers (see chap. 7). In contrast to the Indian supply of engineering expertise, expatriate Chinese professionals and entrepreneurs tend to focus on establishing transpacific manufacturing activities. AnnaLee Saxenian reports that Taiwanese professionals and managers have started up dozens of public technology companies that rely on ethnic and professional networks to form partnerships with firms in the Hsinchu Industrial Park in Taiwan, creating a process of reciprocal industrial upgrading across the Pacific.[16] Other ethnic Chinese from Hong Kong, Southeast Asia, and China have entered the manufacturing end of the computer industry. The concentration of ethnic Chinese in electronics services and manufacturing means that their activities have shaped a latitudinal space that is governed through ethnicized modes of networking and labor recruitment at both ends, on both sides of the Pacific Ocean. It is not surprising that in the economic recession of George W. Bush's first term, Silicon Valley venture capitalists required new companies to involve Asian networks and gain access to Asian labor markets.

Ethnic Chinese command of the transnationalized electronics industry has placed them at the top of the ethnic hierarchy in California as ideal border-crossing and enterprising citizens vital to American business. The new status of cyberhero (think of Jerry Yang of Yahoo) has recoded ethnic Chinese, endowing them with an honorary whiteness that represents a new form of exclusion, in the same way that the model minority citizen initially excluded non-Asian Americans. Indeed, the mobile Asian-American ideal of honorary whiteness has now become a technique of governmentality and is the flip side of post-Fordist ethnicization.

Ethnic Demimondes

Ethnic enclaves have long been associated with immigrant communities in the United States, but, except in the garment industry, they are not usually associated with high-tech production systems. For instance, Peter Kwong has described enclaves in New York's Chinatown that exploit undocumented immigrants from Fujian, who, burdened with debts to the snakeheads (smugglers), must work punishing hours in substandard jobs for years on end just to repay their passage to the United States. "The ethnic enclave, however, is a trap. Not only are the immigrants doomed to perpetual subcontracted employment, but the social and political control of these enclaves is also subcontracted to ethnic elites, who are free to set their own legal and labor standards for the entire community without ever coming under the scrutiny of U.S. authorities."[17] In other words, the ethnic enclave is an immigrant disciplinary model that allows transnational figures to create conditions of indentured servitude for poor and disenfranchised coethnics. In many cases, unlike ethnic patronage systems of earlier generations of immigrants, contemporary ethnic demimondes are not necessarily a steppingstone to upward mobility. Many unskilled ethnic immigrants are hampered by language barriers and, fearing deportation, have difficulty breaking into the wider, unskilled secondary labor markets. Such workers have no benefits and may as well be working in sweatshops in China or Vietnam.

On the West Coast, ethnic-based industries — garment sweatshops, restaurants, and food-processing centers — have continued to proliferate by employing unregulated labor that can be easily pressured into accepting low wages. This is often the effect of a deep dependence on ethnic networks for jobs, and a tight social control wielded by ethnic power brokers to localize unskilled newcomers as a cheap and highly exploitable labor force. In the Los Angeles area, for instance, ethnic Chinese garment sweatshops have been exposed for hiring illegal immigrants (Asians and Latinos) at three dollars an hour for ten-hour days, with no overtime, sewing designer clothes. In an infamous case uncovered in 1995, an El Monte sweatshop forced Thai and Latino immigrants to work for seventy cents an hour. The Department of Labor estimates that at least 60 percent of the approximately 150,000 garment workers in the Los Angeles area are routinely underpaid, but language barriers between the workers have obstructed union organizing.[18] Immigrant employment networks and ethnic enclaves can exert overwhelming power over coethnics desperate for jobs in familiar situations where good command of English is not a necessity. More recently, ethnicized disciplinary mechanisms associated with the garment industry have migrated to the electronics industry.

Silicon Valley may have been the epicenter of what Ulrich Beck calls "reflexive modernization," a second modernization in which most old industrial superstructures are superseded, and the new ones are highly provisional, risky, and unpredictable.[19] In such dynamic and risky environments, Asian managers of electronics-assembly plants have turned to ethnicized practices to extract labor and constitute governable female labor. After all, the dominance of ethnic Chinese managers in the computer industry is a response to "a gradual but strategically important reconcentration of manufacturing activi-

ties in Silicon Valley."[20] I have examined the post-Fordist migration of electronics manufacturing to exploitable female labor markets in Southeast Asia,
but the return of some manufacturing to California is linked to the creation of
unequal working conditions here as well.[21] This post-Fordist reorganization
relies on flexible and segmented regional production networks that stabilize working conditions and wages below those established under union-
represented, Fordist norms. In other words, the post-Fordist return to the
United States is a process of industrial ethnicization, dependent on Asian
managerial networks and flexible, ethnicized practices of labor mobilization
and disciplining.

Post-Fordism in the United States is a response to the rapidly evolving
electronics consumer markets, in which "hot" products such as personal computers and cellphones can be assembled faster and more conveniently than by
offshore manufacturing. Corporate giants such as Intel, Hewlett-Packard,
and Sun Microsystems therefore turn to Asian contract manufacturers in
Silicon Valley to assemble the networks, workers, and labor conditions for
such just-in-time production. Solectron Corporation of Milpitas, founded by
two Hong Kong expatriates, is the largest contract manufacturing business in
Silicon Valley. Electronics-assembly jobs, already framed overseas as labor-
intensive, low-wage, and female, are similarly coded as female and Asian in
California. To keep up with high demands, manufacturing work is routinely
contracted out to smaller companies operated by Asian managers whose
workers are mainly migrant Asian women. Beyond these high-tech factories,
nonautomated work is sent out through Asian shopfloor workers to largely
nonunionized women who are hired as "temporary workers" for ninety days
and are usually paid at piece rate. They can be hired back with no improvement in wages or in contract security and grievance procedures. Through
a series of ethnicized disciplinary institutions — factory, family — shopfloor
workers and their relatives and friends working at home are drawn into an
ethnic demimonde of docile labor. For the management, ethnicity and gender
are also the means for exercising discipline and forging a unified working-
class Asian-American identity. For diverse Asian immigrants, ethnicity and
gender are the criteria for gaining access to such opportunities. Drawn to
production activity through ethnicized modes of gender control, migrants
are rendered governable as docile and loyal workers.

Disadvantaged female migrants of diverse nationalities and ethnicities —
Cambodians, Laotians, Vietnamese, Burmese, Thai, Chinese — lacking linguistic and other skills in the larger market arena, find an ethnicized channel

to job opportunities in high-tech enclaves. They are disciplined through ethnic norms of unequal reciprocity, respect for male authority, and grateful
tolerance of low wages and routine overtime. The carceral logic of sweatshops and the moralized understanding of employer-employee relationships
interact to constitute a unified ethnic understanding of labor relations among
disparate groups of poor immigrants. A labor organizer said in another context that female Asian workers understand relationships with employers in
kinship terms and are unwilling to criticize employers for fear of losing their
jobs.[22] Vietnamese women feel a personal loyalty to Chinese employers that is
akin to intraethnic solidarity. Indeed, the ethnicization of relationships between workers and managers becomes a necessary condition not only for
long-term employment in the factories but also for women employed at
home to gain access to piecework.

It is estimated that at any time, more than a third of the 120,000 Southeast Asian immigrant population in Northern California is employed assembling printed wire boards.[23] Most are home workers who may enroll other
stay-at-home relatives, and even children, to assemble circuit boards and
other components, which involves using toxic solvents. Home workers make
four to five dollars an hour, or forty to fifty dollars per board, work that
involves fusing components and wiring. The work is sometimes paid by the
piece, such as a penny per transistor, and, even with overtime, workers barely
earn the minimum wage. Piecework is not illegal, but it is subject to overtime
laws. In many cases, workers already employed by the same company at
hourly wages are sent home and paid on a piecework basis. In many such arrangements, the labor practices violate laws governing piecework in the electronics and garment industries. Such home-based workers are often underpaid and do not receive compensation for overtime. Almost a third of all
workers in high-tech manufacturing are now employed on such ambiguous
terms of contract and contingency.

Nevertheless, the home workers are recruited and stay with the jobs
because they have found them through ethnic connections and would otherwise not have work because of their limited language and skills capacity.
Working at the kitchen table also reinforces the women's feminine role of
taking in piecework in order to support their families. Family obligations are
thus enrolled in the ethnicized network of female labor mobilization and
disciplining that induces workers to accept the conditions of a scattered,
invisibilized, and casualized labor force. Finally, the ethnicized moral regime
rewards "good" home workers with more opportunities for batch work and
access to factory jobs.

Asian managers are thus honorary whites not merely because of their transnational value-adding activities but also, ironically, because they are able to wield ethnic governmentality over low-cost female migrant labor and thus contribute to America's ever expanding economy. Latitudinal market powers engender electronic sweatshops, becoming a mechanism for the constitution of a common ethnicized working-class identity among varied Asian-American groups, while excluding others. Scott Lash has argued that the exclusion of African-American inner-city populations from information and communication structures is further intensified by blacks' lack of access to the institutions of civil society.[24] But for many low-skilled Americans, access to ethnic networks and susceptibility to Asian cultural disciplining are necessary to gain employment in high-tech workshops.

The post-Fordist ethnicization of computer manufacturing thus contributes to the ongoing undoing of American worker rights. While there is an older established morality of labor dignity, as well as a progressive ideology of worker rights, the floating of labor values down to the lowest denominator is intensified as U.S.-based electronics sweatshops compete with those overseas, in Southeast Asia and in China.[25] The neoliberal logic of exploiting the ambiguities of economic and social orders has meant erasing hard-won battles for labor rights and tolerating American working conditions that historically are poorer for people judged to be socially, morally, and economically inferior, that is, minorities and the latest wave of immigrant workers. The old meaning of citizenship — based on free labor, the succession model of social mobility, and worker mobilization against undemocratic practices — was always contingent at best and always open to subversion by the continual influx of cheap immigrant labor. Since the early 1970s, the systematic "deindustrialization of America," through the export of manufacturing to overseas industrial sites, dismantled the political infrastructure of labor coordination and solidarity on a national scale.[26] In the post-Fordist era, when temporary piecework and sweatshop workers proliferate in latitudinal spaces of ethnic governmentality, an already weakened landscape of worker politics is further segmented and thwarted.

Therefore, despite claims that we have shifted from a disciplinary to a serpentine mode of regulation, the labor markets assembled by mobile managers are diverse. Shaped like an hourglass, the labor pool draws workers at both ends from immigrant streams, differentiated by skills and variously regulated. The low-skilled migrant worker is subjected to both labor and ethnic disciplining that is integrated into virtual self-governing ethnic enclaves largely unregulated by the labor law. In contrast, the expatriate professional is regulated by market forces, induced to be technologically savvy, self-improving, and competitive in the shifting global economy. The interactions between different modes of market governance on the one hand, and situated ethnicized coherence, on the other, are reflected as well in particularized spaces of residence.

Ethnic Securitization

Mobile businessmen and professionals exemplify the kind of ideal neoliberal figures who "maximize their quality of life through acts of choice, and their life meaning and value to the extent that it can be rationalized as an outcome of choices made or choices to be made."[27] But if latitudinal citizenship allows mobile subjects to transcend territorialized citizenship, it is also limited by a narrow range of lifestyle requirements based on risk avoidance and security. Asian business families relocating to Australia, New Zealand, Canada, or the United States have been obsessed about what they call "good education, good environment, and political stability." So while neoliberal risk-taking instrumentality may inform the management of global markets, there is the desire to secure their private lives from risks outside their community. The management of the internal space of the community thus becomes an overwhelming concern, necessary to create a secure zone that is somewhat detached from the risks of surrounding society and even market disruptions. Latitudinal citizenship and communities of securitization are therefore two sides of the same process.

In Silicon Valley, business migrants are mainly concerned about buying nice houses and enrolling their children in good schools; highly paid high-tech workers seem to put more stress on other lifestyle issues such as taxes and a good environment. Homeowners associations have sprung up as a localized form of sovereignty, around which, in an age of free-floating insecurity, concerns about safety of person, family, and personal possessions are paramount. In addition, as business people, many elite Asian immigrants are ideologically conservative and supported Bush in the 2000 presidential elections because of his promise to cut taxes, but they are also worried about his lack of interest in higher education. A Chinese-American mother, the president of a teacher-student association in an affluent suburb, said, "It would be nice if we could cut taxes, but I don't think it would be feasible because of the state of our highways and our education system. I think the voters are willing to pay a bit more for a quality education system and good quality roads." Some Asian-

American leaders wondered if they should persuade Asian-Americans to throw their support behind the "information highway" presidential candidate, Al Gore.[28] In other words, the fierce entrepreneurship of Silicon Valley expresses worries about threats to business, personal property, and the body, about consumption and choices and how they relate to modes of self-regulation and community security.

Others have written about the proliferation of segregated, elite communities in Western Europe. In England, the devolution of political administration has induced the formation of "communities of securitization," which are based on techniques of self-government and community cohesion.[29] Another view maintains that the formation of the European Union has brought about the coexistence of a supranationality based on European citizenship, giving rise to a supplementary citizenship acquired by virtue of residence, giving citizenship an autonomous existence from the state.[30] But in Silicon Valley, the ethnicized, securitized community does not result directly from changes in political governance structures. Rather, these communities are the residential locales of a mobile Asian capitalist elite, the situated personal networks that are articulated directly with latitudinal flows across the Pacific. The community of risk management is constructed as "an extra-political zone,"[31] a segregated ethnicized space of residence, technical know-how, and cosmopolitanism that is a functional node in transnational business networks. These gated, securitized communities are the high-end sites spawned by transnational business networks, and the electronics sweatshops are the lower end. Such residential communities and high-tech enclaves have emerged seamlessly, in connection with the serpentine risk-managing activities of a transnational, ethnic managerial class.

In such a latitudinal landscape, territorialized citizenship rights of access to good jobs and housing cannot be guaranteed. Outside the gated communities of affluent newcomers, ordinary working people have to contend with reduced public support and increased uncertainty. Mike Davis has noted that gated communities inscribe a geography of affluence and poverty directly onto the physical landscape of Southern California; in the northern half of the state the securitization phenomenon has been driven more by cycles of digital boom and burst than by imaginary disasters.[32] There is an acute housing shortage in San Jose, the heart of Silicon Valley. Millions have been spent on civic renovations and redevelopment projects to lure middle-class professionals and high-tech business to the city, while the growing plight of the working people has been overlooked.[33] Thousands of ordinary workers have to make long commutes because they cannot afford housing in the Valley. There is an urban legend that people who make forty-five thousand dollars a year are having to sleep in their cars. An increasing number of working people are homeless, and some spend the night in buses or local shelters. The intensified gap between affluent young professionals (both migrants and citizens) and working families has rippled across Northern California. Thus families in long-term immigrant neighborhoods in San Francisco have been displaced by skyrocketing real estate prices, and the city itself has become "a combination bedroom, office and den for Silicon Valley."[34] Such displacements and upheavals are generated by the dynamics of the high-tech industry, part of the heterogeneous spaces constituted by market networks, labor enclaves, and lifestyle communities.

In short, the transnational and high-tech dimensions of production networks should not distract us from the ethnic and cultural codings associated with the particular sets of actors, interrelationships, and labor practices that have been assembled to extend the frontiers of capitalism. Asian students and scientists — many of them graduates of American universities — participated in the rise of the high-tech industry and were thus well-positioned to forge transnational networks linking Asian labor markets and immigrant workers in the United States. The information industry is supported by networks of ethnic professionals and workers who are drawn from different sites. The effect has been to exclude local populations that cannot be easily trained, disciplined, or managed within established production systems. Ironically, the Asian-American entrepreneurial figure is now excluding poorer citizens the same way the mainstream American citizen initially excluded them. The latitudinal citizenship of Asian capitalists is the flip side of post-Fordist ethnicization and has now become a technique of governmentality for mobilizing and exploiting low-wage workers of color. Because of the flexibility to switch production activities and labor opportunities across multiple sites, power derived from latitudinal markets is a challenge to worker organization at any scale.

Citizenship based on income, the dignity of work, and representation is now mainly achievable only in the securely contextualized service sector, where janitors, nurses, and other service providers have secure jobs that cannot be easily moved. For the low-wage, high-tech workers, however, the expectation of building on the struggles of earlier generations of workers is no longer tenable. In other words, workers who are technically American citizens may not enjoy basic rights because their work rank and location, rather than formal citizenship, determine their conditions of existence. In contrast, transnational entrepreneurs often enjoy rights and privileges regardless of their formal citizenship status.

Mobilities of Capital, Mobilities of Labor

While the "face" and practices of electronics manufacturing are Asian, the capital that drives their location and relocations is mainly Wall Street. Indeed, the latitudinal space of high-tech production includes southern China, where the global concentration of contract manufacturing has also undermined socialist protection for workers. The Pearl River Delta, South China, is home to gigantic labor camps housing tens of millions of migrant workers from all over the country. Here, there are thousands of electronics firms, including American ones such as Selectron and Flextronics that produce computers, cell phones, and consumer electronics for American companies. The vertical specialization in computer products does not produce subterranean, sweatshop conditions. Instead, according to Boy Lüthje, the highly automated system relies on "neo-Taylorist" segmentation and the extreme isolation of workers,[35] the majority of whom are young female migrants making forty to ninety U.S. dollars a month. There are frequent complaints about long working hours, withheld wages, and poor safety, health, and living conditions.[36] Even strong labor rights inherited from the high-socialist era are routinely violated.

In China, ethnic and gendered modes of governmentality are also crucial in disciplining labor. According to Ching Kwan Lee, "localism," or affiliation by place of origin, is especially effective in controlling "maiden workers," since localistic ties are central in recruitment, job training, providing social and emotional support, and assigning favors on the shop floor. Female workers who are from the same province, county, or even hometown as their work supervisors become clients in a localistic patronage system that buttresses "despotic" factory rules and working conditions.[37] The "maiden" or junior status of working women also colludes in factories' treatment of them as temporary workers. For instance, electronics workers are not trained for promotion within the company, and there are few state efforts to stabilize the living condition of migrants by providing full residency rights and access to schools and health coverage. Under such conditions, ethnic patronage operates both as a disciplinary mechanism and as an informal system of social protection for migrant female workers. With their lack of urban residency rights and highly contingent employment status, many female migrants may not even be able to muster a living wage.

Not surprisingly, large-scale, often violent labor demonstrations have erupted in the Pearl River Delta. In the spring of 2004, a violent strike broke out in a Taiwanese-operated factory in Dongguan after the management unilaterally and simultaneously reduced wages and increased workers' hours. A lawyer observed, "The reliable structure of the old society that took care of people from birth to death is gone and now people must depend on themselves to survive. But the new society doesn't provide people with individual rights and legal ways to protect themselves."[38] Thus, in a more extreme situation than that found in Silicon Valley, Chinese migrant workers as subjects of latitudinal ethnicization are politically atomized and prevented from developing independent labor unions.

Contemporary mobilities create particular economic vectors, carving latitudes of sweatshop-based systems in North America or neo-Taylorist governmentality in South China, undermining, respectively, the terrain of democratic or socialist citizenship. The shifting latitudes of globalized production continually disrupt conditions for granting worker rights or for forming worker solidarity. In Silicon Valley, the ethnicized networks and mechanisms of labor both discipline and isolate workers, thus thwarting labor mobilization on any scale. Furthermore, by pitting ethnic enclaves in the United States against China's vast electronic labor camps, workers are exposed to intensified competition over wages. Transnational market power gives the managerial elite wide latitude to employ fluid, temporary labor pools at varied sites.

The reach of latitudinal citizenship and its diverse effects on labor rights thus should make us wary of easy answers to questions of globalization and politics. David Held, Andrew McGrew, David Goldblatt, and Jonathan Perraton, in *Global Transformations*, reject as unduly pessimistic the view that globalization — or the stretching of market-based power — is enhancing the power of capital in relation to labor and the state. They point to "the revolutions in communications and information technology which have increased massively the stretch and intensity of sociopolitical networks" that can be a new political force for "civilizing and democratizing globalization." They suggest that a cosmopolitical project can make accountable those sites of power that escape the control of specific democratic states.[39] But this cosmopolitanism remains an ideal, and, practically speaking, its promise of universal human rights cannot reach millions, even among those who live and labor in advanced liberal societies. Compared to the kind of transnational power rooted in mobile capital that I call latitudinal citizenship, cosmopolitan citizenship is still an institutionally underdeveloped form.

A more radical claim is proposed by Hardt and Negri, who believe that the information and communications tools of capitalism can be appropriated by the multitude to confront the Empire on a global scale. Their one concrete example of a "first political demand" for "global citizenship" is the quest by undocumented workers for full rights of citizenship "in the country where they live and work"[40] (in France). But clearly, what the *sans papiers* are demanding is in concrete terms not global citizenship but national citizenship in France, where they make a living. It appears that by "global citizenship" Hardt and Negri do not mean any concrete institutional form one may associate with Kant's politically meaningful cosmopolitanism; instead, they refer to cosmopolitan thinking and feelings of solidarity between citizens and noncitizens.

But Hardt and Negri offer highly suggestive ideas about the unpredictability and explosiveness of the mobile multitude. The mobile multitude, they claim, represents "an excess of value with respect to every form of right and law." The counter-Empire is not so much an organized mass movement as an unpredictable and uncontrollable restlessness of labor that periodically erupts against Empire. "Mobility and mass worker nomadism always express a refusal and a search for liberation: the resistance against the horrible conditions of exploitation and the search for freedom and new conditions of life."[41] In China's vast labor camps, the restless nomadism of young workers has periodically erupted into sudden labor outflows, threatening to undermine latitudinal forces of corporate power.

In August 2004, a massive outflow of migrants from the Pearl River Delta industrial powerhouse caused an industrial panic. New manufacturing zones have sprung up all over China, so migrant workers packed up in search of better working and living conditions. Overnight, the Pearl River Delta in Guangdong Province was short two million workers, mainly young women, and factories worried about their capacity to keep churning out shoes, garments, and electronics for the world's markets. Suddenly, the specter of labor shortage has begun to haunt export industries in Guangdong and Fujian provinces, the southern core of Chinese industrial strength. After two decades of export-driven industrial growth, the seemingly bottomless pool of migrant labor is reaching a limit, at least a limit of tolerance for low pay and miserable working conditions. There is a new tension between female migrants who demand better work and living conditions, on the one hand, and corporate inducements for labor to keep coming to the established industrial zones, on the other. In the Pearl Delta, companies are beginning to raise minimum-wage rates to the highest national level ($85 a month), cut overtime, raise social welfare benefits, and offer better lifestyle conditions such as English classes, well-equipped dormitories, and recreational centers. An Adidas company offers new counseling services that give female workers tips on romance and birth control.[42] Other factories have become less picky and opened their doors to older and married women. Migrants now have the luxury of weighing the new inducements in Guangdong factories against the wages and the living costs in the Shanghai region, or in booming interior cities closer to their hometowns.

In short, where labor has the capacity to mimic the mobility of capital, especially in the world's greatest concentration of industrial production, it can be effective in circumventing the governmentality of lateral market power. Labor mobility as a form of resistance is enhanced when there are many other competitive manufacturing zones to choose from. But capital is more highly dynamic and fleet-footed; more companies are planning to send high-tech manufacturing to China's interior provinces, where labor is cheaper, or even to Vietnam. Chinese labor will have to travel far to keep up with the corporation's unceasing quest for a particular combination of spatial and labor practices that will raise profit margins — until workers abandon the market to seek better conditions elsewhere.

It thus seems appropriate to conclude that while globalization may lead to the spread of cosmopolitan feeling and consciousness, there is a proportionate lack of cosmopolitan institutions as robust as latitudinal market power to defend the citizenship or human rights of the laboring millions. The dynamism of capitalist networks, always looking for new labor markets to bring into discipline, keeps the location of production activities one step ahead of a restive laboring population. My point is not to end on a pessimistic note. On the contrary, the close analysis of unfolding social realities is itself an optimistic enterprise, since only by examining the actual logics and workings of particular latitudinal systems can we discover how the crisscrossing de- and reterritorializations of capital and labor create fissures and openings that keep latitudinal systems contingent and off balance.

The current debates over diversity and multiculturalism have dwelt on the role of education in preserving democratic ideals in the United States.[1] But what is the role of American higher learning in relation to diversity in the global marketplace? Diversity is often invoked to mean multicultural representation in student enrollment and in a democratic composition of diverse cultural views in education. But when the university student body becomes increasingly multinational, the question of diversity spins on an axis between the ethics of democracy and the techniques of knowledge accumulation. As American universities become global sites for training an array of knowledge skills, a gulf is opening up between moral education and technical education, between education for national citizenship and training for what might be called borderless, "neoliberal" citizenship.

First of all, it seems important to stress that education is a social technology — in the Weberian sense of appropriate means to an end[2] — for constituting subjects in particular spaces of calculation. In modern societies, education is a technology of power involved in the construction of modern ethics and knowledges, the beliefs, attitudes, and skills that shape new kinds of knowledgeable subjects. To put it rather simply, the educational enterprise involves both moral education and technical training. The balance between the two has always created a tension, with stress placed in the earlier years on moral education and in later years on professional skills. This process is intended to form morally normative and economically productive citizens for the nation-state.

In recent decades, leading universities in North America have resolutely expanded beyond the national space to educate elites on a global scale. In colonial times, universities in metropolitan countries trained the elites of their colonies, as well as students who became the ruling class of postcolonial societies. But the educational reach of American universities today is of a different function, less focused on the liberal arts nurtured in the secular-democratic traditions of belonging and more concerned about promoting global expertise and neoliberal values in the world at large. U.S.-based academic institutions are going global by expanding education-abroad programs for U.S.-based students or by opening up branch universities abroad to train foreigners. This dispersal of sites of higher learning intersects with the strategies of overseas elites, who seek to accumulate world-class degrees that will open doors to international careers.

This globalization of the American university goes beyond incorporating multiculturalism or fostering cosmopolitan culture; increasingly, universities have become an extension of world trade. What is at stake is the preservation of the fundamental mission of Western universities. Is moral education that shapes a shared view of modern humanity tenable with a narrowed focus on individualistic careerism?[3] Are deterritorialized values and norms about what it is to be human today—as a calculative actor or a globe-trotting professional—on a collision course with the situated values of political liberalism? By going global, are universities in the danger of stressing the rational ethos—an instrumental and unrestricted quest for self-gain—at the expense of the mission of inculcating liberal democratic values?

Thus, while philosophers and political theorists worry about how political liberalism can be stretched to accommodate cultural diversity in advanced liberal societies, they pay little attention to how their leading universities are also educating an increasing number of foreigners to be knowledge workers, unschooled in the humanities.[4] The framing for my argument is the double movement in American higher education—a shift from a national to a transnational space for producing knowledgeable subjects, and a shift from a focus on political liberalism and multicultural diversity at home to one on neoliberalism and borderless entrepreneurial subjects abroad.[5] First, I discuss the role of moral education in constituting an imagined national community and in structuring the habits and sentiments of a nation's citizens according to ideal values about humanity. Second, I discuss the rupturing of the nation-state as the frame of educational strategies, as American colleges and universities begin to position themselves as global academic institutions, especially in the fields of technology, science, and business administration. Third, I consider how the flexible citizenship strategies of Asian elites have contributed to this global role of American universities in training and grading a range of human talents. This educational nexus shapes a new kind of subject, a neoliberal *anthropos* who is primed for employment in knowledge-driven markets. Finally, I suggest that the globalized university rededicate itself to the democratic logic by becoming a locus for spreading ideals of a cosmopolitan citizenship that can mediate between diverse traditions and communities on the global scale.

Moral Education and the Imagined Nation

We are accustomed to thinking of the nation as a discrete territorial and moral entity. England was the master model of national formation, and most nations continue to rely on the assumption that the *ethnie* — cultural groupings — are incorporated into the state to make a multiethnic nation-state.[6] America as a moral project of state and society was conceived and deployed through the notions of hierarchical race, ethnicity, class, and gender. But this notion of the nation was also tied to a resolutely democratic project that eventually extended across the entire national space. Reginald Horsman has argued, for instance, that the notion of white superiority and destiny founded an Anglo-Saxon formation that defined the biological and cultural inferiority of Native Americans, blacks, Mexicans, and Asians. As the nation progressed, this racial superiority looked outward, justifying the spread of American Christian civilization and capitalism and the transformation of backward regions of the world.[7] During the short span of two hundred years or less, the rise and consolidation of the nation-state — in the West and in the rest of the world — have relied on moral education to produce a set of attitudes and habits, the social forms and the ideal figures that will make coherent the "imagined political community" of the nation.[8] While Southerners sustained white civilization with a romantic nationalism that celebrated historical England, aristocratic origins, social Darwinism, and slavery, Northerners like Ralph Waldo Emerson stressed not racial superiority but humanitarian qualities such as self-reliance in the wilderness and democracy associated with the English idea of the nation and singleness of purpose.[9] Emersonian ideals of self-reliance, which were linked to notions of white Anglo-Saxon entitlements, were central in forming an educated public among the emerging middle classes.

By the early twentieth century, John Dewey conceived of the democratic nation beyond its physical dimensions. Education, he argued, was central in shaping a democratic nation, in the constitution of moral citizen-subjects who cherished the opportunity to work for equal opportunity and to expand the moral frontiers of democracy.[10] The moral power in American education is the enduring tension between a shared notion of human fate and egoistical individualism. But, according to Gerard Delanty, the first model of American university—best represented by Harvard University—was "designed to produce gentlemen and clerics," with the goal of serving the civic community. This moral universe marginalized African Americans, Native Americans, and ethnic minorities who were not yet perceived to be part of the cultural scheme.[11]

For generations of immigrant communities, education was a central feature of assimilation, an institutional form for transforming immigrants and refugees into Americans. Besides the inculcation of American values of autonomy and individualism, the development of a civic nationalism was dependent on the mastery of at least vernacular English.[12] For immigrants and the middle classes, the national boundaries constituted a serious frontier of their educational aspirations, a set of orienting attitudes whereby social mobility through education became fused with attaining the American dream. Indeed, for millions of former slaves and poor immigrants, education was the key that made possible the structure of belief in ethnic succession. Parents toiling in the fields and mills were convinced that their suffering could be converted into educational opportunities for their children, who would eventually achieve their place in the great marketplace of American civic equality. Indeed, as Judith Shklar has argued, from the perspective of the historically excluded—racial minorities, women, and immigrants—the struggle for American citizenship has "been overwhelmingly a demand for inclusion in the polity, an effort to break down excluding barriers to recognition, rather than an aspiration to civic participation as a deeply involving activity."[13] Education was from the beginning tied to the achievement of citizenship vested in the dignity of work, a promise as important as the right to vote.

On a broader level, education to a very important extent contributed to shaping a middle-class citizenry that was generally aligned according to basic values, attitude, and competencies considered desirable in citizens. The basic values of self-reliance, income-earning, equal opportunity, open inquiry, and political representation were instilled in each schoolchild who passed through the American educational system, thus structuring individual disposition and sentiments, a homogenizing effect that Pierre Bourdieu calls *habitus*.[14] July Fourth became the celebration of fundamental American values and an enactment of public culture. Nevertheless, for a long time, these democratic values were inseparable from the domination of the Anglo-Saxon elite.

The project of educating a democratic, white-dominated, Christian nation was based as well on the notion of American exceptionalism, a self-image of American modernity. Uninterrupted rivers of immigrants did not undermine the sense of America as a unique nation that cohered independently of international relations, a country "left alone" by the rest of the world, with no imperialist designs. Writers and historians played a major role as educators in stressing American exceptionalism, and the very idea of American studies itself as a project was defined by the discrete analytical entity of the nation-state. To this day, America's ever deepening enmeshment with the rest of the world is considered under special categories of foreign relations, colonialism, and immigration. The domination of political science and sociology in American studies also reinforces the tendency to study nation-states as distinct units.

In the early 1990s, scholars in other fields began to challenge this view of America as a stand-alone nation-state. A collection of essays, *Cultures of United States Imperialism* (1993), criticized American studies for its denial of American empire and professed innocence of America abroad.[15] The authors called for greater attention to how the internal dimensions of race, ethnicity, and gender are related to the global dynamics of empire building, in all its military, economic, and cultural dimensions. More recently, Arif Dirlik has argued that the Pacific Rim is an American invention, an effect of the strategic, military, and economic designs associated with American hegemony since the invasion of the Philippines in 1898.[16] After all, the major military engagements since — the occupation of Japan, the Korean War, the Indochina (Vietnam) War, the War on Terrorism in Afghanistan, the return to military policing in the Philippines — have been in the Asian theater. But America's enmeshment in the region is also economic and cultural. In the region of the booming economics, American firms set up factories in South Korea, Southeast Asia, and now China, all sites of U.S. investment and future business. American consumer goods, mass media, and educational products are eagerly consumed in Asian cities, even as many in the newly affluent societies resent American political and cultural domination. Since 1965, the majority of non-Mexican immigrants to the United States have come from Asian countries. Indeed, in myriad ways, the Asia-Pacific has become as closely linked to the United States as is Europe, but this joining, this tidal wave, this symbiosis is not reflected in American studies, or in the public's consciousness east of the West Coast. Europe may have given birth to the American nation, but the maturing nation has a dysfunctional conjugal relationship with Asia.[17] Especially since the 1960s, America's emergence as the preeminent global power, its wars in Asia, their repercussions at home, and the increasing influx of immigrants from Latin America and Asia have all shaken the image of the nation as fundamentally white and Christian, as well as the view that education goals are shaped entirely within the national space.

Cultural Diversity and Middle-Class Values

Since World War II and the emergence of the United States as a global power, regimes of education have spiraled beyond these basic functions to include university education for the middle classes, as well as for elites from emerging nations. The intensification of immigration from Latin America and Asia from the 1960s on, including rising rates of foreign students, have increased the number of American residents and citizens who do not conform to traditional expectations of assimilation. Increased immigration, transnational corporate connections, and the internationalization of higher education thus all have contributed to a kind of crisis of American citizenship. As the idea of adherence to a single cultural nation wanes, there is a steady "desacralization" of state membership.[18]

Assimilationist notions of citizenship education are challenged by the demands of diversity and cultural citizenship, and there has been some confusion as to the unifying habits and attitudes of the citizenry. Concomitantly, the demands for cultural acceptance, along with affirmative action mechanisms to increase demographic diversity in major institutions and areas of public life, have shifted discussions of citizenship from a focus on political practice based on shared civic rights and responsibilities to an insistence on the protection of cultural difference as minorities as new waves of immigrants contest with increasing vigor the hegemony of majority white culture.

Since the 1960s, the African-American civil rights movement has inspired struggles for more democratic inclusions among other minorities and immigrant groupings.[19] More recently, in California, Chicano scholars such as Renato Rosaldo have defined cultural citizenship as "the right to be different" (in terms of race, ethnicity, or native language) with respect to the norms of the dominant national community. The enduring exclusions of the color line often deny full citizenship to Latinos and other "persons of color." From the point of view of subordinate communities, cultural citizenship offers the possibility of legitimizing demands made in the struggle to enfranchise themselves. These demands can range from legal, political, and economic issues to "matters of human dignity, well-being, and respect."[20] Rosaldo and others have pointed to the political and economic constraints underpinning claims to cultural citizenship. For instance, laws controlling the "normal" timing and use of public spaces conformed to middle-class norms, but they undermined the civil rights of immigrant workers, who could not avail themselves of the public spaces in the same way because of work schedules and concerns about noise levels. There is a sense, then, that dominant forms of normalization discriminate against the cultural difference of new immigrants, whose cultural expressions are at variance with middle-class sensibility and norms. Similarly, the *immigrant* label has acted against the other newcomers, indefinitely deferring, for instance, the integration of Asian immigrants because of their cultural difference from hegemonic norms of citizenship.[21]

The struggles for a more open and multicultural America, against conceiving it as a single cultural nation—white Anglo-Saxon, (Judeo-)Christian, and heterosexual—have stressed the embodiment of middle-class values more than fundamental values of egalitarianism and equal opportunity. For instance, since the 1960s, gay proponents of what has been called "the politics of recognition" demanded public recognition of cultural diversity. Building on the notion of contribution that earns worthy citizenship, early "outings" of closeted gay individuals were intended to expose to society "worthy" persons who had suffered as a result of social discrimination, bias, and ignorance of their diverse and complex roles. The gay movement also has stressed the more middle-class notions of self-realization and accomplishment as criteria for receiving the full benefits of citizenship. These so-called identity politics thus demanded the right to cultural difference without having to sacrifice full membership in the nation. In Canada, political theorists such as Will Kymlicka argue that liberalism must include the recognition of "multicultural citizenship," since the protection of the claims of ethnocultural groups must be protected in order to promote justice between groups, something which is a matter of both justice and self-interest in liberal democracies.[22] Charles Taylor argues that equal rights are only realized when there is mutual respect for cultural difference, which merely puts into practice the promise of liberalism to nurture the modern, authentic self.[23]

Thus, cultural difference and civic equality need not be contradictory in our multicultural world of advanced liberalism, even though the influx of immigrants poses challenges for the practical task of social integration. But what has yet to be addressed is another set of questions that seems to link acceptance of cultural diversity with middle-class status, and even the embodiment of global norms of professional accomplishment. Especially at the higher levels of American education, colleges and universities, there has been a shift from education as a moral project devoted to democratic nation-building to education as a project of globalizing values linked to democracy, but also to a neoliberal ethos.

The Circuit of American Higher Education

In recent decades, university, college, and high school education in America has become more oriented toward the rest of the world, a process that has led it to expand and make ambiguous the borders of the nation. Area studies were introduced in selected American universities during World War II; today, some form of international studies and education-abroad program is found in most leading institutions. Thus, while the main goal of multicultural education has been to do away with discrimination — based on race, gender, sexual orientation, class, language, and national origin — and to teach a kind of civic equality in intercultural and international milieus, it is also driven by the impulse to prepare Americans not merely to be citizens of the nation, but also to be kinds of global citizens.

For instance, when I was an undergraduate at Barnard College in the seventies, education abroad for undergraduates meant a semester or year in Europe. Since then, there has been a basic shift in the model of education abroad. The goal of studying Western humanities has become merely one of many in a larger project of extensive American university involvement in higher education in most regions of the world. At the ten-campus University of California, for instance, the Education Abroad Program (EAP) is the university's main outreach to the international community, offering students "access to strong academic programs overseas that complement UC campus curricula." Since the first study center was opened at the University of Bordeaux in 1962, more than 40,000 students have studied in over 150 universities in nearly 50 countries. In 2003, more than 3,000 students were enrolled in EAP programs at over 140 institutions in 34 countries, while about 1,000 students from the EAP-affiliated universities abroad attended the University of California.[24] I have been an advisor to the EAP committee on the Southeast Asian region, where undergraduates can elect to spend one semester or a year in universities in Bangkok, Hanoi, Singapore, Jogjakarta, and Manila. Especially since the fall of the Berlin Wall, universities have tried to go beyond the traditional emphasis on deepening American students' knowledge of Western civilization. EAP links with universities in major Chinese cities are growing. The goal increasingly is to expose American students to a level of multicultural sophistication, to allow heritage students to forge links with their parents' home countries, and more generally to prepare the American professional classes who are expected to be operating in globalized sites, whether at home or abroad.

Beyond the concern to give American students opportunities to learn foreign cultures and languages, there is now a sense in top American academic institutions that they must go transnational; that is, they must become truly global institutions by setting up branches overseas. For instance, the study abroad program at New York University is planning to expand beyond its centers in Florence, London, Paris, Madrid, and Prague. A new goal is to support intellectual programs that bring together top academics in a given subject area. I recently organized a workshop on interdisciplinary approaches to the global that was hosted by the NYU-Prague center. Now renamed "Global Education–NYU," the program's website proclaims: "In its continued commitment towards being a truly Global University, New York University plans to open study abroad sites within the next five years in Africa, Asia, and Israel."[25] Plans are already under way to open an NYU-Beijing program. While these study abroad programs are designed basically to provide Americans access to the languages and cultures of the world, there is a sense that these educational channels open up the flow for American values to circulate as well.

Already, foreign students at different levels of training have become a permanent feature of our academic institutions, including high schools. Especially since the early 1960s, accepting ever larger and more diverse bodies of foreign students has been a strategy to increase university prestige, enrollment, and income. The study abroad program is yet another conduit for the influx of foreign students to American universities. American universities are involved in advising and setting up departments in foreign universities. At Berkeley, scholars of Southeast Asia have been advising the University of Hanoi in renovating social science programs. Indeed, these efforts are barely separable from the connections based on the EAP. Berkeley scholars of China are advising the setting up of a new social science department at Chinghua University, one of China's leading academic institutions.

Today, then, the turn toward the global space involves a new kind of risk calculation, an attempt to shape educational programs at home and abroad in such a way as to bring the future under control, a form of institutional reflexivity that responds to the risks of the globalized world and yet is aware that "new types of uncalculability emerge."[26] The traditional goals of higher education — to inculcate fundamental Western humanist beliefs and national-ist values — are being challenged by a stress on skills, talent, and borderless neoliberal ethos.

This global trajectory is most advanced in American business schools, a number of which have set up branches or developed programs to train new managerial subjects based in Asia. The internationalization of American busi-ness schools is most clearly designed to promote a set of American market values, thus shaping the constitution of a particular kind of educated and enterprising subject who works in global cities, that is, a neoliberal anthro-pos. While Europe remains a region where American university connections continue to flourish, moves have been made, especially by American business schools, to forge links with Asian governments and institutions. For instance, the Berkeley Haas School has expanded its international business program by sending teams of MBA students overseas to work for a variety of companies in developing and postsocialist economies. It has established exchange relations with the Hong Kong Institute of Science and Technology. Cities such as Hong Kong and Singapore have attracted many American universities inter-ested in collaborative projects in international business. The Canadian Rich-ard Ivey Business School is well represented in Hong Kong, and it has the largest collection of Asian business case studies in the world. Meanwhile, world-class business schools have converged to make Singapore a hub of global business education. INSEAD, the French business school, is the leader in providing international business training to students from around the world in Singapore. The University of Chicago Graduate School of Business recently established its first permanent campus in Singapore, offering an International Executive MBA, taught by the same faculty that teach at the Chicago and Barcelona campuses. The Wharton School of the University of Pennsylvania has played a major role in renovating the Singapore School of Management along the lines of American business education. Thus, Ameri-can business education has been the leader in generating a global circuit of business culture, focusing on Asia as the region of potentially maximal growth. At least in the transnationalization of American business education, the goal has been to "reengineer" other cultures by promoting business man-agement values and practices.[27]

In short, the higher learning in American universities has been accom-panied by a higher yearning to become leading institutions in global space. Professional schools (business, but also medical, science, technology, and engineering institutions) have become more aggressive than traditional liberal arts colleges in offering global programs and training, especially in emerging cities in the Asia-Pacific. A variety of "twinning programs" now link state universities and technical institutes in China and Southeast Asia. The increasingly global availability of American education puts into circulation both American democracy and the American neoliberal ethos. These programs are part of the risk calculations as universities-turned-corporations seek to make money by going global but also to shape global subjects and global markets. The two figures of the liberal political subject and the neoliberal global subject are also the higher yearning of many aspiring Asian students and their parents looking for "world-class" degrees.

Asian Elites and the American Degree

Since the 1960s, much of Asia's upper and middle class has turned away from colonial metropoles (the United Kingdom, France, the Netherlands) and toward the United States and Canada as sources of globally recognized university degrees. The elites of Europe, Japan, and the developing world have come to view North American universities as places to acquire professional skills and world-class credentials in almost all fields. Among the groups of ambitious, education-driven migrants are those that for lack of a better term I call "overseas Chinese." In recent decades, many overseas Chinese — historically a diasporic group fleeing discrimination and chasing opportunities abroad — have devised a joint strategy that combines the pursuit of educational availability abroad with aspiration to emigrate.

There are approximately 50 million people of Chinese ancestry living outside China, and they are dispersed in 135 countries. Analysts and activists have often referred to this linguistically and culturally heterogeneous population as a single diaspora community, even though it has been built up over centuries of countless flows of first exiles, then migrants, out of the Chinese mainland. Most of the flows from China stem from the late nineteenth century, when British incursions into coastal China, the disruption of agriculture and trade, and famines generated the great south Chinese exodus to Southeast Asia, North America, and South America.[28] In postcolonial Southeast Asia, overseas Chinese are ethnic minorities always susceptible to state discrimination and hostility. The colonial pattern of sending the children of the elite to be educated in British, French, Dutch, and Australian universities was aspired to by many. From the 1970s onward, economic affluence in Southeast

Asian countries, Hong Kong, and Taiwan opened up the possibility for the middle classes to seek educational and business opportunities globally.

I remember as a high school student in Malaysia that the office of the U.S. Information Service (USIS, now replaced by the U.S. Agency for International Development [USAID]) recruited the brightest of us to apply to American colleges. Like our counterparts in Singapore and Hong Kong, we were told that instead of seeking higher education in Great Britain, the colonial motherland, we should consider colleges in the United States, where a liberal arts education awaited us. I was educated in an Irish missionary school in Malaysia, which followed the British system established by Cambridge University into precipitously dividing high school children into arts and science streams. I yearned for a broader liberal arts college experience instead of a narrow professional specialization out of high school. Like many other high school students, we flipped through *Lovejoy's Guide to American Colleges* to make our choice. I chose Barnard College in New York City, from which my sister had already graduated with a degree in art history.[29] A broader reason for ethnic Chinese in Malaysia to apply for education abroad was a state policy that reserved a quota for indigenous Malays in the local universities, thus compelling many middle-class ethnic Chinese and Indians to send their children to overseas universities. In most cases, they considered an overseas education both a glamorous experience and a chance to earn a prestigious degree that would help secure a good job when they returned home, as the majority of them did. Many Malaysians and Singaporeans still preferred higher education in England, Australia, and India because of prior cultural connections.

Things are a bit different in places such as Hong Kong and Taiwan, where daunting academic criteria, not racial quotas, keeps many otherwise smart children from enrolling in local universities. Late in the twentieth century, the impending return of Hong Kong to Chinese mainland rule (in 1998) and political instability in Taiwan spurred many middle-class families to send their children to American high schools and colleges for training in science, engineering, and medicine. Students and their parents are still driven by a complex set of motives. For those children who have not performed very well at home, a diversity of American colleges will give them a second chance. Others seek the latest cutting-edge training, especially in the sciences, at top American universities. More generally, there is in the back of the mind an eventual goal of settling in the United States and bringing the family there. America is still (notwithstanding China's emergence) considered the most developed country in the world, as well as a very safe and stable one. I call this middle-class family plan to seek both education and citizenship abroad "flexible citizenship," since in most cases, the strategy involves locating children in schools in the United States, Canada, and Australia, while the parents continue to work at home while planning to emigrate to join the children.[30] Among the top business families, the enrollment of children in American schools allows as well for a business entry point into the country. For instance, I found many cases where children enrolled in California schools were accompanied by their mothers, who became real estate agents while earning their green cards. Meanwhile, the father, as head of a family business, worked on both sides of the Pacific.

Since the Tiananmen crackdown (1979), thousands of mainland Chinese students have flocked to American universities for training in similar fields. There is a visible shift in ethnic Chinese immigrants into California schools, as more and more mainlanders are arriving to have their children educated from high school on, in order to learn English and to qualify for later admission into universities. For a newly emerging market like China, this is a very expensive strategy in which many resources are lavished on ensuring global educational availability for the single child of the urban middle and upper-middle classes. Plunging into the market is referred to as diving into the ocean (*xiahai*), and many ambitious Chinese link business ventures and professional training with seeking opportunities abroad. Legally, forty thousand leave for the United States, Canada, and Australia each year. Currently, migrants from China are of a higher professional and economic status than earlier ones in the 1980s, and the perception is that the U.S. embassy is raising the bar for skilled immigrants from China. Fierce competition among Chinese professional elites to enter the United States entails making business investments, using family connections, applying to college, or contracting bogus marriages with American citizens. A degree from Harvard Business School or the Massachusetts Institute of Technology (MIT) is part of the global accumulation strategy to reposition oneself and one's family in the global arena of competing intellectual and economic markets.

The influx of Hong Kong, Taiwanese, and Chinese students to North American universities has converged with a growing stream from India, where the upper-middle classes have also begun to turn away from England and toward the United States as the country for educational excellence, at least in the sciences. Thus ethnic Chinese (from many places) and Indians are now greatly represented in the natural science, medicine, and engineering departments of major North American universities. The Engineering Department at the University of Toronto has been called the "Hong Kong Express." At Berkeley, the Engineering Department often uses Cantonese as a secondary language in elevators and corridors. Mandarin is sometimes the language of instruction between graduate instructors and students. But access to American college and university degrees has been available for decades at different levels of expertise. For instance, the University of Hawaii is a major center for training or retraining researchers, civil servants, and army officers from friendly Asia-Pacific countries.

Silicon Valley is a major site for the influx of Asian students, who later flocked to high-tech companies such as Hewlett-Packard, Sun Microsystems, and Intel, where one third of the engineering workforce is composed of American-educated Taiwanese and Indian immigrants. By 1999, one-quarter of the Valley's businesses were run by Asian Americans.[31] Many of these Asian immigrants, who began as university students, have started companies. As I noted in chapter 5, the demand for Asian professionals has been so high that the computer industry put pressure on the federal government to increase the intake of skilled foreign workers (mainly Indians) under the H-1B visa program. It has never been clearer that American universities' recruiting and training of foreign students sustains U.S. high-tech companies, Wall Street corporations, hospitals, and research laboratories. Since the September 11, 2001, terrorist attacks and the amazingly obtuse visa restrictions that the U.S. government imposed in response, the number of Asian students entering the United States has fallen off, many electing instead to study in Europe or Asia. Such "homeland security" moves to strictly regulate student visas has raised a storm of protest from university administrators worried that their science departments will not be filled by students from Asia, and steps are being taken to ease the visa applications of overseas students.

There is already a sizable population of Asian immigrants who entered the United States as students and are now settled in affluent communities. Asian high-tech professionals and families drawn to specific communities with excellent high schools have transformed previously all-white communities. For instance, over the past decade, the ethnic breakdown of Mission San Jose in Silicon Valley has become half Asian (almost entirely foreign born), about forty percent white, and the rest a mixture of other immigrant groups. The high school population is over 60 percent Asian (ethnic Chinese and South Asians), which has increased the competition for getting into top-flight American universities. To some Asian children, the community feels like Singapore. Advertisements for San Jose High School appear in newspapers in Taiwan and Hong Kong, drawing new immigrants, who may rent rooms to establish residency or transfer the guardianship of their children in order to have them enrolled in the high school.[32] Ironically, perhaps, or perhaps not, some of these very same students are sent home in the summer to learn Chinese in Taiwan and Hong Kong. This trend is not limited to Asians. More and more, middle-class Mexican and South American immigrants are also sending teenagers to the home country to learn the language and culture. Well-educated migrants and their children choose aspects of education — high school access to American universities, language and cultural instruction in homeland schools — available in different places to shape a complex scholastic career for their children. Flexible strategies linked to specific educational availability in different countries further normalize the production of flexible, multilingual, and multicultural subjects, as well as their disembedding from a particular national set of values.

There is a danger that the heavy concentration of immigrants with an instrumentalist approach to education will bypass the philosophical underpinnings of American education "in and for democratic citizenship." In an important study, Katharyne Mitchell found that Hong Kong Chinese in Vancouver have effectively challenged the norms of Western liberalism in the local school (values such as equality, pluralism, political participant, and public-private divide) and imposed their view that education is about learning discipline and the acquisition of cultural capital.[33] Some seem to fear that without such "reforms," their children risk being left behind. What is particularly ironic is that while well-off Asian immigrants in North America have tried to dictate a different philosophy of education and political values, poor Asian immigrants and refugees are daily tutored by a spectrum of institutions in the basic liberal values of self-reliance, individualism, and the separation of church and state.[34] There is a tendency among Asian immigrants to focus narrowly on the vocational aspects of American education, a trend that is further exacerbated by fears that the globalization of the university has resulted in an overall decline of the humanities.[35]

Our best academic institutions have responded to the market-driven demands of knowledge and research where the rational ethos is premium. Especially at the level of graduate training, the stress on individualistic skills and entrepreneurial competition often leads to the overlooking of humanistic concerns or cultural values. Robert Reich calls the new professionals symbol analysts and manipulators in a world increasingly running on the production of and access to intellectual property.[36] Recently I was in Hong Kong to catch up with the grown children of the first generation of flexible migrant subjects who sought to leave Hong Kong by 1998. Even more cosmopolitan than their parents, the children — mainly educated in Great Britain and the United States, now work for global companies throughout European and Asian capitals. These "yompies" (young, outwardly mobile professionals) in their late twenties and thirties, armed with degrees from Oxford, Cambridge, Harvard, and other Ivy League universities, consider themselves "global citizens." They maintain a loose network with other Asian, mainly ethnic Chinese yompies from Singapore, China, Malaysia, and India, formed through the global networks of higher education, corporate employment, and favorite vacation destinations. I visited a Hong Kong barrister who met a Malaysian Chinese woman in England when they were both in school; following work relocations to multiple European and Asian cities, they decided to marry and perhaps make their "permanent" bases in London and Hong Kong. But they are free-floating corporate-borne individuals who may dip periodically into these cities for cultural "brain food" in between bouts of global dealing.

The rise of a class of global professionals armed with "world-class" credentials may be good for business and scientific research, but these professionals also embody a new form of global ranking based on human capital, mobility, and risk-taking. As Nikolas Rose has noted of "the enterprising subject," "these new practices of thinking, judging, and acting are not simply 'private matters.' They are linked to the ways in which persons figure in the political vocabulary of advanced liberal democracies — no longer as subjects with duties and obligations, but as individuals with rights and freedoms."[37] The knowledge-rich and globe-trotting subject with unfettered individual liberty has been the product of a neoliberal logic that stresses "the equality of worth,"[38] often at the expense of the equality of rights. When education has shifted from the goal of constituting national subjects allied by common values of equality, pluralism, and free speech, to a global function of shaping free-floating individuals, what are the risks for higher education's ability to define who is a worthy citizen?

American educational availability at the global scale has not necessarily produced a constituency of humanistic values, but it has produced highly trained calculative individuals capable of maneuvering effectively in the fields of corporate business, law, medicine, engineering, biotechnology, and architecture (favorite fields of specialization among overseas Chinese). Their higher yearning is for a kind of global acceptance based on amassing individual knowledge capital, rather than on sharing basic values of cosmopolitan citizenship (e.g., democracy, equality, and pluralism). In this instrumental approach, professional education is a means to a career trajectory that will take students through the upper reaches of global markets. Of course, this educational-expatriate strategy is not unique to overseas Chinese but can be found among elites of all emerging nations. Because the pursuit of knowledge in Western universities by overseas and mainland Chinese has been so striking, they have been used as an ethnographic example of the degree-seeking, knowledge-accumulating professional.

Global Universities and Cosmopolitan Citizenship

Since 9/11, and thanks to the zealous efforts of American embassies and Homeland Security officials, the enrollment of foreign students in American universities has dropped off. Many Asian students have turned in frustration to Western universities elsewhere, especially in Canada, Western Europe, and Australia. The opportunities created for non-American universities to meet the global demand have allowed even Asian-based institutions such as the National University of Singapore to reposition themselves as emerging "world-class" schools. But it is important not to lose sight of the ongoing globalization of American universities, despite this temporary demographic shortfall. All major American universities are poised to become global institutions, and serious discussions are under way about changing not only their student composition but also the content of the curriculum, with a special focus on Asian subjects and perspectives.[39] This temporary drop in foreign student enrollment becomes an opportunity to rethink the role of American universities in the world.

The emergence of the United States as a global power after World War II was paralleled by the transformation of its best universities into global institutions in the areas of science, technology, medicine, law, and the social sciences. American universities have attracted a multicultural, multinational, and mobile population, the very kind of educated, multilingual, and self-reflexive subjects now considered to be the most worthy citizens. Graduates of American universities the world over represent a global standard of professional excellence based on the calculative attitude and practice, articulating with egoistical individualism and self-enterprise in a spectrum of fields. Following this logic of the academic enterprise, it appears that institutions with a central science focus such as Stanford and MIT are models for the university of the future.

There is thus a crisis of the humanities not only at the scale of American education but also at the global scale in which American universities are key players. Higher learning in America has always responded to two kinds of yearning: for the production of a democratic citizenry and for the production of rational subjects. Currently, these two impulses may be in contradiction, since the educational circuit gives priority to creating an international class of calculative actors, not world citizens in the Kantian sense of cosmopolitics. To put it in another way, there is a profound tension and potentially radical disjuncture between an equality of rights that stresses equal opportunity and diversity at home, and an equality of worth that stresses equal opportunity and diversity globally.

Does the neoliberal exception embedded in higher education undermine the ethics of political liberalism? Or should world-class universities be the humanistic sites of exception to calculative thinking and choices? Globalized American education is not merely incorporating a culturally heterogeneous population; it can also be a space of ethical exception for the production of cosmopolitan citizens. The enrollment of a globally diverse student body in American institutions suggests that the global university can become a locus for developing a cosmopolitan ethos. In contrast to other, newer global centers of education, American institutions can be at the forefront of propagating the Kantian view of cosmopolitanism. Kant maintained that it is through the cultivation of the fine arts and sciences that we realize our shared humanity and develop a global sociality based on human fate as a shared enterprise. This kind of world citizenship can only come about if we promote cosmopolitical norms that mediate between the diversity of traditions, interests, and world-political communities.

We need to rethink the political logic of American education as an ongoing struggle for democracy in "a genuinely heterogeneous space" that is at once national and global. Our universities cannot be party to the production of global professional elites who are animated only by a calculative, economistic spirit. The professional degrees for foreigners and Americans alike can be offered alongside lessons on democracy and human rights. Experts in particular would benefit from a view of a shared globalized future that requires conversations, connectivity, and reciprocity across fields, class, and nations. A global project of genuine education can be infused with a sense of moral urgency — so that training in rationalist thinking and ideas can incorporate humanistic values and notions of the cosmopolitical right. Indeed, in the aftermath of 9/11, a turn toward greater development and appreciation of Islamic civilization and cultures is a positive sign of the maturation of the American university as a global center for transnational humanities. By broadening the horizon beyond concerns of the bottom line, instrumental calculation, and unfettered market interests, our universities can set a "cosmopolitan limit," or logic of exception, to the excess of individual liberty.[40]

Outsourcing is a term haunting middle-class Americans, who fear, for the first time, being cast adrift from the great corporate job machine. On a California radio program in 2004, a caller dubbed the current outsourcing of knowledge jobs to Asia a "betrayal" of the public. The rise of the Internet was supported by taxes, she argued, so citizens have a claim on the jobs created by the information industry. Furthermore, this American claim on high-tech jobs is implicitly acknowledged when call centers in Asia require their workers to adopt American accents in order to serve American customers.[1] An African American professor asked what universities beyond elite institutions were having programs funded by high-tech industry. Very few minority students have gained employment in the high-tech boom, she said. "People of color are still waiting for crumbs to fall on their laps."[2] The view that the high-tech industry is American and high-tech jobs belong to American citizens was questioned by a third caller, who identified herself as a social scientist. She rejected blaming foreign workers for job losses. Where, she asked, were American complaints when the "brain drain" from developing countries sent their students and scientists to help American knowledge industries? She bemoaned the fact that "venture capitalists think globally, but activists not enough."[3] Silicon Valley CEOs on the show were happy to describe the necessity of outsourcing jobs that are based on specialized knowledge. They claimed that with offshore outsourcing, companies that wanted new expertise would not need to train their own employees or hire new ones. Instead, they can have skilled workers in China and India bid to offer the services at a cheaper rate. Outsourcing, they argued, saves labor costs and time, and it ensures that new products are developed and get to the market soon. Many small companies might never get started without the economic benefits of offshore outsourcing. The gains for Americans, besides lower prices for goods and services, include stock options for employees in the company.

In chapter 5, I discussed how post-Fordist ethnicized production enforces disciplinary exclusions on workers of color. With the offshore outsourcing of high-tech jobs to Asian professionals, it appears that another Asian-American nexus has opened up, not in the factory jobs but in the realm of knowledge-based work, the kind of expertise that has symbolized twentieth-century American identity and character. Outsourcing may be conceptualized as a form of the "immutable mobile," Bruno Latour's term for global forms that have "properties of being mobile but also *immutable, presentable, readable,* and *combinable* with one another."[4] Here, the immutable market rationality of efficiency, codes, and protocols is drawn together with mobile knowledge and skills, an interaction that changes the claims of American citizenship. As corporations seek lower costs for knowledge workers, entitlements become delinked from citizenship and relinked to the mobile economic and cultural skills in global circuits. Labor arbitrage involves shifting well-paying jobs across borders, a process of deterritorialization that also separates traits associated with middle-class American masculinity, while reterritorializing such features in skilled actors located elsewhere.

Knowledge as Commodity and as Symbolic Capital

Since the early days of capitalism, the commodification of labor power has been inseparable from profound disruptions in low-skilled labor markets; indeed, the very circulation of capital relies on the availability of floating pools of workers who can be easily substituted for one another.[5] During much of the twentieth century, the globalization of capital made labor displacements a routine transnational affair, but it was a phenomenon mainly confined to low-skilled markets. Starting in the 1970s, Japanese and Western firms began to export low-skilled manufacturing and clerical jobs to overseas locales where they could be done more cheaply.[6] As the global center of science and technology, the United States continued to be a citadel of intellectual workers, who seemed immune to replacement by foreign labor markets. Indeed, the steady influx of well-educated immigrants and students after World War II helped to ensure the nation as a secure site of knowledge-driven jobs. American scientific and technical innovation created the information technologies that are the lifelines of cutting-edge industries the world over.

High-paying, knowledge-based jobs symbolize a distinctive form of American middle-class identity, the fruits of personal and family achievement for native-born citizens and immigrants alike. Especially in the aftermath of the Sputnik challenge, science and technology became the area where the United States represented to other societies and to itself its ingenuity, dynamism, and power. In the early industrial era, the Horatio Alger story of the immigrant who goes to college and joins mainstream society shaped the sense of masculine entitlement to middle-class status. Beginning in the 1970s, the digital revolution recast the rags-to-riches story. In the new version of American can-do optimism, ingenuity, and hard work, smart students tinkering in garages can launch a thousand computer companies.

At the height of the dot-com boom in the nineties, Robert Reich (a former U.S. labor secretary) argued that continued growth in the "new economy" required that more Americans become "symbol analysts," people who work with language, ideas, and icons to invent products, designs, services, and markets. These analysts — bankers, managers, consultants, lawyers, engineers, and software programmers — train themselves to stay ahead in the knowledge fields. Symbol analysts, who constituted 20 percent of the American labor force, would safeguard America's continuing prosperity — but even in the 1990s, their inflation-adjusted income had been falling steadily for a decade.[7]

Nevertheless, to many middle-class Americans, knowledge is more than a high-priced commodity, or something you apply at work; it is also a symbol of the promise of American citizenship. To be American is to be self-reliant, self-improving, and technologically savvy, qualities that ensure access to college education and a comfortable middle-class life, with all its accoutrements. We have long admired heroes with scientific talent — say, the astronaut Neil Armstrong, or the discoverers of the DNA, James Watson and Francis Crick — though lately the celebrities have tended to be cyberheroes such as Steve Jobs (and entrepreneurs such as Donald Trump). It appeared that the digital revolution would produce a superclass of high-tech "masters of the universe" who embody scientific prowess and the frenetic lifestyle of the new superachieving American male.

The recent outflows of high-tech jobs have dealt a blow to the ineffable security that links American science and middle-class masculine ideals. By outsourcing, American corporations seem to be betraying a fundamental belief in the entitlements that come with college degrees, and the promise that science is a means to masculine economic and social success. Furthermore, the status of middle-class Americans has been tied to their claims as territorialized citizens, "good" subjects who do not make claims on welfare like less-educated Americans, but only make claims on jobs sheltered from the buffeting of capitalism. But increasingly, educated Americans, like high school dropouts, are becoming exposed to the fluctuations of the global market as the very same companies that launched the digital revolution find labor arbitrage more and more tempting.

Deterritorialization and Arbitrage

Accelerating market-driven flows destabilize not only the job prospects of low-skilled, low-wage workers; new corporate practices are steadily moving up the skills ladder to wear away the foundation of the labor aristocracy. The market's "best practices" are liquefying solid ground, and dissolving with it the assumptions entailed by one's attachment and claim to a national territory. We might think of the nation as a space of territoriality *and* deterritoriality,[8] as a coupling of territorialized home and deterritorialized flows of capital, knowledge, and actors. A whole new ecology spanning different wage zones in the United States and in Asia is sustaining the growth of the information economy. Such de- and reterritorializations of actors and jobs reconstitute the grounds of citizenship, making people vulnerable to corporate decisions that undermine an established sense of what citizenship is worth. Double movements of migrants and jobs between sites have had a dramatic disembedding effect on the accumulation of benefits and claims that we associate with middle-class citizenship in both the original sites of skilled labor and the sites to which jobs are exported.

Arbitrage is a term normally used in financial markets, referring to the practice of buying low in a market and selling high elsewhere. Arbitragers exploit price discrepancies between money markets in order to make a profit.[9] In extreme distortions of arbitrage, wealthy financial traders can directly influence rates of profit by overselling in order to force down the price in certain markets. In the late 1990s, in a case of arbitrage-turned-gambling, New York–based traders attacked Asian national currencies by short selling, precipitating a regional financial crash that threatened to take down economies across the world.

Trading that exploits price discrepancies has existed as long as markets have, but until recently, the term *arbitrage* was not applied to labor markets. The global search for cheap labor in manufacturing, I argue, can be called a kind of industrial labor arbitrage that operated according to the logic of same skills, different prices. As I noted above, in the 1970s, Japanese, American, and European firms moved production to cheap industrial labor markets in

Southeast Asia and Mexico.[10] American blue-collar workers protested the melting away of secure factory jobs. But the steady deindustrialization of America seemed inevitable as working-class Americans adjusted to an expanding service economy, as well as to the idea that America has evolved beyond making toasters and refrigerators. There was and is a widespread belief that America's ingenuity in science and technology would be the basis of its economic preeminence in the world. But skilled labor markets assumed to be the domain of American men soon proved susceptible to global competitive prices as well.

At the turn of the century, offshore operations received a boost from Y2K remediations that sent thousands of lines of code to offshore providers. Suddenly, it became possible for huge segments of business operations to be shipped overseas, opening up opportunities for large-scale and permanent outsourcing of technically sophisticated systems. An outsourcing company coined the term *labor arbitrage* to mean "the ability to pay one labor pool less than another labor pool for accomplishing the same work, typically by substituting labor in one geography for labor in a different locale. The outsourcing industry is now applying labor arbitrage widely; it is transitioning from a novel approach to a competitive requirement."[11] Since labor is a major percentage of any company's costs, labor arbitrage is the new value-adding practice for cutting costs and leveraging gains across different sites of production. American firms are exporting knowledge-driven jobs, mainly in areas such as customer service and financial data processing, but increasingly, jobs in research and development as well. One may say that digital innovations enabled companies to drive down high-tech wages by making alternative, cheaper skilled labor markets more accessible.

Besides electronic communications, labor arbitrage relies on the fragmentation of high-tech jobs into smaller, standardizable, and repeatable tasks. Under Fordism, the production process was decomposed and standardized to increase labor productivity, but such decomposition also allows automated, labor-intensive branches of manufacturing to be exported to lower-wage offshore sites.[12] Today, knowledge is increasingly subjected to a similar form of computerized coding and decomposed into small, rote labor functions. Many everyday business functions—such as data entry, customer servicing, and software development—are easily customized and done in back offices established offshore. The new susceptibility of cognitive functions to a computerized division of labor is what makes labor arbitrage a compelling marketing strategy, since profits can be made by having the same standard-ized knowledge jobs performed elsewhere at a cheaper price. In this digi-talized network, not only cognitive skills are being floated away. Also ar-bitraged, it seems, is some notion of American masculinity tied to technical know-how, as low-cost and high-quality versions can also be found offshore.

The Global Tradeability of Asian Skills

Knowledge is like light. Weightless and intangible, it can easily travel the world, enlight-ening the lives of people everywhere.
— World Bank, *World Development Report 1998/99*

Meanwhile, across the ocean, knowledge economies are emerging at the insti-gation of the World Bank and of homegrown nationalists. In the late nine-ties, on the cusp of spreading financial crises, knowledge became the new answer to the problems of the developing world. World Bank pundits note that knowledge as a free-floating resource is more valuable than material re-sources — land, tools, labor — in playing catch-up in the global economy. The building of skilled labor markets, it is claimed, allows emerging economies to leapfrog over decades of infrastructural development. Developing countries were told to focus on rapidly narrowing the knowledge gap by improving the intellectual quality of their populations through "life-long learning."[13] In emerging economies such as India and China, there is already a major focus on technical and scientific training as linked to national development.

The new stress on human talents has given these regions a boost in the IT field. Over the past decade, the output of scientists and engineers from India and China has been astonishing. Each year, China graduates close to 200,000 engineers, and India almost 130,000. By comparison, there are barely 60,000 engineering graduates in the United States, 40,000 less than in Japan.[14] The vast Asian expertise in science and technology is growing a globally oriented labor force that is easily tapped by industries at home and abroad.[15]

Since the 1990s, India has emerged as a major source of IT workers, who help build its fast-growing leadership in the IT software and business-processing industry. There are thousands of technical institutions in India, among which are seven leading Indian Institutes of Technology (IIT) that are graduating thousands of top-notch engineers each year. These engineers have made the Indian firms Infosys Technologies and Wipro into transnational companies, providing software services to businesses in Asia, Europe, and North America. At present, about twenty-five thousand graduates of IITs are working in the United States, demonstrating the importance of Indian workers to the long-term health of the Silicon Valley economy.[16] These software engineers, who are much cheaper but just as qualified as their American counterparts, are the reason why American companies are outsourcing jobs to India. So, despite the media focus on the attractive Indian woman working in an offshore call center, the target of labor arbitrage is the Indian engineer, usually but not always male, who can maintain business software systems throughout the world, and for a lower salary than American workers. An economist at Morgan Stanley warns that "today's offshore outsourcing platforms now offer low-cost, high-quality alternatives to goods production and employment on a scale and scope the world has never before seen."[17] Let us consider how the Indian engineers first migrated to American computer jobs, and then how the jobs migrated to India. There are two steps in the arbitrage of Asian knowledge workers. The first phase involves the temporary migration of Indian software engineers; the second phase is marked by the steady outsourcing of white-collar jobs to India.

Body Shops in Silicon Valley

There is a synergy between the rise of skilled markets in Asia and the role of Asian knowledge workers both as technomigrants in California and as employees in high-tech ventures outsourced to their homelands. The West Coast is the world's most innovative and influential region when it comes to using cheaper Asian workers in the information industry. The first step toward offshore labor arbitrage was "body shopping," or a system of labor contracting that relocates cheaper skilled labor in a high-wage high-tech market such as Silicon Valley. Throughout the 1990s, leaders in the computer industry pressured the federal government to raise the quota of foreign high-tech workers granted the HI-B visa. Another visa, the L-I, allows transfers within multinational corporations. This visa allows a majority of Indian technomigrants to be brought in as a temporary and cheaper skilled labor force to help fill backlogs of orders. They were subjected to a specific kind of governmentality, that is, by labor-contracting companies, or body shops, that controlled where they worked and when they were paid. As short-term skilled workers on two-year contracts, technomigrants were vulnerable to exploitation, and kept in line by their lack of opportunities to gain American citizenship.

I interviewed a software worker I call Sajit from Amritsar, Punjab, who received his degree from the Guru Nanak Engineering Technology Institute.[18] A few months into his first job in India, Sajit applied to Aviance, a body shop, to be sent to the United States. Aviance obtained his ticket and visa and found him a job in a software company in Houston. When this particular project was completed, Sajit joined the body shop Novetel Network, which operates mainly in California. He claimed that Novetel paid him US$1,200 a month for six months while locating a job for him in Silicon Valley. Meanwhile, still waiting for the job to materialize (or "sitting on the bench"), Sajit was driving a cab, a profession that is dominated by his countrymen. It seemed a flexible way to pick up some money, but it was "hard for an educated man" to take the abuse from some passengers. Sajit was feeling a bit depressed about sharing a small apartment with three other migrant workers in order to save money while waiting for the economy to pick up again. If it did not, they might have to return to India. Meanwhile, he dreamed of the day when he would be free of the body shop and could find work on his own. If an American company took him on as a permanent worker, he could make up to $75,000 a year and have a good chance of getting a green card. But such opportunities are extremely rare, since body-shopped migrants are by definition a circulating low-wage workforce entirely at the mercy of the fluctuating needs of the labor market.

As a mechanism of labor arbitrage, transnational body shops delivered low-cost, skilled labor under conditions of strict discipline. Recruitment practices have included receiving bribes from would-be workers in India, where some candidates buy false papers and diplomas. Once contract workers arrive in the U.S., many are vulnerable to exploitation. Besides controlling their access to jobs and wages, body shops take a percentage of the technomigrants' earnings (from 25 to 50 percent). Furthermore, by holding the workers' visas, the body shop makes it risky for the them to change employers, complain about illegal working conditions, or join a union, since this could jeopardize their prospects for a green card.[19] Body shop operators use the workers' desire to obtain citizenship to intimidate them. An Indian engineer complained that a body shop threatened to send some workers back to India if no contracts materialized. Some were left without money, too ashamed to ask for help from their families back home.[20] Constrained by their fear of losing their temporary visas, some technomigrants can be reduced to a kind of indentured high-tech servitude. Nevertheless, I was told that thousands of Indian programmers considered body shops an important step toward their dreams of becoming Americans, and that by hard work and some luck, they could one day trade their temporary work permits for green cards. Despite the reported cases of abuse, Silicon Valley executives kept up demand for technomigrants during the dot-com boom, paying them much less than long-term employees.

Body shops as a mechanism of labor arbitrage thus index the beginning of the ethnicization and lowering of earnings for high-tech work diffused across borders. The visa and employment programs that favor Indian technomigrants because of their skills and body-shopped availability in the computer industry constructed the ethnicity of software engineers as Asian or associated South Asian men with the performance of cheaper high-tech jobs.

According to labor organizers, the real issue for importing technomigrants was not the lack of qualified Americans, including those of African-American and Latino ancestry, but that companies have had trouble finding engineers and programmers willing to accept the salaries offered. Due to the body shops' control of high-tech labor circulation, computer jobs are becoming a form of ethnic specialization that further disqualifies non-Asian American minorities from jobs in the high-tech industry. Clearly, the neoliberal rationality of cheap labor substitution does not include investing in or training native-born American minorities, preferring to ship in already skilled Asian workers under a form of labor substitution. South Asian technomigrants recognize their role as "cybercoolies," being paid much less for the same work than mainstream American software engineers. But by the beginning of the twenty-first century, body shops began to be phased out, and a more stringent business visa came to replace the temporary work visas, allowing only a few well-placed immigrants to work in the high-tech industry.

Sending Jobs to Asian Cybercenters

Following the September 11, 2001, terrorist attacks, and with a persistent economic recession, the bloom has faded from Silicon Valley as a site of employment. Asian expatriates and technomigrants have been leaving as work opportunities dry up. There has also been a steady decline in the numbers of Asian students entering the country to attend American universities. Post–September 11, tighter immigration rules have dissuaded many Asian students from coming to the United States. At the same time, America's preeminence in the science fields is being challenged by the large numbers of technical institutes and science centers in South and East Asia. The decreasing supply

of Asian knowledge workers is so serious that the National Science Foundation sounded an alarm about America's shortfall in graduates in science and
technical fields, combined with rising numbers of departing Asian experts.[21]
In late 2003, Andy Grove, chairman of Intel Corporation, appealed to Washington policy makers to transfer a tiny amount of agricultural subsidies to
universities, but his plea fell on deaf ears, and education budgets continued to
be trimmed everywhere.[22]

But the greatest challenge to the American computer industry is not so
much the declining supply of Asian knowledge workers in the United States
as India's emergence as a site for high-tech jobs. Expatriate Indians shifted
from operating body shops in Silicon Valley to setting up high-tech centers
in India. Conditions that favored this move to Asia were in part prepared
by American companies, which foresaw the logic of relocating high-tech
jobs abroad.

In 1991, the Indian government began systematically to dismantle tariff
and export controls. Soon, Jack Welch of General Electric spearheaded the
drive to develop high-tech labor in India. GE formed joint ventures to make
medical instruments and contract the development and maintenance of software by workers in India. The company was also among the first to initiate
backroom work and call centers in India. Contracts from GE boosted the
revenues of India's largest software company, Tata Consultancy Ltd., beyond
the billion-dollar a year level; GE also facilitated Tata's overseas expansion to
develop high-tech labor markets in China[23] and Eastern Europe. In short, GE
played "a starring role" in India's high-tech emergence by making early investments that helped fuel the technological and service sectors in India,
making it a cheap source of expertise.[24]

Within a decade, Indian IT companies have emerged as the global leaders
in back-office or business-processing expertise. High-tech centers include
Bangalore, which has over a hundred software companies with strong connections to Silicon Valley firms. Asian expatriates in the United States have
returned home to build up the IT economy. One estimate put the number of
"returned nonresident Indians" in Bangalore at thirty-five thousand.[25] But
clearly, the outflows of Asian computer expatriates and of American jobs are
irreducibly linked to the cost-cutting measures of American corporations,
taking advantage of the ease with which they can shift from high-cost to low-
cost skilled labor markets.

American managers view India and China as new providers of knowledge
workers who offer the same quality for lower cost, thus creating an opportunity for companies to maximize profits by relocating offshore. The wage

differences for like quality work are huge. The chief executive officer of a major offshoring company (Everest Group) notes that an Indian call center worker with a university degree earns under eight thousand dollars a year, while his or her American counterpart with similar experience typically earns fifty thousand dollars plus benefits and overhead. The gross savings for companies that participate in offshoring is frequently over fifty percent.[26] As the U.S. economy recovers from recession, Silicon Valley venture capitalists are requiring the outsourcing of up to half of a firm's workforce as a condition for funding it.[27] Major Indian software companies have grown to the extent that American consulting firms such as Accenture are setting up offices in India in order to compete with Indian counterparts. The Indian dominance of this field is expected to gain from the half a million Indians expected to be in back-office jobs worldwide by 2006. Meanwhile, American competitors such as IBM Global Services and Computer Services Corporation were expected to erase a total of eight hundred thousand American jobs by the end of 2005, and almost 3.5 million by 2015.[28] In short, the ethnicization of high-tech workers, the reverse brain drain, and the rise of low-wage cybercenters in Asia have converged, making global labor arbitrage a relentless logic in knowledge-based industries.

Arbitrage of Americanism?

Labor arbitrage as a corporate technology is challenging Americans' cherished belief that they are citizens of the world's leading scientific nation. This has been expressed by two leading high-tech executives. While many male business leaders in California have defended offshore outsourcing as a logical economic policy, the most articulate framing of the issues in cultural terms has been done by female chief executives. Carly Fiorina, the former CEO of Hewlett-Packard, remarked in defense of outsourcing: "There is no job that is America's God-given right anymore. It is interesting to me that so many people talk about China or India or Russia as being a source of low-cost labor. Truthfully, over the long term, the greater threat is the source of well-educated labor. And if you look at the number of college-educated students that China graduates every year, it's close to 40 million. The law of large numbers is fairly compelling."[29] It seems that Fiorina felt she need not mention the shortage or future supply of American knowledge workers, because the situation of the American labor market is becoming irrelevant in the global depression of high-tech wages.

Another former CEO, Carol Bartz of Autodesk, was more candid about the profit motive: "When you can get great talent at 20 percent of the costs, it isn't about waving the American flag. It's about doing what's right to have a good company. We would be irresponsible if we didn't find a way to get our costs in line with what other people are doing. I have enough belief in open markets to believe that there will be other things for our people to do here."[30] Bartz explicitly stated that the American entitlement to knowledge jobs is in jeopardy, and her suggestion that there will be alternatives to high-tech jobs is left ominously vague. Fiorina and Bartz chose to question directly American beliefs in God-given entitlements and flag waving. They brusquely dismissed such deep-seated sentiments as outdated in a world where growing skilled-labor markets cost one-fifth as much as equivalent American labor. Both executives played the role of the iconic strong female figure who appears in a time of crisis to shore up middle-class masculinity, only this time they are actually dismissing "masculine" birthrights as irrelevant in an era of globalization. Suddenly, the college-educated American male is not only threatened by downward mobility, his ideal masculine role as main breadwinner is further imperiled.

Have Asians Become More Flexible?

Outsourcing thus involves not only a displacement of jobs but also a displacement of American middle-class values and entitlements overseas. The relocation of knowledge was facilitated by Indian professionals who seek to bring "America's best practices" to new business and government projects in India. A new casualized work ethic links floppy hair, jeans, and rolled-up sleeves to the introduction of e-commerce and e-government. While salaries are lower than those earned in the United States, returnee executives can enjoy a higher standard of living in India, complete with servants and chauffeurs. Former Silicon Valley denizens recreate American middle-class lifestyles, including gated communities and sport utility vehicles. These individuals embody in Asian environments, where the availability of cheap labor serves U.S. corporations, the can-do, technologically savvy, and entrepreneurial figures celebrated in American neoliberalism.

The most aggressive outsourcing of "American" jobs has been in second-tier jobs that capitalize on Indian skills in technical as well as in cultural knowledge. At Bangalore call centers, Indian workers perform a kind of Americanism. In order to make their American customers feel at home, they acquire American names and try to neutralize the influence of their mother tongues by trying out Midwestern accents. They are prepared to offer snippets of a fictional American background, family stories, geographical facts, and characters in TV shows and sports.[31] Thus labor arbitrage not only finds substitutable but cheaper labor overseas, it also requires Asia-based workers to assume virtual American personalities.

While values of self-improvement and entrepreneurialism have long shaped notions of what it means to be American, the rapidly shifting conditions of skilled employment now also include the capacity and potential to become a border-crossing professional. Cross-cultural skills, alongside knowledge skills, are important components of global marketability in a world of shifting nodes of hypercapitalism. South Asian professionals seem to display this flexible response to a variety of globalized work environments. Their geographical and cultural flexibility allows them to accumulate wealth, rights, and honorary white status in the United States. At the same time, as "nonresident Indians," these mobile high-tech actors are able to consolidate and expand economic and social power in their home countries. Thus the South Asian knowledge worker comes to represent the disarticulation of citizenship entitlement from its territorialized base and its connection with tradable skills as deterritorialized claims in a spectrum of market zones.

Knowledge is weightless and ubiquitous, no longer the monopoly of middle classes in advanced capitalist countries. Indian workers in the technological fields — broadly defined — constitute only one million of their country's more than one billion citizens. China's middle classes are only 350 million people in a total population of a similar magnitude. These islands of Asian expertise in oceans of national underdevelopment have arisen to challenge Western monopoly over knowledge and skills required in contemporary circuits of capitalism. In the space of a decade, Asian professionals have rapidly acquired technical and cultural knowledges that make them globally marketable and competitive with U.S.-based engineers. Below is a graphic representation that actually underestimates this challenge to the "American" workforce.

In July 2004, the *New York Times* printed a cartoon "graph" of "America's Shortage of Quality Jobs" (fig. 1). There is a pun in the use of "shortage," indicating ceilings (in jobs and skills) as well as the height of Asians (the figure on the left) compared with Americans (the figure on the right) depicted in the diagram. Asian men are represented as 10 percent as skillful as Americans, and costing 10 percent less than American men. This representation of the changing stakes in competing skills markets hints at, but does not

Figure 1. America's shortage of quality jobs. Cartoon by Leif Parsons. *New York Times*, July 25, 2004. Copyright © 2004 The New York Times Co. Reprinted with permission.

show, the actual differences by industry and by occupation that are remaking the landscape of knowledge industries. If one were to narrow the comparison to the skills in question — engineering and automated high-tech work — then the Asian figure would be as tall or taller than his American counterpart, while the cost differentials would remain constant. Asian workers are also rapidly catching up in research fields in the biotechnology industry. The stakes are much higher than depicted for Americans to hold on to their job entitlements.

On the same page as the cartoon, six letters submitted to the newspaper grudgingly accept the outsourcing of well-paid American jobs, but they also bemoan the lack of government and corporate help to cushion the blow for American workers. After all, at least a quarter of the American labor force is losing its capacity to provide for its basic needs. This is clearly identified as a threat to the middle class: "Although wage differentials between countries present excellent business opportunities for multinational companies, and may create some high-paying jobs within the United States, the bulk of our middle class will continue to experience downward pressure on wages until the wage gap closes. Why should the middle class accept these policies?" If we continue to ignore this issue, a day of political reckoning is inevitable.[32]

But middle-class workers, still adhering to the older view of America as an enclosed political and economic space, are currently focused on protesting the outsourcing of jobs as "un-American." There is a basic assumption about the entanglements of nationalism and capitalism, a citizenship belief that is being undermined by the globalization of information-based jobs. A major response to the sense of displacement and betrayal by corporations is disdain for foreign ways. As a result of complaints about Indian service and accents, the computer firm Dell closed one of its Indian call centers. New Jersey is planning to pass a bill to block outsourcing to India, even though high-tech jobs are also leaving for China, Ireland, the Philippines, and Canada. A white-collar labor war is brewing as American unions—TechsUnite.org (Calif.), the Alliance of Technology Workers (Wash.), and "Rescue American Jobs" (Ohio)—pressure politicians to outlaw the shifting of state jobs overseas. As part of the post–September 11 resurgence of nativist nationalism, more displaced workers are demanding legislative restrictions and tax constraints on the outsourcing of white-collar jobs. Meanwhile, the negatively received news about outsourcing has moved off the front pages, which are still dominated by post-9/11 concerns about terrorism and corporate scandals.[33] This vanishing from the public consciousness gives the impression that outsourcing has gone away, but nothing is further from the reality. The territory of national citizenship and the territory of labor arbitrage are pulling away from each other, cutting well-educated Americans off from the ever receding world of high salaries.

Masculinity and the Job Machine

Labor arbitrage is thus nibbling away at the foundation of American knowledge economy and reworking American ideals of masculinity. Middle-class professionals find themselves vulnerable to the same shifting currents of global labor markets that have long affected poor working Americans. Ironically, outsourcing dislocates American professionals in the very spaces in which they are the presumed heirs to Americans' global lead in information technology and innovation. Outsourcing disrupts the capacity of middle-class Americans to get good paying jobs, to accumulate capital, and to realize the good life. There is a growing insecurity as American middle-class men find themselves in direct competition with Asia's middle classes, expensive brainpower competing with cheaper brainpower, becoming subject to the valuing and devaluing of their status as moral persons by the switching mechanisms of the profit machine.

Clearly, a new set of expectations now confronts the well-educated American male as this new wave carries jobs overseas. In the 1970s, the economic boom fueled a trend whereby men began to turn away from the 1950s masculine ideal of chief breadwinner. Feminists have critiqued this shift in masculinity as a prolonged phase of youthful indulgence and a flight from domestic responsibility.[34] But there was still the expectation that college-educated men would be able to get well-paying jobs when they were ready to do so, if only to pursue a comfortable single lifestyle. But by the 1980s, the erosion of solidly middle-income jobs—in the transportation and computer industries—had cut further into the norm of masculine respectability based on a good salary and homeownership. Katherine S. Newman calls this process "falling from grace," as laid-off middle managers and air traffic controllers found that "they could still be evicted from the American dream." The loss of guarantee of a good job meant a "broken covenant" that stripped men of their self-respect; the loss of access to a good life was further compounded by the deprivations and insecurity suffered by their families. Many were bewildered and no longer sure what the "cultural rules" were for reversing this downward slide.[35] The dot-com crash in the late 1990s further exploded the myth of easy male entitlement to a good life.

We are now at a historic moment when new rules are set by the neoliberal exception, which enforces the internalization of ideals of "self-responsibilization." American neoliberalism is now articulated by the Bush administration as "every citizen an agent of his or her own destiny." American liberty is tweaked to mean freedom *from* state protection and freedom to respond autonomously to the turbulence of global markets.[36] The "master-of-the-universe" trope is a register for a new male ideal that can transcend the loss of guarantees of high-paying jobs at home. But this figure mocks the laid-off engineers and managers who, in the prime of their lives, are often unable to find jobs with the same salary or benefits as their old ones.[37] There is a rising tide of bankruptcies among middle-aged, middle-class Americans.[38] Being jobless or bankrupt at middle-age seems to imply the loss of key values of being American—self-reliance, self-sufficiency, competitiveness, and respectability. Growing irrelevance to new trends in the global economy cuts at the heart of middle-class America. There is a profound irony here because a short decade ago, Robert Reich complained that the symbol analysts in the new economy were becoming increasingly isolated from the rest of America through intensified segregation by job, income, residence, education opportunity and achievement, privatization of services, and a less progressive taxation system.[39] These qualities perhaps describe the current conditions produced by nonresident Indians in their homeland, not a middle-class America under siege by progressive job losses despite education and hard work, and losing a sense of who it is and what it can be.

For the younger generations, an era of greater uncertainty and lowered expectations looms. Some worry that educated Americans will be eligible only for geographically fixed service jobs such as sales. Not only are they losing their cutting edge as preeminent symbol analysts, they may be becoming less globally competitive as well. Americans are less flexible and hirable, because they are geographically based in a high-wage country. Over time, as diverse kinds of cognitive functions and skills flow out, the homeland itself may be affected. A commentator points out, with some exaggeration, that "a country whose work force is concentrated in nontradable domestic services is a Third World country."[40]

The late twentieth century of American values of education, innovation, and entrepreneurialism are have now been adopted by elites the world over. Colin Gordon has argued that the "neo-liberal *homo economicus* is *manipulable man*, man who is perpetually responsive to modifications in his environment." Furthermore, this calculative, self-enterprising subject is required to acquire skill, aptitude, and competence in order to build up human capital; in short, to be self-enterprising.[41] Most Americans think that they monopolize such "quintessentially American values," and that these values constitute the ethical foundations of what it means to be American. But Asian knowledge elites, like those from Europe, Russia, and Latin America, have also acquired neoliberal capacities and traits, but in far larger numbers. In addition, they possess cultural skills to be more flexibly relevant to diverse global zones in a way that many American professionals and businessmen, long dominant in global markets and dependent on native mediators, cannot. Increasingly, in a world of labor arbitrage, global cultural expertise is part of being a risk-taking entrepreneur in global circuits.

Global labor arbitrage has wide-ranging implications for the American middle class, which, held hostage by a globalized economy that sends high-paying jobs abroad, finds itself on suddenly shaky economic ground. There is betrayal beyond the strictly economic losses. If indeed the Protestant ethic makes work a calling, this Weberian claim[42] is most likely to be found among middle-class Americans for whom diligence and rationality are impersonal social virtues. Following Weber, we have long assumed that the economic ethic — or a calculative and methodical attitude toward the acquisition of skills, competitive gain, and market activities — is a fundamental necessity for participation in the capitalist environment.[43] But Weber did not live to observe the incredible dynamism of contemporary capitalism that can exclude some categories of calculative actors. Increasingly, their skills are unmarketable if they do not include neoliberal elements of manipulability, and therefore they cannot be equally valued in fluid market conditions.

Global arbitrage threatens to remove the social order of things in which the middle-class subject has long lived, casting him out of the economic cosmos that defines the ethical coordinates of his status as an independent actor. Increasingly, middle-class American men, like educated women and men everywhere, are obliged to acquire features of manipulability as free agents navigating a borderless world. But, rooted in a set of work attitudes and habits long framed by American capitalism, middle-class professionals are insufficiently manipulable. The knowledge economy presents an interesting paradox, deterritorializing white-collar jobs while territorializing American citizens. It is true that American senior managers and young MBAs are flocking to Asia to manage corporations (see part IV), but these constitute a fraction of the American middle-class population that is unable or unwilling to leave the home country and compete directly with Asian engineers and technical workers in lower wage zones. There is a basic belief that conditions for their reproduction as middle-class citizens cannot be deterritorialized in the world's wealthiest country. Even as conditions for making the American dream have slipped outside the territory of the nation, many Americans cling to a notion of entitlement and privilege that is resolutely place-bound. Being "American" and doing "American" jobs have proven to be truly tradable qualities, but "real" Americans may not be so marketable across globalized sites after all.

Are we in a post–Protestant ethic moment when the instrumental rationality that is a basic ideal of American citizenship has become so tradable that the mere possession of calculative skills no longer guarantees remaining in the game of modernity? Has the country given up "the ghost in the machine," and has the spirit of rational ethos and flexibility migrated east? Labor arbitrage is the latest technique to exploit time-space coordinates in order to accumulate profits, putting into play a new kind of flexibility that makes the American worker ineligible in some high-tech domains. We thus see a widening gulf between America as the preeminent site of rational citizen-subjects and the critical mass of highly skilled workers emerging in Asia. Will American workers have to give up their image as heroes of late-twentieth-century capitalism? The more profound betrayal is perhaps not the loss of American entitlements to well-paying jobs but rather the sense that American men have become less competitive with elite Indians and Chinese, or that they have become excepted from the spaces of neoliberal optimization that have shifted to Asia.

PART IV

THE EDGE OF

EMERGENCE

For decades, Singapore has called itself "an intelligent island," in an archipelago of presumably less intelligent places. But keeping one step ahead in the intelligence game is no longer sufficient defense against the risks and opportunities of fast-flowing technologies and venture capitalism. In the aftermath of the Asian financial crisis of 1997–98, the leaders of the city-state understood that a "New Singapore" needed to capture innovative technologies and foreign experts to spark new dynamics of intellectual growth. At a National Day rally, the prime minister declared, "Today, wealth is generated by new ideas, more than by improving the ideas of others. . . . That is why we have to bring in multi-national talent, like the way we brought in MNCs [multinational corporations]. Like MNCs, multinational talent, or MNTs, will bring in new expertise, fresh ideas and global connections and perspectives. I believe that they will produce lasting benefits for Singapore."[1] Among these lasting effects unspecified in the prime minister's speech are the risks entailed in the new meaning of being Singaporean.

As I discussed in chapter 3, the postdevelopmental moment in Southeast Asia makes the control of the population a key strategy for linking up with global circuits of capital. But whereas Malaysia relies on cheap labor to attract foreign investment, Singapore is repositioning itself as a hub for accumulating international expertise. Singapore was a nineteenth-century creation of British merchant enterprises and immigrants from Asia and Europe. As a postcolonial island nation of under four million people (of whom over half a million are foreigners), Singapore is famous for being run like a giant corporation. For decades, the economy ran on the management of domestic savings and the attraction of foreign direct investments through massive tax exemptions.[2] The domination of government-linked corporations and multinational firms has made Singapore an Asian "global city" if one bases this designation on foreign investment flows, cross-border contacts, and the percentage of the population that is online.[3] This so-called Asian tiger model — based on a mix of export-oriented manufacturing, high rates of saving, and a high rate of foreign investment — allied with an efficient government has made Singapore one of the richest countries in the world (the per capita income is on par with Canada's). But the 1997–98 Asian financial crisis rattled the government sufficiently for it to consider the tiger model as potentially crippling. New global pressures to deregulate markets, the China challenge, and reduced earnings from manufacturing spurred a major effort to "reinvent" Singapore by transforming the city into a node of a global knowledge-driven economy.

Authoritarianism and the Neoliberal Exception

The Singapore case is larger than the island itself, since the pairing of neoliberal logic and authoritarian control in Asia has produced some of the most radical experimentations with social engineering. The larger issue suggested is that the neoliberal exception invoked by authoritarian regimes does not rely on the same kind of technologies for problematizing and governing the population in relation to space. In chapter 4, I analyzed how the Chinese socialist state deployed zoning mechanisms to demarcate special zones for experimentation with market reforms. Here, in another context of Asian authoritarian rule, the neoliberal exception allows Singapore to experiment with an elastic notion of the scale of the nation and its citizenship.

Neoliberalism as exception is a "technicalization of politics"[4] that recasts politics as mainly a problematizing activity, one that shifts the focus away from social conflicts and toward the management of social life. Governmentality at a level of specificity refers to different styles of reasoning and problematization that are fundamentally concerned with transforming situations of uncertainty into calculative strategies.[5] The reduction of politics to identifying problems and making technical interventions in order to shape human conduct has wide implications for the new meaning of human being and the social. The interrelationships linking problematizing activity, calculative choice, and everyday conduct transform and give value to human beings and social life.

So far, such theoretical formulations have been resolutely focused on evolving sites of neoliberal modernity in Western settings.[6] Theorists have not yet paid sufficient attention to emerging sites of globality where neoliberalism as technique and ethos creates new spaces and new valuations suggesting a new style of space-time manipulation. In Southeast Asia we find an innovative use of neoliberal logic at three registers: the transformation of links between internal and external spaces, the orchestration of knowledge flows, and the linking of knowledge and entitlements. First, a site like Singapore redefines itself not within an established urban system but in relation to an emerging network of symbiotic flows. Second, by pulling together elements from disparate sites, the hub intertwines its future with that of global organizations. Third, network participants — technologies, firms, and experts — set new norms of innovation and flexibility for citizens. At stake in the fabrication of a niche of technoethical diversity is the reorganization of society and of citizens.

Baroque Ecology

For decades, the Economic Development Board (EDB), Singapore's administrative brain, came up with five-year plans that recalculated global risks and the island's position in strategic streams of commerce. In the late 1990s, a new strategy emerged to break radically from the island's geographic, demographic, and intellectual confines. The blueprint is state policy, not subject to real debate. "We aim to build a vibrant and effervescent enterprise ecosystem, where large and small companies can thrive and leverage on [sic] innovation and intellectual property to create value."[7] More than a hyped-up economic program, this blueprint entails a reimagining of the nation as a platform in a chain of knowledge production. It seems to draw inspiration from "the science of complexity," which holds that networks or interactions between diverse elements can give rise to nonlinear dynamics that can be spun into gold.[8] As a *Harvard Business Review* article put it, "Stand-alone strategies don't work when your company's success depends on the collective health of the organizations that influence the creation and delivery of your production. Knowing what to do requires understanding the ecosystem and your organization's role in it."[9] In Singapore Inc., we have a case of management theories informing social engineering as policy makers mobilizing market expertise and scientific research to transform Singapore into a hub for biotechnicity. Singapore now positions itself as the hub of "a wider Asian region of 2.8 billion people within a flight radius of seven hours" that is also well connected by sea and by digital links.[10] In this curved space, more than the propinquity of "healthy" organizations is involved; the propinquity of "healthy" citizens is also at stake.

I use the term *baroque* or *complex ecology* to describe the spatial formation that repositions the city-state as a hub in an ecosystem created from the mobilization of diverse global elements — knowledge, practices, and actors — interacting at a high level of performance. This approach to the outside is influenced by theoretical biology, which identifies fractual spaces in living systems. The reasoning is that each site can produce its own niche by combining flows of values and actors in order to create a particular synergy. An ecological analogy to what Singapore seeks to become would be the tropical canopy that is defined as much by the traffic and exchange between different populations as by the state of dynamic criticality their interactions engender.[11] The flows and nodes linking diverse populations create an irregular space that crosscuts conventional borders. Niches or nations of stabilized populations are drawn into flows; varied populations thus brought into interaction produce a baroque ensemble of diverse qualities.

Besides the spatial dimension, the baroque quality is also defined by the combination and recombination of diverse flows and actors. The corralling of global technologies and talents attracts collaborations with international companies and research institutions. The Singaporean ecosystem puts into play multiple domains, technologies, and actors so that their futures become intertwined in a network of sustainability. An EDB official informs me that in the transition from authoritarian taskmaster to venture capitalist, the state adjusts "the invisible hand," "giving the right ingredients but not actually control[ing] things." He uses the gardening metaphor: the EDB seeds schemes and provides fertilizers, thus acting as a catalyst to allow different organisms to thrive in the ecosystem.[12] Venture capital and infrastructural development invite collaborations with an array of industries, research bodies, and foreign experts, thus creating a synergy that fosters economic opportunities and intellectual accumulation.

The predictability of niche performance requires a complex reorganization of ethical norms. The close interactions between foreign experts and citizens are expected to engender higher rates of competitiveness, creativity, and knowledge value. Flux and effervescence are the unavoidable effects of such choreographed entanglements. "Ecosystems," we are reminded, "are typically distributed along the critical boundary separating stable from unstable dynamics."[13] The assemblage of venture capital, research institutions, and foreign actors is poised between systems of stability and instability. In Singapore, the biological field of the national oikos is now resituated within a baroque ecology that has reordered internal and external relationships along the lines of scientific expertise and entrepreneurial innovation.[14]

A rift is opening up between home and dwelling, between the rootedness of Singapore as a home country and new norms of citizenship represented by the knowledge anthropos. New regimes of human worth distinguish between foreign experts and local ones, those possessing intellectual capital and those who do not, setting into motion a new flow of ethical criteria and human consequences that put into jeopardy what it means to be Singaporean today. I will illustrate the changing ethical guidelines of subject formation in two overlapping areas of transnational biotechnicity.

The Technopreneurial Network

When knowledge is treated only as commodity, the university is transformed into "a free enterprise zone," a site of investments by knowledge enterprises or universities from around the world. The National University of Singapore (NUS) has become the hub of institutional links with various foreign programs in information technology, business management, engineering, and the biotechnical sciences. This knowledge configuration is intended as a system that combines academic excellence with creative entrepreneurialism, that is, that fosters a set of practices called "technopreneurialism." By forming partnerships with American and European institutions, Singaporean policy makers hope to shake up the complacent, academic, by-the-book approach to knowledge, and to ignite a sense of knowledge as an exciting thing that can be converted, with the right amount of entrepreneurial zeal, into intellectual capital. In addition, headhunting campaigns attract foreign professors and researchers—the prime catch being individuals with an MA or a PhD, about thirty-five years old—to come and work in Singapore, thus adding to its store of expertise. Furthermore, through propinquity and interactions between foreign experts and citizens, administrators hope that a culture of "technopreneurial" practices will blossom among Asian students more accustomed to being told what to do.

A key partnership in the high technology field is the Singapore-MIT Alliance (SMA). Formed in 1998, the SMA is devoted to training Asian students in advanced engineering and new computing technologies. The faculty is comprised of MIT and local professors in fields such as materials science, computation, manufacturing technology, molecular engineering, and computer science. The program has recruited dozens of top students from China, India, and Asia-Pacific countries, who are given generous scholarships to study in Singapore and, it is hoped, in time contribute to its talent pool.

The SMA boasts to being the largest interactive learning program in the world, a new paradigm "to promote global science & engineering education and research."[15] To accommodate the schedule of experts from the United States, the academic year has been adjusted to the American semester cycle. Students have the option to spend one semester at MIT in Cambridge, Massachusetts. It is hoped that these young scientists (with MAs and PhDs) will develop spinoff companies based in Singapore. To foster that development, foreign students on full scholarships are to become permanent residents. On graduation, foreign students will have guaranteed employment and high salaries, as well as invitations to become residents and citizens.

The goal is to have a student body that is more than one-fifth foreign, making the NUS a major hub of science training that will feed workers into the biotechnology network. It is perhaps no exaggeration to say that the state considers scientific knowledge as the new frontier on which the nation will be defended and strengthened. At a recent symposium, the Singaporean minister of defense hailed the SMA's core program, which will allow the attraction and retention of "the finest regional talent, along with the generation of an exciting ecosystem of research and idea creation."[16] The SMA represents the largest of many joint science projects with Western universities.

Science programs merely nurture a pool of engineers and researchers; the other half of the knowledge configuration is served by a network of business schools that will complete the training of scientists as entrepreneurs. There is a surprising cluster of name-brand business schools in Singapore — including INSEAD, the Wharton Research Center at the Singapore School of Management, and the University of Chicago — to instill in students an "enterprise" mindset. As the hub of an effervescent enterprise system, Singapore wants to be a "business incubator" or an environment where student entrepreneurs can obtain funding to play with their "marketable ideas." Again, the goal is to generate a synergy between students and entrepreneurs and to nurture whiz kids who spin off ideas into start-up companies. Can the strategic network of academic and business institutions replicate Silicon Valley entrepreneurs in Southeast Asia? To extend the "environment" of entrepreneurship, the NUS has set up colleges in Silicon Valley and other high-tech zones where Asian students can experience "technopreneurial" practices at work. For instance, NUS engineering students have enrolled at Stanford University, with the aim of getting internships with Silicon Valley firms. In a glowing write-up, a third-year material science student who was heading for Silicon Valley enthused that "we are young and not risk-averse." Through the internship program, "we hope to experience first-hand how a start-up works. The practical experience will be invaluable."[17] Another subsidiary, NUS America Inc.

will place students in internships with technology-based companies, giving Singapore-based students access to the best American programs, including biomedical institutions in the Philadelphia area. In short, the knowledge ecology that has been forged is meant to shake Singaporeans out of their conventional ambition of working for multinational corporations and instead become knowledgeable, risk-taking entrepreneurs who help attract investments from global firms. By force-marching university students up the value-chain, Singapore's leaders hope to make it "the Boston of the East."

The Biopolis Web

The engineering web is linked to the growth of the "Biopolis" complex, where bioinformatics and biosciences will be developed (see fig. 2). Now at its second stage of growth, a few billion U.S. dollars have been funneled into development of the biomedical sciences. The government has been investing in American and European companies in order to have them locate their research facilities in Singapore. An important nexus in the biotechnology field is the Johns Hopkins–Singapore Company. Techniques and patents developed at Johns Hopkins University in Baltimore will be used for research into various diseases endemic to Asia, with the hope of developing new therapies and diagnoses. Senior Johns Hopkins professors manage laboratories with links to the NUS and the national hospital. They train students and scientists from Singapore and beyond to undertake research on potential cures for diseases such as diabetes and cancer. A genome institute provides lavish grants and facilities for diverse pharmacology and animal research, thus drawing foreign scientists to locate their projects in Singapore.

The biomedical complex projects itself as a new venue for stem-cell research, without the monetary and ethical limits that may constrain such work elsewhere. There is also access to Asian biogenetic materials that can be used for developing customized therapeutics, thus opening up new drug markets for "Asian" diseases ignored in Western countries. Singapore thus positions itself as the ideal site for testing drugs and developing treatments tailored to Asian patients. The head of the Genome Institute says, "Genetic research today is global. . . . In Singapore the relevant resources for human genomics research are the ethnic diversity and high quality clinical databases."[18] Thus the biomedical system corrals not only foreign experts — such as the Scottish scientists who cloned the sheep Dolly — but also the genetic materials of the Asian populations that pass through Singapore's medical establishments.

Figure 2. The Biopolis complex in Singapore. Notice the botanical design of street lamps.

The constellation of laboratories and companies therefore constitutes a biofeedback loop, harvesting the population's biogenetic resources in order to sustain it. There is a transnational process of converting public value to "biovalue."[19] New forms of "biosociality" and ethical technologies come into play around issues of biological corporeal and moral vulnerabilities.[20] In this as in so many other debates, the authorities take the initiative to frame discussion and preempt serious debate. A government-appointed ethics committee has forged "a common moral approach" among Singapore's diverse religious and ethnic communities to questions about being converted into biogenetic resources. While some groups may object to the use and creation of embryos, the bioethics spokesman proclaims embryonic research as "a sacrifice for a larger good. . . . We need to express our respect for the embryos as potential human beings. This respect is expressed . . . in the form of strict regulation of such tissues as embryonic cells."[21] Stem cells are to be derived from embryos unused in fertility treatments, and research is to be entirely oriented toward treating illness. It is agreed that human cloning is morally wrong. It is not clear whether the sacrifice called for is to benefit Asian health or Asian wealth, but clearly it is impossible to disentangle the two. A new kind of biosociality requires the domestic population to turn against its own deeply held beliefs —

in Malay culture, for instance, there are ethical reservations about surgery and organ transplant—and to yield up genetic tissues for transreligious commingling. The ethical questions of what it means to be cultural beings are now framed within the transnational artificial environments dominated by the interests of global pharmaceutical firms.

The terms *nursery* and *incubator* so much on the lips of Singaporean technocrats now take on new meanings. They promote technologies for hatching not only new kinds of enterprising, knowledgeable subjects, but also new biogenetic forms from the population, that is, subjects and biovalues to be harvested by global companies, while plunging society into new kinds of ethical dilemmas. We will now turn to two major areas of citizen dis-ease that are opening up: the privileges of expatriates who are widely perceived as a "flow-through" population and the intensified calculations regarding one's life chances in this knowledge ecosystem.

Reengineering Citizens

Singapore has always been an immigrant society and since independence in the late 1950s has made social engineering a touchstone of stability and growth. Population growth and inflows were regulated to maintain a population distribution that is over 75 percent ethnic Chinese, with the remainder mainly a mix of ethnic Malays and Indians. In the early decades of industrial development, immigration was largely dominated by Malaysian Chinese professionals and workers from across the causeway.

By the 1980s, Singapore had become an affluent country (often compared to Switzerland), and the government introduced measures and tax incentives to encourage couples to have "three or more children if they can afford it." The pronatalist policy failed to stem falling birthrates, and a new "baby bonus" program provides generous financial support for second and third children up to six years of age.[22] At the same time, there is growing resistance to marriage and parenthood, especially among the well-educated ethnic Chinese majority.[23] Attempts by the state to arrange dating services and courtship venues have made little difference in the number of professional women who remain single (men tend to marry much younger, less-educated women).[24] At the same time, tens of thousand of Singaporeans study or live abroad, adding to the shortfall in skilled labor. As it is, Singaporean students are performing at the highest global levels in mathematics and science, but they do not yet form a critical mass of professional skills. The government attempts to enforce "a constant replacement ratio" for those who leave, substituting them with foreign experts.

The Asian financial crisis intensified the governing logic of "developing people," and the strategic focus shifted from population growth to recruiting skilled workers from the Asia-Pacific region. In 1999, an international head-hunting program was launched to recruit university students and professionals, especially from India and China. An official told me that the Ministry of Manpower is charged with adjusting the population mix of locals and foreigners; its website proclaims that it is "dedicated to developing a talent capital, passionate about people development." The current population includes half a million foreign workers, of whom one-fifth is highly skilled. The technology of immigration depends on a set of rules that are "focused on more skills, more privileges [at the top], and more control [at the bottom]." He added that "the market determines the economic value" of the immigrant worker. The instrument is the employment pass system, which grades skilled foreigners according to an intricate three-tier system of employment passes. The top criteria are professional qualifications, university degrees, and specialist skills; professionals, administrators, entrepreneurs, and investors are mostly highly valued. Foreigners are also graded in terms of their basic monthly salaries. The expatriate (a term applied to all white-collar and skilled foreign workers) can obtain permanent residency easily, depending on a point system measured according to skill and income. They can bring their families and buy condo properties. More and more, there is a focus on bringing in mainland Chinese students and professionals, who besides their skills possess the "right" ethnicity.

Low-skilled foreigners are also desperately needed, but they are subject to rigorous control. A work permit system is used for low-skilled migrant workers from Southeast Asia, who are brought in on two-year contracts. Needed in construction, manufacturing, services, and domestic work, migrant workers cannot change jobs and have absolutely no chance to become permanent residents. They may renew their contracts for up to ten years, with preference given to "foreign domestic workers" because of the high demand from local and expatriate families for household help. Surprisingly, there is no minimum wage for other migrant workers. Nevertheless, the inflow of low-skilled labor is tightly controlled by a levy imposed on employers. The goal ultimately is to reduce the number of migrant laborers to the absolute minimum.

Foreign talent in glamorous biotech companies is complemented by renewed stress on ordinary citizens' becoming competitive workers in the manufacturing sector in a time of global uncertainty. Ordinary people are required to embark on life-long learning and constant skill improvements in order to provide higher value-added as well as unique products and services. As a result of such retraining, companies like Hewlett-Packard and Cisco Systems now have new products developed, designed, and produced in Singapore. To maintain an edge in high-end manufacturing, workers are urged to think of themselves in a new social compact with employers and the government to increase social capital in the country. The campaign to build new capabilities and new mindsets has moved beyond workers to other targeted groups, such as homemakers and senior citizens, who are urged to acquire basic IT skills to complement language and arithmetic ability. Subsidized and multilingual classes are offered in many training centers throughout the island. The goal is for all Singaporeans to have basic computing and Internet skills in order to improve their employability "and in turn develop Singapore into an e-Inclusive society."[25] Those Singaporeans beyond such regulations are thus excluded from the IT-vision of "the New Singapore." The majority of citizens are being brought into line to provide a support system for the high-powered clusters of finance, engineering, and biotechnology devoted to the building of intellectual property.

The Ethical Debate

The emerging nexus of knowledge domains represents a new ethical regime assembled around claims to intellectual excellence, scholarships, employment, and valuable citizens. While reliance on skilled foreign workers is not unknown in other countries (including the United States, as I discussed in chap. 7), in Singapore foreign talent represents an unusually large share of the total population, and the government has demonstrated an extraordinary capacity to mobilize local opinion in favor of expatriate populations as a permanent feature of tiny Singapore. Deploying a combination of biopolitical and economic rationalities, officials and spokesmen argue that in a time of declining birthrates and global uncertainty, there is no other choice but to rely on foreign assets.

Thus state officials defend the foreign talent policy as vital to the economic growth of the nation. The deputy prime minister has pointed out that without foreigners, Silicon Valley would not be Silicon Valley, and London would not be London: "If Singaporeans were to throw out foreigners, there would not be regional headquarters here, half of whose staff are foreign; nor multinational corporations[,] . . . 40% of whose workers are foreigners."[26] He cited the example of Singapore Airlines, sixty percent of whose pilots are foreigners.[27] Economists from the Ministry of Trade and Industry claim that in the 1990s, 41 percent of the GDP "was achieved on the back of the inflow of foreign human resources, especially skilled manpower with employment passes (about 37 percent)." The low birthrate and the lack of a direct substitution between the skill profiles of locals and expatriates support the prime minister's claim that "the need . . . to attract these foreign talent will be a matter of life and death" for the nation. The report claims in triumph that despite the growing debate, 64 percent of those surveyed in a recent Gallop poll agreed on the necessity of importing foreign talent, notwithstanding the mounting layoffs.[28]

In response, the political opposition and Singapore Workers' Party has promoted a "Singapore First" rule that would only give foreigners jobs not filled by locals. There is fear of a zero-sum game, that expatriates will replace qualified locals, or that they will be replaced in the labor market by "mediocre" foreign talent. The opposition also called for raising the qualifying pay level for an employment-pass holder, that is, so that the influx is limited to the upper reaches of the professional and managerial category. Some returnees from Great Britain argue for a system similar to one there, where preference in employment is given to British citizens, with foreigners only getting jobs that are unfilled. Officials have responded with the argument that there was no simple one-on-one substitution, as locals and foreigners do not necessarily have the same professional expertise or skills profiles. Thus foreigners are valued for their technical skills but also for "asset ambiguity," or the kind of border-crossing talent that can capitalize on differences in various domains of worth.[29] Can the Singaporean citizen offer an equally wide spectrum of skills?

Again, the technocrat seeks to shape a new ethics of citizenship that goes beyond traditional excellence in ethnic-driven commerce. An official from the Ministry of Manpower told me: "Competition is a fact of life. This is an open economy in which global links predominate." He argued that the Chinese merchant figure of economic competition based on kinship- or ethnic-based relations (*guanxi*) must be buried once and for all. This is a new turn against the pioneering Chinese trader model celebrated a decade ago.[30] What is needed, the official stressed, is "the international risk-taking entrepreneurial figure who is beyond the Chinese merchant model. In the postindustrial society, [there is] the need for a Western attitude of risk-taking, a need to mix guanxi with Western global practices." In short, he is pronouncing the end of the family business in the economy, of the notion of local Chinese commercial activity, that is, naturalized by the activities of the family firms and networks, which are ad hoc, grassroots formations. Instead, capitalism now has to be planned by the state, or at least coordinated through an assemblage of resources, personnel, ideas, and techniques to shape the economic terrain that is entirely oriented toward producing goods and services for the world, and through which expatriates must flow in order to add to the value assets of the city-state.

Reengineering Life Chances

The new baroque economy, with its multiple clusters and scales of production and services, has introduced an increasing sense that the comfortable foundations of the old tiger nation have tilted radically, splintering the life chances of citizens according to new sets of criteria. Older rationalities about ethnic Chinese culture, administration, and market relations have become obsolete, and locals, no longer sure of their footing, have started talking about the roots of citizenship.

Among the many new discourses is an attack on the attitudes and practices of the suddenly old Singaporean corporate culture, which looks positively antiquated in relation to the calculative rationality of the new economy. Heretofore, a scholarly official class has operated government-linked corporations, controlling large amounts of national savings and enjoying an oligopoly sponsored by the government. An economist from Morgan Stanley observes that the civil servants turned corporate managers do not have the appropriate skills, creative values, and innovations of enterprising American IT culture. These technocrats should be replaced by "tomorrow's risk-taking New Economy entrepreneurs" who can convert these corporations "into genuine enterprises."[31] Even employment with multinational firms is not sensible, since corporations teach technical skills but not entrepreneurial risk-taking and the capacity to hive off homegrown companies.

The culturalist discourse about Asian values as the ballast stabilizing Singapore's success has also become tarnished. A bureaucrat at the EDB, telling me about the rapid shifts in state reasoning, confides that "to be a planner is a dream in Singapore." The government appeals to "the rational mind" and backs up its plans with a fine track record of delivery. Whenever it falters, it quickly gets back on track. The public has been socially conditioned to "instinctively go along with accepted wisdom." In the 1980s, during the boom times, the national discourse centered on good Asian values, and leaders could substantiate claims with double-digit growth figures. There was widespread acceptance of rules and regulation in exchange for the comfort and security of "an air-conditioned nation."[32] During the post-1997 recession, the "shared values" talk was abandoned. The Ministry of Information and the Arts whipped up a new slogan — Singapore Vision 21 (in reference to the new century) — to provide the psychological defense and buzz words needed to orient the population to the idea of a knowledge-driven economy.

This would require a shift from an educational rationality that has stressed the "stuffed-duck" (force-feeding) approach to one that was more "American," to ethics that stress independent thinking and risk-taking. Singapore has built its past achievements on cultivating industriousness, dedication, loyalty, and teamwork in its students. Now all levels of the education system need to instill initiative, creativity, critical thinking ability, and entrepreneurialism. At an NUS-MIT symposium, Morris Chang, chief economic officer of a manufacturing company, noted that the region "has strong advantages over the West" in diligence, loyalty, and teamwork, and engineering graduates are willing to take up careers in manufacturing. However, Asian graduates lack curiosity, innovation, and independent thinking, which are perhaps more crucial in the knowledge-based economy. Chang expressed ambivalence, however, fearing that his recommendations would be viewed as counter to traditional Asian values, but he insisted that a calculative and creative approach was only necessary in the workplace and need not spread to the family and society, where Confucian respect of individuals and collectivities should remain the norm.[33] In Singapore there is a pervasive belief that the cultural ethics can be protected from the risk-taking, cut-throat attitude and behavior being foisted on the young in the new economy.

But such culturalist knowledge is undercut by the new economy's stress on risk-taking market behavior. I had coffee with a stressed-out young employee at DBS Bank who had just spent a long day shifting around millions of U.S. dollars every minute. He complained that foreigners brought in new skills relentlessly driven by a bottom-line calculation. Another young Singaporean told me that whereas in the old regime job security was guaranteed by relations with the bosses, now performance was what counted. The bottom-line calculation applies everywhere, so that even the smallest mistakes are unforgivable, and officers are driven to assume more risks, take bigger positions, and tolerate wider margins of wins and losses. Employees like him talk about the old breed of British-trained bankers, comparing them to the foreigners who are better paid. The focus has changed from trading to getting customers, to expanding business through sales profits, to make DBS very risk-taking and very competitive. "We are to be more daring and aggressive, to take bigger positions, and make back losses." If he cannot keep up with the pace of winning back yesterday's losses, he will be out of a job soon.

In short, for Singaporeans, the politics of comfort have shifted, and many have become impatient with the red carpet rolled out for foreign expatriates. Expatriate fund managers, professors, and scientists appear to enjoy comfort with minimal controls, while locals are in distinct discomfort and are feeling "invisibilized." Indeed, the scale of risk has widened, since citizens feel that they must compete with foreigners not only overseas but also at home. The state headhunting agency beckons expatriates with the claim, "The country provides a fertile ground for breeding creativity." Talented foreigners such as scientists and musicians are identified as actors who can make life in Singapore "like an allegro. Fast, furious and fun"[34] (see fig. 3). The contrast is between exciting, risk-taking, creative, and talented foreigners, on the one hand, and narrowly trained, security-conscious citizens constrained by Confucian ethics of deference and groupthink, on the other. Expatriates are expected to help train locals in cutting-edge fields. But the two-track system intended to whip up effervescence in the ecosystem is also eroding the firm ground of citizenship.

The logic of regulating the flows of desired and undesirable populations has had the effect of displacing the host society. In the "flow through" populations, there are those who are desired as citizens but they do not stay long enough: many expatriate workers are on five-year contracts and the vast majority from Western countries and Australia do not intend to seek citizenship. An American working in a media company said that although Singapore was a great place for an American who wants to be a global manager in Asia, he was tired of the fact that "local identity seems all wrapped up in economic values." He is married to a Singaporean but plans to leave, after making a bundle of money. Most Western expatriates want to leave after three to seven years. The permanent residents mostly likely will come from mainland China and among Indian students who have been lavished with scholarships and places in the university, forming the core of an elite scientific-technical class. Then there are those who desperately want to stay but are excluded: the Filipina maids, the Thai construction workers, the Indian day laborers, none of whom have been allowed to apply for permanent residence.

"Life in Singapore is like an allegro. Fast, furious and fun."

For a man who usually lets his baton do the talking, Lan Shui is effusive in his praises.

"Singapore has this unique ability to combine its traditional Asian heritage with contemporary Western influence. The country provides a fertile ground for breeding creativity."

Born in China, Lan Shui honed his musical talent at the prestigious Beijing Central Conservatory and Boston University. He has already enjoyed great success as a young conductor with the highly acclaimed Baltimore Symphony Orchestra and Detroit Symphony.

Renowned for its economic achievements and efficient infrastructure, Singapore is also making its mark on the global scene as a vibrant arts capital. As Music Director of the Singapore Symphony Orchestra since 1997, Lan Shui is thrilled with the exciting pace of artistic growth in Singapore.

If you want to be a part of this buzz, visit www.contactsingapore.org.sg/time today. It could be another important stage of your career.

Singapore. Your world of possibilities.

Contact Singapore

OFFICES: BOSTON • CHICAGO • SAN FRANCISCO • LONDON • SYDNEY • CHENNAI • HONG KONG • SHANGHAI • SINGAPORE

Figure 3. A conductor from China cavorting in the new symphony hall, Singapore. Courtesy of www.contactsingapore.org.sg/time.

For locals who do not aspire to be elite professionals or managers, there is a sense of reverse bumiputeraism or nativism. *Bumiputera* refers to the native-born Malay majority in neighboring Malaysia who get preferential treatment in all areas of the economy, politics, and education. In contrast, some Singaporeans, who have long felt superior to Malays in Malaysia and in Singapore itself, now feel themselves to be second-class citizens. Students are concerned about career chances, and some believe that they must compete with foreign students for university scholarships. For instance, the NUS-MIT program awards scholarships to dozens of foreign Asians who also receive fee waivers and other perks in education and employment. Singaporean professionals feel that they are losing out to foreigners, who seem to be preferred by the government-led corporations and private industry. The majority seem won over by the state argument that expatriates add much needed value to the entrepreneurial economy, but they fear competing within ever widening scales of markets and geopolitical space.

With the rhetoric of Singapore as a global city, state authorities are privileging the globally marketable subject who must be induced to spend time in Singapore. An official boasts that "in the 1970s we competed with Sri Lanka. In the 21st century, we compete with Tokyo, Sydney, Hong Kong, London, and New York, but it is cheaper to do business here." Already, the city is making plans to accommodate additional population growth of over one million by 2015, making the city into a high-density "Manhattan-style" island linked by connector parks and underground malls and mass transit.[35] A little under a fifth of the new residents are expected to be expatriates. A committee of academics and professionals urge the government to consider building a "softscape," or cultural areas centered on heritage buildings and historical neighborhoods in order to foster "a sense of rootedness in Singaporeans." This is a limited recognition of the fact that many are feeling increasingly invisibilized by the traffic of professionals and managers in an emerging ecology of expertise.

In this latest feat of self-reinvention, Singapore repositions itself as the hub of a knowledge system that spans national borders. The dependence on inflows of foreign actors has split homeland and dwelling. The bifurcation between a virtual digital ecosystem, on the one hand, and an oikos being divested of its immediate past, on the other, has inspired feelings of inauthenticity. The quest to be an enterprise ecosystem undermines a sense of political moorings. Locals have begun to reflect on what it means to be a citizen, because expatriates seem to have citizenship status, to be cajoled into becoming citizens even when reluctant to do so. Expatriates are now referred to as "citizens without local roots," while those who are technically citizens are beginning to feel unrooted. A young man looking for a university scholarship pointed out that expatriate permanent residents do not have to perform national service. All native male Singaporeans must spend at least two years in military service, submitting to the ultimate measure of citizenship, a project to build solidarity and loyalty, though it is clear that the island cannot really protect itself. Young men are put into the army during the two to three critical years when they are ready to launch themselves into high-powered careers. Only doctors can delay army service. This is a further source of resentment of expatriates, who are not obligated to national service yet who enjoy state largess, scholarships, and employment in the new spaces of calculation. The specter of effervescent

citizenship induces a sense of being renativized, of becoming subaltern subjects, as in colonial times where colonials, not locals, were the citizens. At
the same time, a new mode of subjection makes locals potentially available
as biovalues for global companies. This predicament attests to the separation
of national oikos and national anthropos, between mind and body, as the
fragile island struggles to situate itself in the shifting networks of information
technology.

So neoliberalism, as a form of government enterprise and a mode of governing practice, enters into a peculiar relationship with political authoritarianism in this fast-evolving situation. For Singaporean technocrats, Silicon Valley
entrepreneurialism represents the acme of neoliberal practice—calculating,
entrepreneurial, and risk-taking. Singapore depends on international institutions and actors to instill these new technopolitical obligations of a self-
enterprising citizenry. This "technopreneurial" exception challenges the
earlier unified model of intelligent citizenship. Ordinary citizens are now
expected to develop new mindsets and build digital capabilities, while professionals are warned that they must achieve "technopreneurial" attitudes and
skills or lose out to expatriates and be reduced to de facto second-class status in
their own homeland. Clearly, a citizenship based on value-added human capital suggests that not all citizens are intelligent enough, or risk-taking enough,
to be similarly valued. A media official reminded me that Singaporeans are
accustomed to being told that they are to compete with foreigners on their
own home turf. It's a matter of merit, not race or ethnicity, she claimed. "If
you're no good, you're no good. The job goes to better educated people," no
matter where they are from.[36] The rhetorical emphasis has shifted from the
older form of ethnic governmentality that favored the ethnic Chinese majority. It is also no longer enough to be well-trained, hardworking, and law-
abiding. The "Asian values" discourse is dead, replaced by enunciations of the
effervescent ecosystem. The moral calculus in this knowledge ecology requires
a worthy citizen both to excel at self-management and to be globally competitive and politically compliant. As citizenship criteria are set according to the
shifting contours of a baroque ecology, citizenship itself becomes as effervescent as intelligence itself.

CHAPTER NINE

A Biocartography:

Maids, Neoslavery,

and NGOs

The underpaid, starved, and battered foreign maid, while not the statistical norm, has become the image of the new inhumanity in the Asian metropolis. The following cases illustrate the range of assaults on Indonesian maids by well-off households in neighboring countries:

— In 2002, an Indonesian maid in Malaysia was found to have been held as a "sex slave" for nearly two years by a government employee.
— In the same year, an Indonesian maid who had been starved and repeatedly tortured by her Singaporean employer died from a final blow. The employer was sentenced to eighteen and a half years in prison and twelve strokes of the cane.
— In early 2003, a Hong Kong housewife, who "filled her afternoons with golf lessons, facials, and hair treatments," beat her Indonesian maid until the maid's liver ruptured. The housewife was later charged with assault and is serving a three-and-a-half year sentence.
— In July 2004, photographs in the newspapers of a foreign maid with extensive burns on her face, breasts, and back exposed a harrowing tale of torture. Nirmala Bonat, a nineteen-year-old from eastern Indonesia, had been repeatedly scalded with hot water and burned with an iron by her employer. The images of Nirmala's wounds aroused a sense of national shame. The prime minister apologized to her publicly, and some lawmakers called for imposing a life sentence on the employer *before* her trial.[1]

In addition to the above cases of maid abuse and disfigurement, there are other incidents that remain murky and concealed. For instance, over the past five years, about a hundred foreign maids have fallen to their deaths from Singapore's high-rises. The main causes cited were the maids' slipping off window sills while cleaning the outside glass or hanging laundry to dry on bamboo poles. Others suspect that maids "imprisoned" in apartments were trying to escape or to commit suicide.[2]

The frequency and ferocity of abuses of foreign maids index a brewing human rights crisis as neoslavery emerges in Southeast Asia. Over the past decade, having a foreign maid in the household has become an entrenched entitlement of middle and upper-middle classes throughout Southeast Asia. Foreign domestic helpers from the Philippines and Indonesia compete to cook, nurse babies, clean bathrooms, and perform other bottom-drawer chores for middle classes throughout the region and beyond.[3] There are approximately 140,000 foreign domestic workers in Singapore,[4] 200,000 in Malaysia,[5] and 240,000 in Hong Kong.[6] As an expendable and underpaid servant class, they have become key to the maintenance of the good life in affluent Asian sites. It has been said that these are countries where "the middle classes have no idea how to cope without a maid."[7]

The number of cases of abuse by employers and recruiters remain small, compared to the total number of female migrant workers. Nevertheless, although there is no easy way to assess the actual number of attacks on foreign domestic workers, the gruesome nature of the violence that has come to light reflects a widespread attitude toward foreign domestic workers as subhuman. "Maids as slaves" is "Asia's hidden shame," a novel mix of rising affluence and mounting abuse that exposes the "vulnerable millions" of young women on the move.[8] Low-skill foreign women circulate in zones of exception that support the citadels of Asia's new rich.

Ethicopolitical Spaces of Humanity

Social theorists have argued that the paradox of humanity is its birth in the nation-states, an inscription of the particular in the universal.[9] Giorgio Agamben's concept of bare life points to the seemingly contradictory situation whereby sovereignty is predicated on the exclusion of living beings not recognized as modern humans.[10] Observers note that categories such as migrants, refugees, and illegal immigrants have been defined in ways that make their rights claims external to citizenship and the law.[11] Agamben maintains that the logic of exception constructed "a zone of indistinction . . . in which the very concepts of subjective right and juridical protection no longer made any sense. . . . power confronts nothing but pure life, without any mediation." The juridico-legal division between a zone of citizenship and a zone of bare life, while compelling, is a static and restrictive model, although in the end

Agamben seems to be searching for a politics that is not founded on the biopolitical fracture, or oscillation between the two poles of inclusion and exclusion.[12] In contrast, a temporal conceptualization of the politics of exception would recognize that the state system interacts with other ethical regimes that also operate along a continuum of inclusion and exclusion, though without mapping onto the same division between citizens and bare life. We should not discount shifts in the lines dividing the human from the inhuman, the virtuous from the evil that are crystallized in the interplay between the sovereign exception and other systems for valuing and devaluing bodies.

Another binary model that should be challenged is the strict division between human rights and situated ethics. Nevertheless, some make the extravagant claim that a "human rights culture" now prevails. Michael Ignatieff argues that "the existence of a single normative rights standard leaves no room for . . . moral and political evasions" in non-Western countries. The human rights discourse, he maintains, provides "a moral vernacular for the demand for freedom within local cultures."[13] This approach envisions a universal standard of the moral good that will provide the language for articulating human freedom in a range of presumably "bad" cultures in the global south. Ignatieff seems to discount the relevance of the great religions that have long existed as universal systems of civic virtue. Indeed, only by recognizing the relevance of the "moral and political" elements that Ignatieff dismisses as mere evasions can we study how moral problems are posed, claims articulated, and resolutions arrived at a particular milieu.

Such dichotomies, between the licit and the illicit, between a universal human rights regime and local cultures, are simple abstractions with little relationship to actual ethicopolitical negotiations on the ground. Instead of a rigid division between zones of humanity and of inhumanity, I propose that the space for problematizing the human is a milieu constituted by a nexus of multiple ethical regimes. A situated constellation of citizenship regimes, moral systems, and NGO interventions defines the space within which the translation and transmission of human rights discourse proceed. Because the site of problematization is shaped by diverse systems of value, it cannot be claimed that only human rights creates a moral vernacular, as if situated ethical regimes have nothing moral to say in the matter of labor and life.

In Southeast Asia, interrelationships among labor markets, nationalisms, and moral economies crystallize conditions of possibility for diverse notions of the human. The neoslavery of migrant women emerges out of a postcolonial intersection of racialized nationalism, neoliberal strategies, and disjunctive moral economies based on kinship and ethnicity. In postcolonial nations built on founding or dominant races, questions of who is considered human or subhuman are still inscribed by ethnic biases or hostilities.[14] This racialistic opposition is reinforced by moral schemes that are skeptical about the attachability of mobile, alien women detached from their own moral communities. The biopolitical concerns of the wealthier nation to secure middle-class entitlements depend on the availability of foreign others, creating an environment of class privilege and bias that tolerates slave-like conditions for poor female migrants. Thus, in addition to the biopolitical fracture, ruptures between racial and moral economies further complicate notions of who can or cannot be considered a morally worthy human being.

Into this knotted tapestry of situated power and ethics, local NGOs introduce an ethical debate on the plight of female migrants, articulating political claims for their moral dignity beyond a condition of neoslavery. It is widely assumed that NGOs, as actors in the global public sphere, operate as watchdogs of human rights vis-à-vis the state.[15] But in practice, NGOs, both local and transnational, have had to engage the nation-state in a variety of practical ways shaped by the nexus of variables. Can NGOs, in their actual representations of excluded populations, operate independently of relationships to the nation-state and to the market? Is the discourse of human rights effective for bringing about social improvements, or do NGO interventions require translations of their humanitarian goals into situated ethical notions about the common good? Because NGOs work in a fluid space of contending regimes, their negotiations on behalf of the politically excluded are contingent, and the resolutions are at best ambiguous.

As practitioners of humanity, NGOs make both technical and ethical interventions, since their work is fundamentally about managing the risk and security of marginalized populations by giving them value. In order to make claims on their behalf, NGOs define and sort out different categories of excluded humanity, in order to give them resources that *may* be convertible into entitlements and rights. Such ethical work of giving moral value to the politically excepted has an increasingly spatial dimension. NGO interventions entail mapping of spaces of sheer survival that challenge the political spaces of inclusion and exclusion demarcated by individual nation-states. Such techno-ethical strategies are necessary for redrawing the map of moral inclusion.

My argument here is in two parts. First, I discuss how the disjunctures between nations and moral economies create conditions that foster neoslavery for some foreign maids. As "transient aliens," foreign domestic workers are subjected to a household-based disciplinary regime and to techniques of securitization at the national level. Because they are mobile women, foreign domestic workers are not considered attachable to moral economies despite their role in reproductive labor. As a migrant population, female foreign workers are considered to be undesirable aliens as well as a threat to the security of the host society.

Second, interventions into this specific milieu of household-based neoslavery must first address the moral economies of the new middle classes. In Malaysia and Singapore, NGO interventions stir ethical reflections on the moral obligations of employers by invoking situated ethical norms that can protect the welfare of female foreign workers. NGOs align the bodily integrity of migrant women with their availability as a cheap labor, thus projecting their biological claims on a regional scale.

Biopolitical Otherness

The Moral Economy of the Female Migrant : The emerging cross-race, cross-ethnic economy of female migrant workers intersects with multiple moral economies rooted in kinship, religious ethos, and ethnic communities. Conceptually, a "moral economy" is a web of unequal relationships of exchange based on a morality of reciprocity, mutual obligation, and protection.[16] In anthropological terms, moral economies involve substantive relationships of exchange that are governed primarily by morality (whether peasant, religious, or "cultural") or by ethics governing a particular vision of the good life.

Moral economies in villages and urban milieus are the fundamental stimulus for the outflows of young women as migrant workers in Southeast Asia. Young, mainly unmarried women are central to the capacity of the family, community, and even homeland to sustain a level of development otherwise not available without remittances from abroad.[17] Labor migrations responding to the moral obligations of family and kin have created opportunities for organization by state agencies as well as labor syndicates that seek to channel migrant women to overseas markets.

The Philippines is famous for supplying the world with nannies. Whereas other Southeast Asian nations seek to position themselves in manufacturing chains and knowledge webs, the Philippines' neoliberal strategy has been to transform the country into a labor-brokering nation. An overseas employment administration program makes contractual agreements with foreign countries to hire "the great Filipino worker." The government advertises in global news magazines, claiming that "Filipino workers . . . were born with a natural ability to adapt to many cultures and even delight in discovering new ways to improve their craft."[18] Labor recruiters for overseas markets stress the flexibility and docility of female Filipino workers. At the same time, the state appeals to women to seek overseas jobs as a patriotic duty of "modern day heroes" whose overseas earnings are needed by the country.[19] There is thus a process of feminization of migrant labor, as well as a masculinization of their national roles, as soldiers and "ambassadors" who must not betray the national image of their country as the home of global workers.

NGOs play a crucial role in training and indoctrinating would-be migrants, focusing in particular on self-management techniques that instill proper attitude and conduct abroad. Feminist NGOs offer lessons linking overseas employment with Catholic feminine values. Using terms such as "empowerment," NGOs foster a moral connection between free choice in seeking overseas employment and the young women's sense of moral indebtedness to their families and duty to sacrifice for them. With rape and even murder a real risk faced by workers overseas, NGOs give advice on balancing the vulnerability of their working lives and their families. They must protect the precariousness of their own families, not forgetting to send money home to their relatives and hometowns. At the same time, they should be "friendly but not familiar" with overseas employers, not "sexually available" but on the contrary assertive and confrontational with men who proposition them.[20] Thus, NGOs play a crucial role in reinforcing the moral economic justifications of overseas employment and in sustaining the moral economy of the family, all the while teaching female migrants to be free economic agents in overseas markets. The massive, informal outflows of migrants from Indonesia to more developed neighboring countries have been less organized. Village families have been sending their daughters — often by perilous routes operated by criminal syndicates — to Malaysia or Singapore, where they can earn ten times the wages they can make at home. The government is not directly involved in the organization of the maid trade, relying instead on moral economic systems to mobilize young women from towns and villages, and on NGOs to train them for overseas work. Dar Rudnyckyj reports a *calo* system of labor recruitment that exploits the notion of moral indebtedness and obligation. Calo agents advance cash to would-be female migrants, thus binding economically and morally to circuits of labor recruitment.[21] Female migrants are collected in camps where NGOs train them in the "techniques of servitude" that include stock English phrases of compliance, keeping to a time schedule, and the use of modern appliances. These two regimes of female out-migration are in competition across the region.

Differences in nationality and educational levels will come to color how they are morally assessed in the receiving sites. Filipino maids—English-speaking, frequently college-educated, and exuding a sense of Western style —reign as a kind of labor aristocracy in the regional and global domestic service industry. The Philippine state and NGOs also promote the "export value" of their female migrants as responsible workers who are professional and worthy of respect.[22] In contrast, the Indonesian authorities and NGOs have not (yet) undertaken a campaign to sell the virtues of their female migrants. But nevertheless, in both countries, NGOs enhance the capacity of the state in making female migrants available for employment overseas,[23] where they are exposed to conditions of violence and neoslavery.

Incarceration and Securitization : The interplay of moral economies, state policy, and NGOs has created conditions whereby tens of thousands of female migrants are sent across ethnic, religious, class, and national boundaries. The circulation of transient female labor engenders both biopolitical availability and biopolitical othering. Under two-year contracts, these "temporary aliens" become part of a revolving labor pool that sustains thousands of middle-class households in affluent neighboring countries. The contingent legal status of foreign workers reinforces their "biopolitical otherness"[24] as noncitizens and lower-class subjects in tension with upwardly mobile Asian identities. The very biopolitical availability of foreign maids for sustaining a high standard of living becomes the reason for their exception from the good life and the body politic. In the host society, foreign domestic workers are subjected to two technologies of control: a housebound form of labor incarceration, on the one hand, and a technology of securitization that treats them as potential political threats, on the other.

The influx of foreign domestic workers to the sleek, high-rise cities— Singapore, Hong Kong, Kuala Lumpur—is a vital prop to the new entitlements of the growing middle classes.[25] These cities are competing to achieve global-city status, and satisfying the demands for cheap domestic help is part of the bargain with two-income families. A high standard of living is considered impossible without one or even two foreign maids to take care of household chores as well as of children or the elderly. Having a maid at home is a social right, like access to good schools, housing, shopping malls, and leisure, all entitlements of the middle-classes bent on buying their way to the good life. But even as the host country finds itself more intimately entangled with poor neighbors who participate in the reproduction of family life, disciplinary mechanisms and ethical exclusions invest the foreign maid with a biopolitical otherness in the public and domestic realms.

Foreign maids are sent to be confined in the households that employ them. In Hong Kong, Singapore, and Malaysia, contracted foreign domestic helpers can apply for the renewal of contract but not for citizenship. In Singapore, work permits confine foreign domestic workers to "duties of a domestic nature," exclusively within the confines of employer's home.[26] In Singapore and Malaysia, there are no rules regulating the work conditions of foreign nannies. The Singapore employment act "prefers to leave the free market to determine the wages and other conditions of service for foreign maids because it is too impractical to impose standard terms."[27] Only in Hong Kong do foreign maids get special work visas that ensure a minimum wage and days off. In practice, in all three sites, the majority of foreign maids are not guaranteed good working conditions, minimal earnings, or rest days.

The unregulated nature of domestic employment is based on a logic of incarceration. The employer controls every aspect of the foreign maid's life. It is common practice in Singapore and Malaysia for the employer to hold the maid's passport and work papers, on the pretext of preventing her from running away, but in effect confining her within the household. The employer thus gains a de facto ownership over the foreign domestic, who is thus made vulnerable to exploitation of her labor and sexuality. Such incarcerating control over an individual who can be subjected to abuse is a form of neo-slavery.[28] Furthermore, even benign employers in these countries do not as a matter of norm give regular days off to domestic workers, thus effectively imprisoning them in the house and in the endless round of housework. Given such conditions, foreign domestic helpers are often reduced to the status of nonbeings, with no legal claims on their employers and society at large. Also, because foreign women are admitted into the country specifically for domestic employment, there is widespread public skepticism as to their right to a public presence in the affluent cities.

When the maids are allowed days off, Hong Kong and Singapore limit where they can go and when they can go there. Public gatherings of foreign domestic workers are restricted to Sundays and certain urban spaces. The conditional tolerance of their public presence enhances the hypervisibility of foreign maids as an embarrassing Third World presence in upscale metropolitan sites. In Hong Kong, Filipina maids gamely resist such public exclusions by regularly staging street festivals, costume pageants, and parades to establish their claims to a public presence in the host society.[29] Filipina workers enjoy some kind of glamour derived from their English-language skills, a kind of "trophy" maid status that enhances their employer's prestige. Nevertheless, in Hong Kong, any Filipina-looking woman is hailed as "foreign maid" (or *fan-miu* in Cantonese), in a process of interpellation that frames an individual as "always already" a subject of ideological construction.[30] In Singapore, domestic workers are frequently referred to as "menials," a term that reinforces their association with lowly, filthy work. Symbolically, then, foreign domestic workers are reminders of a too recent past from which Singaporeans and Hong Kongers have escaped by scaling the heights of urban living. Singaporeans consider foreign maids in public a "social nuisance" and even those who tolerate their presence avoid their weekend enclaves, which are associated with dirt, noise, and chaos.[31] There is a synergy between a racial/dirty personal profiling and a racial/dirty spatial profiling, a sense of the contaminating presence of the transient but ever present foreign female labor force. So, despite the gloss of Westernized cultural skills, Filipina maids operate as a ubiquitous, contrastive racial or alien other to the dominant ethnic Chinese populations in the two metropolitan sites.

At a regional scale, the ethnoracial differences between middle-class employers, mostly Chinese, and their domestic helpers is projected onto the relationship between the glistening cities and their poorer and "darker" neighboring nations. The scramble to become "global cities" has led to the reinforcement of laws against public expressions of racism in Hong Kong, Singapore, and Kuala Lumpur, but these rules do not apply when it comes to the treatment of foreign migrants who perform a variety of "low-skill" or "unskilled" jobs avoided by local citizens. But the daily intimate association with these "backward" racial others threatens to subvert the self-image of well-heeled Asians, who themselves have so recently sloughed off menial labor and paddy fields. There is a suppressed fear that the increasing presence of poor migrants will blur the ethnoracial distinction of the nation, which in postcolonial Asia is based on ideological constructions of race, kinship, language, religion, and culture.

As I have suggested, Filipina domestic workers as a category are better treated than Indonesian maids in Southeast Asia. Filipina domestics, many of whom had worked as teachers or nurses at home, command the highest wages in the region. They are viewed as a kind of status symbol for well-off families and expatriates in Asian cities. While some Filipina maids have been victims of rape, as a group, they are less likely than Indonesian workers to be routinely mistreated by their employers and by the police. The Philippine government has bilateral agreements with host societies that give some measure of protection to Filipino workers, so that, in cases of abuse, their chances of obtaining compensation and justice are greater than for other categories of foreign nannies.

Other foreign female workers—from Indonesia, India, Sri Lanka, and Thailand—are frequently viewed as a migrant population likely to have been trafficked and enter the host society illegally. There is indeed a huge and not easily controllable system of labor smuggling that ferries low-skill Indonesian workers to Malaysia. There is a widespread perception of Indonesian workers as a source of petty crime and social ills such as prostitution and AIDS.[32] They have been accused of practicing a kind of radical Islam not generally welcome in the country. These perceptions of Indonesian laborers generally also color the treatment of Indonesian women who enter seeking work as domestic help.

While most Indonesian maids in Malaysia are recruited under a two-year contract, they are all tarred by the perception of being "illegal." Their relative lack of skills, compared to Filipina maids, reinforces their negative image. They are also under constant surveillance, suspected of being family wreakers and prostitutes, and in public they are frequently threatened with violence. Indonesian maids are subjected to frequent checks by the police. Public intimidations include police destruction of their documents, demands for bribes, or even gang rape. Unprotected from labor exploitation and non-payment of wages, foreign maids in Malaysia are given no mechanisms for the redress of abuse. The Indonesian diplomatic service has not been able to help beyond providing shelter for dismissed migrants who are awaiting deportation. Where foreign maids are concerned, Malaysians tend to be "pro-employer and antiemployee" with the result that abused migrants are criminalized,[33] while crimes against them go unpunished in the vast majority of cases.[34] The situation in Hong Kong is slightly better, but employers charged with maid abuse often avoid punishment.[35] Singapore has set up a procedure for maids to complain about abuses they suffer.

Foreign domestic workers are thus situated in a transnational field of labor exchange and traffic that strips them of the most basic political rights. In addition, they are frequently treated as a threat to the social body. Securitization techniques include the manufacture of ruptures that provoke panic and fears of political disorder.[36] Indonesian migrants, frequently targeted as a threat, are, on occasion, subjected to mechanisms of international penology. During economic downturn or social panic, a cascade of "emergency" acts reworks the divide between internal and external enemies. For instance, in the aftermath of the Asian financial crisis in 1997–98, close to nine hundred thousand migrant workers, the majority of them female, were expelled from host nations.[37] In Malaysia, campaigns such as "Operation Get Out" pushed migrants to nearby Indonesian islands that acted as holding stations. There, migrant women survived by providing sexual services to tourists from Singapore and Malaysia. The combination of routine police harassment and transnational securitization measures gives the host society great flexibility in keeping borders open or shut to migrants, depending on the economic climate or public moral outrage. Indonesian workers are always assessed in terms of their probability of being illegal, criminal, and a threat to the host country. It is no surprise therefore that Indonesia has come to see itself as a "coolie nation" that makes available its own citizens as cheap workers for richer neighboring countries. The incarceral logic thus imprisons foreign female workers in employers' households, but the logic of securitization keeps them in constant motion as a transient labor pool. An editorial in the leading Singapore newspaper comments on the expulsion of Indonesian workers, observing that "if we must grow calluses on our hearts, so be it."[38] Indeed, foreign maids have a precarious claim on the moral economies of the host society.

Disjunctive Moral Economies : In addition to these political controls of disciplining and securitization, the host society also erects moral barriers to the presence of foreign domestic workers, who are considered a necessary evil to maintain the household, which must be constantly vigilant to protect itself from the menace they pose. This moral ambivalence underlies social demands for strict controls over foreign maids. The employer comes to have unrestricted personal power over the foreign domestic helper, including holding their passports and work permits as well as determining their wages and work and living conditions. But while such privatized power gives the employer wide latitude in dictating the hours of work, there is a difference between a slave owner and a slave driver who feels no compunction in repeatedly abusing the foreign domestic worker.

Incidents of torture and murder of maids escalated following the Asian financial crisis. In Singapore, the authorities do not deal with the problem of maid abuse through legal protection, but on a case-by-case basis. The government recently introduced a half-day orientation for new employers of foreign maids, with the hope that employers can be socialized to treat their foreign maids with respect. Such mechanisms do very little to prevent violence against maids, which continues despite severe punishments for criminal acts of employers. Perhaps recognizing the limits of such legal action, an official pleaded, "It is vital that employers respect their domestic maids and look after them properly, as invaluable helpers in our households, and not as slaves or chattel."[39] We are thus in a situation where a distinction is made between creating exploitative working conditions and abusing the foreign worker, between being a slave owner and a slave driver, i.e., a paper-thin wall that is no barrier to arbitrary violence against maids.

The biopolitical otherness of foreign domestic workers is mapped onto the ethnoracial politics surrounding the production of life and traced through the disjunctive terrain of ethics through which foreign domestic workers circulate. The status of foreign maids as an external ethnoracial servant class makes employers profoundly ambivalent about foreign maids' crucial role in the material and social reproduction of middle-class families. Tensions between a perception of foreign maids as racially and socially contaminating and their involvement in intimate family care engender complex mechanisms of internal exclusion. Three factors contribute to an explosive situation whereby an ordinary household employment of foreign female labor can escalate into neoslavery.

First, among ethnic Chinese populations, there is a historic practice of servitude that constructs the unattached, mobile woman as an unprotected category. Many in Southeast Asia are familiar with the *mui-jai* (in Cantonese) or bonded maidservant who faithfully served a single family throughout her life. In the early twentieth century, mui-jai were young, unattached girls who could be bought and sold as a form of dowry for concubinage, prostitution, or slavery. The mui-jai was therefore an essential outsider, marked by her kinless state and thus assigned a slave status. A more pejorative term was *yong-yan*, an individual for the personal use of the owner. The mui-jai could only overcome her social condition by becoming attached through kinship to the employer's family. "A woman was nothing unless she could be validated through kinship relations [as wife or mistress] with a man."[40] The enslavement of poor, unattached young women was a pervasive practice throughout the British colonies in Southeast Asia. In 1921, the new professional class in

Hong Kong led the fight against the mui-jai, in the name of modern progress and support for female liberation.

It is therefore ironic that some of the attitude toward mui-jai, or bonded maidservants, seems to have survived among the new middle classes in Hong Kong, Singapore, and Malaysia. As unattached female migrants, domestic workers are seen as moral outsiders, despite their reproductive work and incorporation into the household. The domestic worker's externality to kinship is what marks her as a kind of slave, making her highly vulnerable to physical abuse. Furthermore, unlike earlier generations of mui-jai, who were by and large ethnic Chinese like their employers, contemporary domestics are ethnic others and therefore impossible to transform into kin. The moral unattachability of foreign domestic helpers makes permanent their exclusion from kinship considerations and obligations that once were extended to outside women brought in to work as servants. The Filipina or Indonesian maid is an unalterable alien to the moral economy of many Chinese families.

Second, from the perspective of the employer, the short-term employment of the foreign maid creates a sense of being "cheated" by the maid's leaving after she has been trained to cook Chinese food and perform other chores specific to Chinese domestic life. Thus, in many complaints voiced by mistresses, and in many of the abuse cases, foreign domestic help is described as a drain on the family resources. Given the economic investment in her upkeep, the mistress thus feels it urgent to extract the maximum service from the helper during her short employment contract. According to Christine Chin, female employers in Kuala Lumpur frequently refer to their foreign maids as "garbage" or "slave." One employer summed up her distrust of foreign domestic helpers in the phrase, "love to hate them, hate to love them."[41] Despite the foreign maid's contribution to household maintenance, she is also perceived as an outsider who can waste family resources such as food, utilities, and money, and even betray affection from the host family.[42] With the relationship to the foreign maid reduced to one of necessary evil, there is often little room for affection or for developing a sense of moral obligation, so that in extreme cases, employer resentment is expressed violently.

Third, the mistress sometimes views the foreign maid's presence in the household as a double-edged sword. The maid's material and emotional labor are props of the host family's well-being, but the presence of an exotic young woman in the household stirs worry and jealousy of her sexual allure. The many cases of seduction or rape by male employers contribute to a widespread hostility to the maid's sexuality, a negative view of her as neither kith nor kin, but a potential home wrecker.[43] In Malaysia, middle-class women share stories about the "sexploits" of their maids, as well as their potential threat to the family as carriers of sexual diseases.[44] Such extreme mistrust minimizes the chance that an employer will develop a sense of moral obligation to the foreign maid or a desire to protect her. Female employers are more likely than male to view the maid as a potential economic and sexual threat, and they are also more likely to oppress foreign domestic workers.

In Malaysia, even the moral economies of Malay Muslims and their Indonesian maids, while having in common Islam, race (*bangsa*), and similar *kampong* (village)-derived cultures, do not always guarantee good treatment for the latter. Domestic workers from Indonesia are viewed as "social pariahs" undeserving of public sympathy. They are commonly perceived to be perpetrators of moral and sexual crimes who should be locked up in "depots" and deported.[45] The limits of Malay moral economy indicate that national and class divisions break down the extension of ethnic-based moral obligations to poorer coethnics from overseas. There is thus a convergence of language and national bias, with the nationality of the foreign worker recast as a racial otherness, making it less likely that a sense of kinship obligation and mutuality can be extended to foreign domestic workers. In short, the ethical exclusions of foreign maids contribute to the widespread view of their moral inferiority, a kind of suspension of moral obligation that permits their treatment as subhumans, or bare life.

Indeed, the detachment of poor migrant women from moral economy is most concretely inscribed by the technologies of sterility. During the two-year contract, the foreign maid is not permitted to have sex or to marry a local citizen. To ensure that she will have no biological recourse to citizenship, the foreign domestic helper is tested every six months to check for HIV and pregnancy. Pregnancy results in the termination of the employment contract and expulsion from the country. Meanwhile, there is no regular health coverage for foreign maids, and any support for their health care is left to the discretion of their employers. There is thus a total suspension of the female worker's biological rights during her overseas employment. She cannot express corporeal desires. She is hired to perform reproductive services for the host family but excluded from reproductive activities of her own. This denial of her reproductive role vis-à-vis her own family has led to the transnational relay of family care. Filipino maids working overseas hire poorer women in their home villages to care for their own children.[46] In short, within this realm of biopolitical otherness and disjunctive moral economies, migrant women's legal, moral, and biological statuses are highly contingent, making them vulnerable to the harsh working conditions, rapes, beatings, and disfigurements one associates with neoslavery.

Remapping the Ethical Terrain

A Milieu of Ethical Reflection : Modern situations of inhumanity become the milieus within which ethical reflection on modern humanity arises. In Asian locations, some critics, following Jürgen Habermas, have pointed to the "democratic deficit" in public life.[47] For instance, a study of the mistreatment of foreign domestics in Singapore identifies the lack of a lively civil society.[48] But while that may well be the case, the model of the public realm is an abstracted space that does not take into account the diverse elements and contending visions, of which democracy is only one element, that shape the political and spiritual visions of the good life. Furthermore, the radical democracy model seems to predetermine only one outcome—full democratic citizenship. But when we investigate the actual unfolding situation for resolving the migrant worker problem, specific milieus of humanitarian crisis shaped by various elements—politics, markets, and ethical systems—also crystallize conditions of possibility for an ethical reexamination of the issue and for a search for ways to revalue the politically excluded. Communitarian theorists have pointed to the centrality of cultural norms and practices in any conception of the public sphere. But in any one milieu, debates must take into account situated political and ethical reasoning about the public good, especially the kind of moral thinking about sheer life.[49] Below, I will consider the role of NGOs as they enter into the fray of middle-class entitlements, disjunctive moral economies, biowelfare, and market calculations that surround the plight of foreign domestic workers, and through which the ethical treatment of aliens crystallizes.

The growth of the foreign maid' trade coincided with the rise of the discourse of "Asian values." As I have discussed elsewhere, the discourse arose in the context of the economic boom of the "Asian tigers," fundamentally as an ideological claim that capitalism in Southeast Asia was a kinder and gentler system in which collective interests were not displaced by unfettered individual interests.[50] Thus tied to nationalist development, the narrative of Asian values became part of the governing process to draw moral support for development despite social dislocations. The talk of a "caring society" in Malaysian and Singaporean claims that wealth accumulation need not be incompatible with kindness operates as a kind of regulatory discourse that lines citizens up behind development projects. The treatment of migrant workers, who are crucial to national development, has never been addressed by Asian values discourse, nor has the plight of migrant domestic women who have become indispensable to middle-class life. Nevertheless, the gap between the "caring society" and the treatment of foreign maids cannot be entirely attributed to state developmentalist ideology. Ethnic-based moral economies reinforce the common view of foreign maids as people from coolie nations who are politically and morally unattachable to the host society. In order to intervene in this constellation of values regimes, feminists must articulate an alternative geography of moral accountability.

NGOs: Mapping a Biocartography : A common view about migrant workers is that the host country should award them citizenship in recognition of their contribution to the national economy.[51] But in Southeast Asia, NGOs that intervene on behalf of foreign maids do not demand that they be granted citizenship. In fact, the majority of foreign migrant workers do not want citizenship in the host country; they want moral legitimacy and market access. At the same time, competition for foreign jobs among labor-exporting countries precludes insistence on human rights for their migrant workers. Thus, while NGOs may formally invoke UN conventions to claim rights for migrant women and their families,[52] their interventions respond directly to the specific conditions in the space configured by labor markets, biopolitics, and divergent moral economies.

It is useful to think of NGOs as a form of social technology that, like other kinds of governing entities, defines "objects, rules of action, [and] strategic games of liberties."[53] NGOs give moral value to bare life by defining the maids' biological existence in relation to political space. NGOs thus gain power over the politically excluded and exercise the power to regulate, frame, and represent their interests to various parties. For instance, in Singapore, some church-based NGOs "govern" foreign maids by helping them submit to their lot through religious disciplining and forbearance. "What we do is help them [the maids] cope using the Bible. . . . We don't encourage complaining, because that's not Biblical. So you either learn to forebear, or seek alternative solutions."[54] Church-controlled NGOs thus create a religious space for inducing self-discipline among foreign maids.

But NGOs in Malaysia operate in a different direction, by mapping a different geography of claims for female migrants that crosscuts the space of the nation-state. This space is scaled at the level of regional migrant flows and is intended to bridge disjunctive nations and moral economies that devalue the moral status of female migrants and tolerate conditions of neoslavery. These NGOs discover that a space of migrant claims to sheer survival can benefit from aligning the claims with neoliberal interest in cheap labor.

Biowelfare : The respatialization of migrant claims at a regional level is suggested by the commonality of dangers encountered by migrant women in many national, racial, and moral economic contexts. NGOs throughout Asia have collected data on the array of abuses that female workers suffer in the course of their migration and work in host societies. Migrant women are highly vulnerable to being trafficked, raped, deprived of their earnings, and infected with HIV. The labor conditions are defined by the three-D jobs (dirty, demanding, and dangerous) and the three-D stigmas (disease, depravity, and drugs). NGOs remind the public that a majority of migrant workers are female who provide "the cheapest, most flexible, and most docile labor . . . for dirty, demanding, and dangerous jobs which locals shun."[55] The extensive documentation of abuses inflicted on female migrant workers at the regional level exposes the hypocrisy of official claims to be "the caring society" (in Malaysia) and the "educated society" (in Singapore). Such self-representations do not come with legal and moral protections for foreign female workers, whose circulation enables neoliberal standards of living.

Using "the media as their ally," feminists broaden the ethical debates on the treatment of foreign domestic workers, also challenging the Malaysian state to increase the protection of migrant women.[56] Reports on the abuse, maltreatment, torture, and even death of migrant women have provided ammunition in negotiations with local authorities to make medical coverage part of the work contract for female migrants. One outcome has been stricter control over agencies that recruit and transport migrant workers. But there is nearly unanimous support for the government's position that foreign maids should not be given citizenship.

Therefore, a major strategy of NGOs is to change public perception about the moral obligation to support and protect the migrant women who have contributed to the realization of the society's middle-class dreams. Press reports of maid abuse have increased public awareness of the problem, bringing shame and horror to Malaysians, who are accustomed to viewing themselves as a warm and hospitable people. The director of a women's shelter in Malaysia said that people need to realize that "poorer people who are working for you also have rights. This is not slavery."[57] The focus is on the mobile female body and its vulnerability to enslavement. What kinds of claims can be made that will shift the perception of the migrant female body from a site of a biopolitical otherness to one of biological claim?

Talking about undocumented workers with AIDS in France, Didier Fassin maintains that "the *suffering body* proposed in the name of common humanity is opposed to the illegitimacy of the *racialized body*, promulgated in the name of insurmountable difference." The discourse of the suffering body, he argues, has created "bio-legitimacy" as a new legal claim whereby health and illness become legitimate ground for awarding citizenship to the asylum seeker.[58] In Southeast Asia, NGO discourses of the "enslaved" or "at-risk body" of foreign maids is not proposed in the name of common humanity in order to gain citizenship. Indeed, Southeast Asian countries and their populations are very firm in their beliefs that it is legitimate for the state to discriminate against aliens in favor of its own citizens. Thus, NGOs are not invoking human rights as a legal status; they are appealing to basic cultural values about the moral worthiness of women's bodies. The focus is on *biowelfare*, an ethical claim that skirts the issue of political rights by focusing on the sheer survival of foreign female workers. Only by invoking cultural understanding and compassion, not abstract rights discourse, can the moral legitimacy of alien women's bio-security be persuasive to the host society.

The biowelfare of foreign domestic workers, as "women at risk," is an even more fundamental claim on Asian ethics. The bodily integrity of women, the female body confronted with potential violence, is something that can elicit greater moral sympathy from Asian society than demands for gender or migrant rights. In the course of their work, migrant women are exposed to violence and life-threatening diseases and have little or no access to health services. The foreign maid, NGOs remind the public, is not a machine; she also requires rest, and a limit to overtime labor. Feminists ask why, if Singapore is such a civilized society, maids are treated as "emotionless and slavish working machines" and not as human beings.[59] In the absence of enforced laws requiring maids to have rest days, feminist NGOs are now insisting on employers' moral obligations to let their domestic helpers have days off for "rest and relaxation" or to attend to religious services. The language avoids demanding "worker rights," stressing instead the moral and health benefits from time off, since the foreign worker should not be treated like a slave-like thing. After all, migrant women and foreign maids are frequently also mothers and nurses, life-givers and life-nurturers that are cherished in Asian traditions.

By focusing on the at-risk female body, NGOs compel Asian middle classes to acknowledge the vulnerable female body and their own honor as host society to secure the biowelfare of their foreign workers. Islam, Hinduism,

Buddhism, and Christianity all stress special protection of the weak and vulnerable, especially women and children. The religions also support moral traditions of hospitality to foreign visitors in a region long shaped by international trade and migration flows. Advocates of migrant workers thus stimulate a coherent reflection on ethics into which the public is drawn. In other words, they suggest ways to reconsider the situation of the domestic worker, whose very biopolitical availability denies her bodily security and human dignity, reducing her to a slave-like status. NGOs raise questions such as whether living the good life (in the material sense) should entail the mistreatment of less fortunate others. Although foreign maids have no citizenship, their enslaved, threatened bodies challenge the modernity of Southeast Asian societies, suggesting a backward slide to feudal dependency on slaves.

In contrast, the healthy and secure body of the foreign maid can only redound favorably to the higher standard of living enjoyed by well-heeled Asians. Such ethical reflection will repair the marred face of Asian affluence and perhaps stimulate the recovery of a sense of Asian hospitality, one that combines the value of the life of the female migrant with the moral economy of Asian families. The questions posed are tied to wider moral questions of how Asians should live, and how they should treat others who provide their daily comfort and family security. The calls for Asians to return to the heart in their treatment of migrant others induce them to rethink, in both political and ethical terms, the daily activities that support families and the nation. Can middle-class employers break from their sense of entitlement and complacency, reenvisioning their relationships with foreign maids as a kind of moral economy, that is, as ethical relationships that minimally secure the biological health of migrant women? In the absence of legal rights protecting the foreign helper, can her biowelfare be guaranteed through the moral economy of the family?

Biowelfare refers to the rights to life and bodily integrity, which have been called "the first genre of human rights," the fundamental elements of individual rights.[60] But the moral demands for biowelfare by Asian NGOs are not antecedent to claims for full-fledged legal rights for migrants to become legal citizen-subjects. The question remains whether this kind of strictly moral claim for migrant workers can be reinforced through market reasoning.

Market Rights : NGOs are not content to simply promote the biowelfare of female migrants, they want foreign domestic workers to be truly free economic agents as well. As I discussed above, some NGOs have taken on the role of making available contracted labor migrants for overseas markets. Now, in order to be effective protectors of abused migrant workers, other NGOs ramp up the claims of migrant workers to job freedom in overseas labor markets. Although the foreign domestic helper is not as glamorous as the globetrotting corporate warrior of neoliberalism, she is also a risk-taking subject, someone who crosses mountains and oceans to reach a labor situation where her biological and economic well-being is highly uncertain. So NGOs are linking the demand for a healthy migrant body to a kind of neoliberal calculation, claiming that foreign workers should enjoy freedom of residence, employment, and family life, that is, the conditions of social reproduction that are enjoyed by foreign professionals in Asia. Foreign domestic workers should have the right to reside in the host city, to bring their families, and to change jobs or find other lines of work. This right of market access and freedom to operate across the region is very different from demands for citizenship.

In surveys conducted by local NGOs, the vast majority of female migrant workers say they are not interested in becoming citizens of Hong Kong, Singapore, or Malaysia. No more than ten percent express a desire to settle in the host country, and most of these are migrant women who have married local people.[61] What migrant workers want is legal residence, as well as unrestricted movement back and forth to home country. For Filipino workers, the demand for residency rights and easy mobility also ensures that the Philippines can continue to be a labor-exporting country. Indonesian domestic helpers also feel that migrant rights of residence abroad will enable them to contribute to the development of their country. The Asian Migrant Center, a Hong Kong–based umbrella of migrant-oriented NGOs, is currently fighting for the right of foreign domestic workers to be temporary residents in the city of employment and to work and move between Asian cities without the limits imposed by the contract system.

The ethics of healthy and unharmed migrant bodies becomes the ground for their claim to free competition in regional labor markets. Furthermore, the health and security of the female migrant is unavoidably entangled with the well-being of her family left back home. Claims for the integrity of the migrant body and for freedom of choice in the regional marketplace will make migrant workers (and their families) less vulnerable. At the same time, this alignment of gendered biological security and neoliberal logic also highlights the economic benefits to the host society. Health security and market flexibility will ensure that the foreign servant class continues to be available to affluent Asians, but under better material, moral, and economic terms. The demand for migrant biological welfare is thus embedded in economic inter-dependency between the sending and the receiving countries.[62]

Such NGO reasoning thus creates an ethics of exception for foreign maids, making a good moral economic argument for why, despite their status as aliens, they deserve biological justice. By inscribing a biocartography of migrant workers, NGOs reterritorialize their moral claims at a regional scale. Unfortunately, given the contingencies of the forces at play, NGO governance can only safeguard the biological security of migrant women by foregrounding their capacity to serve the insatiable demands of the neoliberal sector. For the moment, such moral bargains provisionally maintain migrant wages below those of citizens of the employing countries.

We need to maintain skepticism toward claims that NGOs are building the institutional skeleton of a "global public sphere." We have seen that NGO activities are situated within particular constellations of power and ethics; their interventions can actually generate new moral hierarchies. In action, NGOs have not so much converted the globally excluded into humanity with legal rights as redefined and reordered different categories of the human in connection with various moral systems, markets, and the state. This is because specific NGO problems are crystallized by and their interventions take shape through situated constellations of economic, political, and ethical relationships. NGOs thus are not the actors of a "postnational constellation," in the Habermasian sense of an emerging global civil society,[63] for two reasons.

First, in Southeast Asia, NGOs are demanding moral guarantees of biological welfare, not rights of citizenship for migrant workers as members of a global humanity. Even if they formulate their demands in terms of "migrant rights," there is no juridical institutionalization of migrant rights outside national treaties between sending and receiving countries, and even these are minimal and easily thwarted by the host society. The shocking case of Flor Contemplacion, a Filipina maid executed in Singapore for causing the deaths of the child in her care and of another maid, raised questions of the sending country's capacity to protect the individual rights of its citizens in the host country.[64] Rather, within the Southeast Asian matrix of economic, moral, and political economies, NGOs invoke a value shared by various ethical regimes: the female body deserves moral status and physical protection. Such an ethical reasoning can bypass if not displace the ethnoracialized stigma of foreign domestic workers as alien and illegitimate bodies. The biowelfare claims construct a moral status that may reduce brutal attacks on and disfigurements of foreign maids. But given the current nexus of nationalisms, migrant labor, and moral economies, it is not clear that claims of biowelfarism will lead to formal citizenship in the host society.

Second, the NGOs are not postnational: although "nongovernmental" strictly speaking, they often play a variety of roles on behalf of the nation-state and become somewhat party or subject to national agendas and capitalist interests. NGOs in labor-exporting countries are part of the institutional infrastructure that supports the state development strategy of making migrant workers available overseas. At the same time, other NGOs protest the dangerous and violent conditions of migrant employment and movement, seeking a kind of basic security and freedom for migrants as mobile workers. NGOs thus directly or indirectly subcontract for states and work with market interests. Such connections to strategic political and market institutions, and enmeshment in normative structures, actually make NGOs more effective in pursuing grass-roots causes.

My ethnographic discussion shows that NGOs in operation are not autonomous entities entirely devoted to an abstract notion of universal democracy. Rather, the NGO modality in action is one of complex attachments and detachments—embeddedness in cultural affiliations but solidarity with the plight of migrant workers; links to the nation and capitalism but contingent ties to notions of common humanity; use of situated ethical beliefs but rare mention of human rights; and investment in regional attitudes toward migrant women more than in abstract ideals of global humanity. As actors intervening in particular milieus, NGOs are vulnerable to regulation and manipulation by the state, the media, and public opinion, even as they struggle to build an ethical solidarity between foreign domestics and their affluent employers. For the millions of intrepid young women traveling far from home in order to support their own families, the geography of labor circulation becomes the unstable ground of their claim for biological security.

This formulation of situated attachment and detachment is a different modality than the concept of "detachment" proposed by the "new cosmopolitanists," that is, distance from particularistic ties and disinterested affiliations based on universalism.[65] The point is not that there are no "new cosmopolitanisms" but rather that NGO missions must be translated and negotiated within particular alignments of institutional power, and the ethical outcomes are not solely predetermined by human rights. In order to be effective at all, NGOs must work with and thus become subjected to the conjunctural force of overlapping political, moral, and economic systems. Furthermore, most

NGOs in the South receive funding from transnational NGOs based in the Netherlands, Denmark, Sweden, the United Kingdom, and Canada and are thus also subjected to the governance of a universalizing human rights regime that often pushes human rights agendas without dealing with the practical problems of millions of impoverished people living on the edge. NGOs are caught betwixt and between transnational and situated regimes of living, trying to safeguard lives as well as living conditions. NGOs try to negotiate in the interstitial space among diverse ethics regimes.

Third, the concept of constellated ethical systems challenges Agamben's pessimistic view that bare life exists in a zone bereft of any possibility of moral intervention.[66] NGOs' interventions on behalf of noncitizens and the politically excluded operate in a realm of diverse traditions that can be tapped for ethical principles that cherish and protect life. Humanitarian work relies on the interplay of rhetorical claims and counterclaims, constantly translating values across a range of exceptions, always making the special case for bringing in one more baby, one more torture victim, from the ambiguous edge of humanity. The temporal dimension of NGO labor is one of continually undoing the binarism institutionalized in citizenship, or the conceptual separation between rights and ethics. When we recognize the fruitful interplay of diverse forms of virtue, we know that there is no permanent zone of indistinction; there are only endless ethical challenges to established dichotomies of the human and the nonhuman, or of good and evil.[67]

CHAPTER TEN

Reengineering the

"Chinese Soul" in

Shanghai?

Standing on the roof, we looked at the silhouettes of the buildings lit up by the streetlights on both sides of the Huangpu River, especially the Oriental Pearl TV Tower, Asia's tallest. Its long, long steel column pierces the sky, proof of the city's phallic worship.

The ferries, the waves, the night-dark glass, the dazzling neon lights and incredible structures — all these signs of material prosperity are aphrodisiacs the city uses to intoxicate itself. They have nothing to do with us, the people who live among them. A car accident or a disease can kill us, but the city's prosperous, invincible silhouette is like a planet in perpetual motion.

— Wei Hui, *Shanghai Baby*

The study of global business has rarely paid attention to the actual work entailed in introducing management ideas and practices to Asian sites — the interruptions, articulations, and tensions attendant on the emergence of the metropolis in the world economy.[1] Rather, there is a widespread assumption that neoliberal knowledge flows smoothly into new contexts and is seamlessly internalized by recipient authorities and citizens alike. This view is influenced by the theory of "the global city." Saskia Sassen has claimed that global cities such as New York, London, and Tokyo are best conceptualized as strategic nodes in a transnational urban network. Global cities are the source of corporate power, knowledge, and rules that are disseminated to emerging countries, where "second-tier" cities such as Shanghai become launching pads for the adoption of neoliberal practices for doing international business.[2] While the general outline of such an infiltration of global corporate knowledge and rules is persuasive, the hypothesis that global capital claims will be received compliantly by the host city and its population needs to be investigated rather than assumed.

The Global Manager's View

Another perspective shifts the analytical attention from the macro level of global circuits to the level of actual business thinking and practices in confronting global sites. For instance, Susan Roberts has looked at business school manuals to discover the proposed styles and techniques for creating the "new global manager," who is expected to steer a course through the risks and diversity of various market sites.[3] Strategic management guidelines are an example of what Nigel Thrift calls "the practicalities of business" that should be the stuff of investigation. How do business knowledge and practices become mobilized to solve a host of problems relative to competence in different business locations?[4] Business schools, global managers, and management gurus are the main actors in spreading business ideas and practices, and yet they are often frustrated when they try to "reengineer" local attitudes and behavior to conform to global corporate norms. Indeed, when I first went to Shanghai to study the introduction of global business management, American managers were unanimous that their "number one problem" in Shanghai was not the Communist Party, nor the uncertain supply of electricity, but "human resources," the white-collar Chinese worker. Changing what they call "the software" of Chinese employees was more difficult than reengineering a computer, since foreign companies have had to deal with a host of individual agendas, styles of creative entrepreneurialism, and ethical interests.

While fractions of the Chinese ruling elite remain ambivalent about market reforms, they have kept their eyes on the prize of Shanghai, the star in the renascent Chinese firmament.[5] Keeping in mind this link between the neoliberal exception and patriotism, I will analyze the ambiguous attitude of white-collar workers to foreign corporate demands. Chinese employees of foreign firms maintain a stance that is not as explicitly obsequious as workers in other Asian sites because it is aligned with a larger national profile. Unlike the rest of East Asia, China has not launched its market reforms "by invitation" to foreign corporations; Beijing has been careful to retain its autonomy and its bargaining rights.[6] This unbowed attitude has not been lost on Chinese workers, who are discovering their own energies and ambitions.

My approach examines how Western business knowledge and practices are transferred to Shanghai in two major ways. First, I discuss attempts by American companies to instill management thinking and behavior among their white-collar employees. Business knowledge funneled through firms is focused on disciplining Chinese employees to be team players, not entrepreneurial figures. Frustrations encountered in attempts to "reengineer" workers are expressed by managers in terms of the opposition between Western business "rationality" and Chinese cultural "irrationality." Chinese employees, they complain, are not easily amenable to corporate guidelines and norms. The workers appear to be driven less by company discipline than by individualist careerist moves in a turbulent job market.

Second, Western management knowledge is entering not only through American companies but also through returning Chinese expatriates who have been educated abroad. These are cultural entrepreneurs who selectively deploy business management in combination with cultural forms in an individualistic, instrumental manner. These figures play with Western and Chinese elements in a logic of self-fashioning and in a strategic marketizing of cultural forms. The double-coding of their personalities and business projects is a mix of cultural pride and commercial detachment. As entrepreneurs in the latest wave of cosmopolitanism, Chinese returnees now have the authority to determine and interpret transcultural flows and meaning.

Third, we will see that neoliberal techniques interact with Chinese notions of *guanxi*, or moral economic understandings of interpersonal relationships. While managers think that rational management practices will eventually erase guanxi-influenced action in the corporation, Chinese employees disagree. Guanxi becomes repositioned within business management, a form of ethical reasoning that deflects business rationalities, bending them to accommodate workers' social obligations to relatives and friends outside the corporate world. In short, global management strategies to reengineer personalities in the new Shanghai milieu must continually recreate themselves in the light of the entrepreneurial individualism of Chinese subjects and their entanglements with guanxi exceptions. At the same time, the rationality and efficiency of management technology is electively absorbed by entrepreneurs and workers who want to control the form of Chinese capitalism.

Reengineering Corporate Players

American managers in Shanghai readily agree that the training of Chinese science and engineering graduates is "world-class" and that the best university graduates and most talented people stream into Shanghai to find jobs with foreign companies. But in the mid-1990s, the managers encountered a baffling problem: the new knowledge class in China generally did not display an attitude or behavior recognizable to the managers as "business intelligence." "Why do we need consultants on human resources? According to a management trainer, 'People are the greatest controllable element in China; not market, not politics!'"

The managers noted with dismay that bright Chinese university graduates lacked the "modern, rational, and fair-minded" attitude that is desired in corporate employees. They mentioned widely observed employee behavior such as not following company rules, guidelines, and goals; nonresponsiveness to feedback; and difficulty with teamwork. These qualities were summed up as a problem with authority and learning on the job and an inability to work together to solve a common problem. International business responded to what it saw as a corporate crisis in managing Chinese employees by importing management trainers and techniques. Global business practices promote "intelligence about competence within specific problem spaces," and the spread of management techniques, business schools, manuals, and media to the Asia-Pacific is central to this process for cultivating reflexive management.[7] Management gurus stress the importance of the new business knowledge, which will help Chinese workers reflect on what it takes to become self-managing actors. Self-management is encouraged by teaching employees to develop reflexivity, a kind of thinking that reflects on business problems and is fed back into everyday practice. Global companies want elite Chinese workers to render themselves governable, not by Communist Party dictates but according to corporate norms of self-initiative, self-responsibility, and self-engineering.

Business trainers claim that Chinese personalities, even "souls," must be "reengineered" like computers "for the global age."[8] Management workshops give lessons on how to "rewire" Chinese attitudes and outlook to produce a new "market-oriented mentality"[9] — that embraces values of self-motivation and self-improvement aligned with the corporate vision. "Reengineering" was first used by management gurus in the 1990s in proposals for the radical streamlining of corporations to make them more agile in global markets.[10] But in China, management experts invoke "reengineering" not so much to promote leaner and meaner companies but to prompt Chinese employees to be more focused on continuous "quality performance" and rational action in their workaday lives.

In business-speak, intelligence is the capacity to think, plan, and act in a "rational" way, according to specific goals such as increasing and maintaining company profit margins. Here business managers are invoking a Weberian notion of rationality, of capacity for rational consensus, cost-benefit calculations, and other techniques of the modern enterprise. Fundamental rationality is based on the objective, calculative application of rules. In contemporary corporate situations, employees are expected to reason and self-manage according to such calculations large and small in the interest of a common corporate enterprise.

To encourage rational compliance with the larger corporate project, American managers in the 1990s promised competitive salaries, quality interpersonal relations at work, and a clear promotion path. Management workshops trained participants to focus on "life values" that would promote their careers and to internalize self-governing practices that foster reflexive thinking and team spirit. Such inducements did not work for many of the ambitious, self-propelling Chinese MBAs, who displayed a kind of calculative behavior entirely focused on realizing their own self-interest. This highly individualistic form of entrepreneurialism, which elsewhere would be recognized as a "neoliberal" value, did not work for corporations that sought a rationally organized workforce devoted to company goals. Western managers misrecognize the self-enterprise of Shanghainese professionals as Chinese culture or guanxi, rather than as a precipitous embrace of neoliberal values of self-management and risk-taking. They point to the high degree of calculative, self-interested behavior among corporate employees as the consequence of "cultural misunderstanding" or as adherence to the practices of a "diffuse" culture. In contrast, managers argued, Westerners operate according to the norms of a "specific" culture, meaning rational planning and performance that is directly linked to company goals. Thus foreign managers in Shanghai discounted self-enterprising behavior—the Shanghainese professional has loads of that—and instead talked about the need to "reengineer" Chinese thinking and behavior along lines of corporate reasoning. Reengineering has become a metaphor for converting Chinese employees from particularistic cultural beings into self-disciplining professionals who can remanage themselves according to corporate rules and practice.

The Cultural Experts

Managerial knowledge is thus concerned not only with disciplining white-collar workers but also with producing reflexive, corporate subjects. To international firms, such management training is desirable but not essential for the cosmopolitan workforce in Hong Kong. Shanghai, however, as the new metropolis of Chinese globalism, seems in urgent need of global lessons in business flexibility and reflexivity. A business professor notes that "the lack of local talent in China" is a tremendous constraint on the growth of international business: "The pool of locals who possess the requisite business skills and mindsets are in acute shortage."[11] A Chinese worker bearing a technical or business degree is "an unfinished product" and has to be subjected to training programs to be turned into a "manager of the future." Consultancy firms based in Hong Kong have been streaming into Shanghai in order to "coach management and coach workers" so that they will acquire the necessary "intellectual management skills" and "social skills" to work in a global firm. Let us meet two culture experts devoted to reengineering "Chinese personalities."

Dr. Heyman, a British subject who became a naturalized American, is in his early fifties.[12] He used to be a professor of cognitive psychology in Texas. After his marriage to a Taiwanese woman, he stumbled on the big problem for global firms in China: how to transform the new generation of white-collar workers. Heyman does not speak Chinese, but he sees himself as an expert on intercultural communication and training. In 1993, he set up the first management consultancy in China. His goal was to "bring American corporate culture to make a hybrid culture." A few years later, his company joined a multinational consultancy firm with eight thousand employees in thirty-one countries.

The "sad state" of social communication in China, Heyman says, is "created by culture and China's unique history." More specifically, the management evolution is from "a command economy to a more market-responsive one, plus political control. . . . And the GPCR [Great Proletarian Cultural Revolution] is still part of the culture." His evolutionary model claims that the growth of a rational, management style is hampered by the political culture that grew out of Maoism. The high technical training inherited from socialist constructionism is not matched by equivalent management skills. Heyman cited an assessment of forty technocrats who displayed "a built-in hierarchical model" that leads to "bad management." White-collar workers, especially those from state-owned enterprises and joint ventures, tend to punish rule breaking and yet are uncomfortable criticizing a subordinate's performance. At the same time, in the view of Western business consultants, Chinese workers display a lack of communication skills, self-presentation, and politeness in their interactions with subordinates, which are said to reinforce the latter's lack of initiative and sense of responsibility to the company. Heyman claims that this mix of political and cultural styles has led to demands for business consultants like himself. Many transnational firms partly blame their low profits on the lack of a rational managerial force in China. The problem is so widely recognized that companies now have special budgets for training and translation. Heyman's company has trained about a thousand managers in Shanghai. He identifies three key problem areas:

— *face*: a kind of defensiveness that often results in not telling the truth, in not taking responsibility for action, in taking offense at being given direction, and in a lack of initiative.
— *team work*: "The Chinese are excellent only in physical projects, like building roads. But intelligent management skills are lacking, because they have never had role models."
— *"silo model" of control*: "The top-down government control has induced a 'wait to be told what to do' attitude. Locals are good at guanxi to get things done, rather than show leadership."

Heyman wrote the first foreign-based training manuals for sale in China. In contrast to the knowledge-based and case-study method popular in the United States, Heyman's approach is action oriented and based on small steps. Trainees are gradually introduced to incremental changes in organization, attitude, and behavior over the course of a few days. Applying a modeling survey, Heyman found a positive correlation between desired behavior and education, and a negative correlation with age. He expects that over time, there will be more internalization of rational procedures. Heyman sums up his approach this way: "We train people on how to bring about change; intelligent problem solving in a creative context." Clearly, he sees himself as doing great social good by training Chinese workers in "leadership" skills, the acquisition of which he believes were blocked by Chinese values concerning "face," guanxi, and authority. Chinese flexibility and initiative in interpersonal relations are not considered the kind of social skills that can facilitate corporate problem solving.

Another kind of management training focuses less on the need to adopt rules of corporate behavior and more on gently inducing the Chinese employee to become a reflexive subject, capable of self-management. Ethnic Chinese trainers are popular for helping workers manage the social interface between Chinese social norms and American managerial expectations. I interviewed a Taiwanese woman I call Flora Kang, who works for a major Boston-based firm.[13] Kang visits the United States regularly to collect ideas about human resource management that she can apply in China. Her firm mainly advises foreign finance companies operating in China, where the stress is on "achieving customer service." When we met for our interview, Kang was dressed in a brocade Chinese dress (*qibao*) with slits down the side, and a matching set of jade jewelry. Her face was immaculately made up, and she gestured elegantly. Her main role in the company is to localize successful American concepts and stories in China, but she regrets that many people are skeptical that these concepts will work. She sees herself as a cultural translator, converting American messages into Mandarin and tailoring them to the local power settings. Kang's "knowledge-based" approach works on the attitude of Chinese clients before proceeding to their behavior. She stresses the usefulness of knowledge and self-reflection to her clients as a way to free oneself from the problems usually identified by foreign companies (defensiveness, lack of initiative, awkwardness in social relations). Her workshops define the directions and norms for clients to attain desired performance; they are first motivated and then tested to see if they reach the goal. She identifies three kinds of changes that are especially important in helping Chinese individuals adjust to American work environments.

— *Resistance to feedback*: Chinese workers are uncomfortable reviewing the performance of subordinates and about being evaluated for past performance. What management considers objective assessment is often viewed as threatening, as being taken "hostage." For Chinese clients, "constructive feedback" is considered an expression of foreigners' tendency to focus on conflict. Kang believes her first step is to reassure Chinese employees that suggestions made by management are neither a form of punishment nor a sign of breaking relations. She stresses the need for Chinese employees to understand that management corrections are not a black-and-white final assessment but an ongoing, dynamic process of continual adjustment to feedback. Only when the workers understand the reflexive process involved in management, she claims, can they develop a sense of accountability and interest in improving future performance.

— *Need for "soft skills"*: "Because locals are used to taking orders, they are not so good at social relations." There is also what she delicately calls the "hygiene problem," which is also a major gripe in the foreign hotel industry. Her coaching includes personal cleanliness, greeting customers with a smile, making light conversation, presenting one's business card, and learning to circulate at parties, with a drink in hand. Her manuals draw on Harvard business school texts, but they simplify the case studies and practice sessions. She spends much time getting her clients to engage in role-playing and demonstration as a way to think through their interactions in uncomfortable situations.

— *Planning priorities*: Kang criticizes other management consultants who measure Chinese subjects in terms such as "motivation," "discipline," and "quality" in order to judge them as lacking a "rational" approach to the organization of time, data, and responsibility. Instead of focusing on their purported "irrationality," Kang's technique is to get workers to think about how to spend time at work and how to distinguish between business and private interests. Human resource managers are of course aware that Chinese workers are "demotivated" by global practices such as the stark differences in salaries for expatriates and for locals. Thus when managers accuse Chinese employees of not understanding the importance of keeping schedules and for ignoring company deadlines in favor of family matters, Kang understands that workers are signaling their lack of investment in their companies. Managers complain about such "failures to internalize procedures," but their Chinese staff often feel justified in believing that their "own practice is more efficient."

Kang's job is to bring the thinking of Chinese employees closer to management norms and expectations and to teach them to think of the possible effects on their own careers of their noncompliance with company rules. She makes them more aware of the need to be responsive to client expectations and to think globally. She retranslates "acting locally" not as adhering to Chinese preferences and norms but rather as making more cross-cultural connections with foreigners and developing a greater awareness of how non-Chinese, nonlocal matters can affect employment chances.

Heyman and Kang represent two management modalities — one aimed at changing behavior to conform to corporate governance, the other at producing a self-conscious, reflexive corporate subject. These business consultants see themselves as vital to the "transfer of learning" necessary for China's new knowledge class. International management firms, not the Communist Party, are the new legislators of Chinese humanity, working not through political browbeating and a crude reward and punishment system but rather through the micropolitics of corporate training sessions that both cajole and induce workers to make themselves over into reflexive corporate subjects suitable for global markets. The pervasive demands of globalized economic systems act very strongly on the elites, the executives, and those who wield power at the intermediate level. The disciplinary mechanisms are also intended to get them to think of themselves as part of the company's "global family."

But clearly there is a disarticulation between corporate goals and the relentlessly "self-interested" practices of Chinese professionals. Indeed, what managers view as irrationality and intransigence are ultrarational maneuvers to take advantage of an insatiable demand for corporate talent. In this heated job market, male professionals become impatient after one year in a company and begin looking for another position where they can earn more money or learn new skills. They also dislike working as employees, especially under a foreign employer. The overriding goal for professionals is to use new knowledge to start their own companies in competition with foreign investors in the global marketplace. A neoliberal instrumentalism has been internalized, fueled by a sense of China's rising economic fate and a lingering desire to throw off Western market domination. I would argue that male corporate employees learn management knowledge without entirely succumbing to its corporate discipline. Chinese men especially are driven by a logic of entrepreneurial self-fashioning that seeks to control markets and forge a different kind of Chinese capitalism.

The Cultural Entrepreneurs

There are now many Chinese expatriates educated in Europe and the United States who have internalized some of the values sought by Western companies. All consider themselves Chinese patriots, owing their loyalty not so much to the government as to their vision of the Chinese nation, its cultural integrity, and its making of a modernity different from those found in Western societies. They have different ways of expressing their roles as cross-cultural mediators whose work also contributes to the fashioning of a Chinese modern subjectivity tied to the conversion of new knowledge capital and social status. These people one meets by hanging out with the well-educated and well-traveled, many of whom spend their evenings in Xintiandi ("New Heaven and Earth"), the refabricated neighborhoods, restaurants, and nightclubs in the former French Concession.

This is where I met Lin, a chain-smoking, thoughtful, and lean man in his thirties, dressed in tight black turtleneck and jeans. Educated in cultural studies in Paris; he prefers Bourdieu to Foucault. His interest is really in French literature. Lin has been back in Shanghai for a couple of years. He is still single, which is unusual for elite men of his age. Lin is fluent in French but does not speak English, and he is mildly scornful of the United States. At first glance, one may think that Lin is a Francophile misfit back in China, but he was recently hired by a Shanghai TV station, to a position in charge of cultural affairs. He intends to use his position to shape the cultural forms that he thinks should be part of a Chinese modernity that is distinctive, rooted in Chinese history and literary sensibility, but he is not likely to bend easily to a state-dictated version of what Chinese culture is all about. He seemed offended at such a suggestion, confident that his specific blend of cultural capital and political connections will enable him to shape public culture without the direct interference of the Chinese Communist Party.

Television is one site for the production of modernity; the other is restaurants and bars, where global managers, their clients, professionals, capitalists, and hangers-on congregate and "decompress." I was given a list of bars and restaurants in Xintiandi where the new professionals gather with foreigners in their leisure hours. I was introduced to Tang, a professional-turned-entrepreneur in his early thirties who runs the most fashionable restaurant in Shanghai.[14] Born in the city soon after the GPCR, Tang emigrated as a teenager and later studied mechanical engineering at the University of Southern California. He gained experience working for American companies, then decided to return home and help shape the new urban scene. With financial backing from a Hong Kong restaurant group operated by Australian and British expatriates, Tang wanted a high-end eatery that would cater to the expatriate-cosmopolitan crowd in Shanghai. It is the first night spot in Shanghai to be located in a park, "like the Tavern on the Green" in New York City. Decorated in knowing fashion, the restaurant is filled with art deco icons — furniture, light fixtures, and design motifs — taken from the Shanghai nightlife of the 1930s. Outside, a billboard with the image of early modern Chinese ladies beckons. Inside, we are served Asian-Californian fusion cuisine. The customer is immediately greeted by a wall-to-wall mural of a naked, buxom young woman supine against a drapery backdrop, her image doubled on the other side of the room by a mirror above the long, gleaming bar (see fig. 4). The features of this figure are Asian without being Chinese, her body Western but odalisque in pose. The effect is an updated art deco Orientalism inspired by Ingres. To Tang, the mural captures the image and the self-ironic attitude he deploys for the technocorporate elite: hybridity, California consumer culture, affluence with a touch of decadence, rather like the Asian and Western elements intermixed in the Singapore sling from the bar. He told me the full-bodied image "represents freedom, East-West cross-currents, and

Figure 4. Nightclub odalisque: Chinese cosmopolitanism today. Photo by Lisa Hoffman.

some sexiness." The nightly crowds are international, mostly white expatriates with young Chinese women dressed in daring outfits, who come to mix,
drink, and dance.

A description in the novel *Shanghai Baby* captures the scene perfectly.

> There were plenty of fair-haired foreigners, and lots of Chinese
> women, their tiny waistlines and silky black hair their selling points. They
> all had a sluttish, self-promoting expression on their faces, but in fact a
> good many of them worked for multinational companies. Most were col-
> lege graduates from good families; some had studied abroad and owned
> their own cars. They were the crème de la crème of Shanghai's eight
> million women, but when they were dancing they looked tarty. God
> knew what was going on in their minds.[15]

At first glance, one is reminded of colonial Shanghai, where foreign merchants and Chinese warlords ruled the flesh trade.[16] But here are Chinese
career women, not bar girls, in action. Clearly, the female nightclub habituées
are self-styled entrepreneurs, packaging their managerial skills with orientalist
bodies, offering a new kind of transnational talent and performance that is a

Figure 5. Hotel mural of early modern Shanghai.

double attraction for foreign investors (as we will see below). The point is to participate in global business but also to control it through self-advancement and even patriotic capitalism.

Tang has creatively assembled the conditions of this globalized interweaving, where corporate talent is infused with distinctive Chinese elements. He has been featured in newspapers as one of the leading lights of the new Shanghai trying to recapture the glamour of the city when it was "the Paris of the East" (see fig. 5). He is quoted in a newsmagazine as saying: "The rest of Asia is so dead. I'm convinced that I came back to the right place at the right time."[17] In person, Tang is modest, and he seems effective in the local scene. He managed to wrest permission from local authorities to build his restaurant in the park, something quite unprecedented. He sees his patriotism in terms of devotion not to a pure Chinese past or the recent socialist transformation but rather to reviving the cosmopolitanism that flourished in colonial Shanghai. Clearly, I am invoking not Kantian cosmopolitics but rather cosmopolitanism in the conventional sense of a situation of transnational elements, worldly experience, and cross-cultural expertise. Tang's passion is for creating the kind of elegant international culture that will position Shanghai

Figure 6. The Marxist duo: figures from an earlier cosmopolitanism. Photo by Lisa Hoffman.

in the new century. He professes to be too busy for marriage. He has started a new magazine — which will be free — about "what's in and what's out in Shanghai" — a version of the *Village Voice* but without the urban politics. New York City, the current financial capital of the world, is a partial model but only in order to overtake it as a new, Asian financial capital.[18] Returning Chinese expatriates such as Tang are producing the urban milieu for an emerging transnational class linked to global commerce and overseas education.

At the end of the evening, I walked through the wooded park (a miniature, dusty Trocadero) and exited at the other end, where I discovered a fused statue of Marx and Engels looming in the dark (see fig. 6). An earlier cosmopolitanism seems to be in eclipse. But there is a kind of continuity in managing the oscillation between Western and Chinese cultural knowledges in the current process of global localization. Since the early twentieth century, Chinese intellectual embrace of Western "scientific" knowledge has entailed recasting foreign ideas in a Chinese context so Chinese intellectuals can see their country as "modern" without being "Western."[19] For instance, Mao famously differed from Marx in identifying the revolutionary class among peasants, not proletarians.[20] In contemporary adoption of Western forms, returnee Chinese expatriates have picked up professional skills as well as a consumerist sensibility that gives them a more knowing playfulness with our expectations of "the West" and of "China." Especially in the high-end consumerist milieus, one finds a riotous juxtapositioning of Western and Asian cultural elements that oscillates between embrace and distance, intimacy and detachment, an orchestration of markets that Chinese entrepreneurs effect with a commercial ironic detachment. The difference from the earlier period of cultural cosmopolitanism is that Chinese elites now have the authority to determine and interpret the significance of capitalist ideas, goods, and enactments, including parodic forms of self-orientalism.[21]

Furthermore, such involvement with and detachment from Western ideas and practices are not considered to contradict patriotism.[22] Support for one-party rule in China is widely viewed as crucial for maintaining the stability that allows capitalism to flourish and China to become more powerful.[23] The young people, especially women, seem to believe that it is possible to combine a capitalist savvy with patriotic possibilities, to embrace neoliberal rationality by resituating it in a different, globalized cultural matrix.

Twenty-Somethings Traveling at Warp Speed

But in the corporate world, Western managers are obsessed with trying to control their Chinese employees, with transforming them into Western corporate subjects. Global management invests its hopes in college-educated Chinese still in their twenties, especially young women. This under-thirty age group came of age after Tiananmen (June 1989) and after Deng Xiaoping's 1992 speech "To get rich is glorious." A Hong Kong manager sardonically comments that this group's "commitment is to survive and make money, and not to criticize the government."

Whereas the older generation was shaped by the political upheavals of recent Chinese history, this young urban generation is being shaped by the converging forces of global consumer markets and the managerial technology. Unlike their shell-shocked parents, the young professionals are said to display a thirst for learning, career development, and opportunity, including management roles. Foreign corporations compete to hire graduates of Fudan University's management school, as well as MBAs from business schools based in Shanghai. Companies take advantage of the freedom to recruit qualified applicants of specific gender, age, and even looks who will reflect the international corporate norms. The corporate headquarters I visited—housed in high-rise towers featuring marbled lobbies decorated with Chinese antiques — were staffed by local young people who could have grown up in Singapore, Hong Kong, or California. Their openness extends to adopting foreign ideas and practices. Most are single, friendly, and efficient. Young women are often dressed in expensive Armani suits, wear makeup, and display relaxed social and sexual mores.

There is a slight gender skewing in multinational employment. American managers favor young women over young men, if they have comparable qualifications. The managers believe that young women are better with foreign languages, are more presentable, flexible, and willing to become aligned with foreign corporate interests. The director of a German firm based in Pudong, Shanghai, told me that Chinese women are "more careful, reliable, stable" white-collar employees whereas men tend to leave the company after learning skills. This observation coincides with the view of her male Chinese manager in the company whose role is to coordinate company relations with the customs house, a job that gives him a large measure of autonomy and an external link to Chinese authorities.[24] He considers women "more appropriate for lower management positions because they want stable jobs, and then [to] find husbands. Most men always think about the next position, in another firm. After one year, they want to leave because it seems a waste of time already invested. They always want to expand their salaries. They do not think they can rise within the ranks; they want to be hired as manager. As men, they think they ought to have the top position." Male professionals favor jobs where they enjoy autonomy as Chinese men, such as positions in joint ventures where they deal with foreigners as partners, not as subordinated workers. Is racial masculinity at stake in this reengagement with the world?[25]

Foreign firms believe their future lies with Chinese twenty-somethings who are hungry for foreign knowledge that can advance their careers and improve their standard of living. A manager in an advertising firm observes that these workers have a strong desire to become "international, worldly persons" by learning from corporate culture. They are people that business consultants like Heyman most want to bend to the demands of global capital: "The young are more relationship-oriented and process-oriented; they are traveling at warp speed." Here Heyman does not refer to the relationships of guanxi, but rather to an openness and susceptibility to Western notions about interactions and norms in the workplace and in the urban social scene.

Young people are considered the main reason for the rising rate of divorce in Shanghai, which many blame on the new sexual promiscuity among young women, depicted with fearless candor in *Shanghai Baby*. The novel was banned and burned throughout China, without any impact on the shifting values of urban culture. Women are considered more willing to advance by becoming mistresses of rich men or by focusing on their careers to the detriment of their marriages. Others break off their marriages in order to take up relations with foreigners.[26] Fast young women entangled with foreign men seem an iconic image of the intoxicating swirl of fast capitalism in Shanghai. The novel was rejected partly because Zhou suggests that despite Chinese men's claims that they are at the cutting edge of change, young Shanghainese women are more empowered — erotically alluring and socially adept — than men in playing the aphrodisiac game of global emergence.

When I asked a Hong Kong manager whether there is anything "Chinese" about these young people, he replied, "Chinese culture continues to live in the heart — in family relations, in filial piety."[27] This ritual invocation of Confucianism is typical and seems to fly in the face of the high rates of divorce and family breakup. Or maybe something more sophisticated is indicated, in that the strategy for personal power (through acquiring new knowledge associated with foreign firms) is not necessarily incompatible with an ethic that continues to sustain primary social relations, between children and parents (if not husbands and wives) and between relatives and friends who may have been differently served by the economic boom.

Refashioning Guanxi

There is some evidence that less elite professionals, even as they are being subjected to the daily bombardment of corporate management and consumer culture, have trouble freeing themselves from the guanxi expectations of their relatives and friends. Below the new cosmopolitans — managers, engineers, and accountants — is a second tier of technical workers who interact daily and directly with shop-floor workers. As employees of foreign companies, they are the ones who daily translate Western corporate policies and meaning to their Chinese compatriots. I received a tantalizing glimpse of how the technical workers recast corporate practices by giving equal or unavoidable attention to guanxi claims of relatives and friends.

Ms. Bao is a research assistant at a European business school in Shanghai who promotes and yet disagrees with the goals of the international business school in changing Chinese society.[28] She is critical of its "contradictory" focus on cross-cultural understanding. The training of MBAs puts all the emphasis on Western methods, while Chinese culture is treated as an obstacle course that must be negotiated. She points out that in Chinese society, Confucian ethics, especially as expressed in guanxi, is very important. It is ironic that foreign professors (Americans and British) teach the business ethics without any method to deal with guanxi. Foreign managers think of guanxi as corruption (backdoor [*houmen*, in Mandarin] stratagems), but they themselves rely on guanxi to establish and consolidate links with state-owned enterprises (for joint ventures) or with officials to access business contracts. As Bao sees it, guanxi has deep roots in China and cannot be eradicated. What is significant is that its moral worth has changed in recent conditions of market opening.[29] In her view, guanxi had a bad connotation under Mao because it referred to the system of clientelism linked to the system of political classes. Members of the Chinese Communist Party were power brokers who monopolized guanxi, or the relationships that provided a conduit for the exchange of patronage from above to the supply of goods and services from below. In the era of market reforms, the market has opened up a new domain of worth to challenge the political sphere of value. There is now a diversity of decision makers and power wielders, and guanxi bubbles up from below. "This new horizontal form of guanxi is more diluted," Bao claims. She seems to differentiate the older guanxi of instrumental patronage and clientelism from what she sees as the new, diffuse links arising from multiple sources involved in the transfer and conversion of values across various domains. As Bao asks, "The question is, how is guanxi worth now."

Indeed, the rethinking of guanxi (after all, is there a more self-conscious quotidian weighing of exchange and accountability?) and its redeployment reflect new strategies to interweave fragments of the social world rent by employment in global companies. Bao argues that the question foreigners should ask is "How [do we] mix guanxi with the Western system of doing business?" This is a practical problem that foreign firms doing joint ventures with state-owned enterprises have been grappling with for years. The overall responsibility to workers in state enterprises means that Western practices of quality control often must take a back seat to guanxi considerations, such as taking care of workers who have become unproductive.

Bao's friend Liu, who is a quality control supervisor at General Motors (GM), notes that "everyone's in a big pot; we a responsible for each other. Individual responsibility is very new."[30] Liu sees fundamental differences between Western and Chinese cultures. "In the West, everybody's equal, and talent and performance are the only judge of a person. But in China, the confidence and trust of a friend, i.e., social obligation and responsibility, are just as important." In his everyday life, Liu deals with the conflict between objective Western norms and Chinese guanxi practices, and he feels that Western managers err by focusing only on technical skills and ignoring the importance of social values. He thinks that punishing people for their errors is a mistake because this will lead them to hide their future errors. GM does a number of things to eradicate guanxi, but these efforts have failed. They test the technical skills of applicants and see if they can work with bosses before hiring them. GM pays higher salaries than local firms in order to discourage workers from engaging in "guanxi," here meaning using their personal connections to engage in shady deals with outsiders. For instance, at Liu's workshop, "guanxi sometimes leads to purchases of low-quality equipment, at the same or at a different price." In his estimation, only a quarter of such actions are ever caught. But Liu thinks that even though firing workers for getting kickbacks is strictly legal, it is "not reasonable." In his view, GM managers simply think that "money talks." He mimics American talk: "Let's get him, he's the best!" American managers will make the first assessment of applicants, testing them for their technical skills. But their Hong Kong employees will say, "You don't know Chinese culture. If there is not consideration of guanxi, you cannot get people!" There is usually a huge number of applicants for any one job, and the problem is how to select the few. Here guanxi steps in and makes the final cut, choosing applicants on the basis of friendship or payback for past favors to coworkers. Liu puts it this way, "In the final analysis, everything [else] being equal, you have guanxi, you're in!" In Liu's view, this method, which combines Western rational-technical standards and Chinese guanxi, is "a reasonable system. Even if the most qualified person can get the job, guanxi remains important. A clever manager will not employ a stupid employee, but only one who can make profits for them. But he will still prefer those who 'have guanxi with me.'"

In other words, you hire someone with different kinds of worth (production and social), and the benefits will accrue to both the technical performance and the social relations in the workplace, and beyond. A narrow Western view of production worth blinds Western managers to the kind of benefits gained from paying attention to the social values of workers as well. While there is recognition that some kinds of guanxi practice has been used for kickbacks and other corrupt behavior, the corporate system cannot ignore the importance of how Chinese people define social worth, based on Confucian ethics, specifically the value of being accountable to coworkers and to relatives and friends. Just as the foreign corporation participates in a trade-off with the Chinese authorities, meeting the political requirement to keep defunct workers on the roll in exchange for the right to joint ventures, so Chinese workers view their economic power gained from working in foreign firms as a resource for gaining social value in the public sphere. In these ways, guanxi practices — as relations for the transfer of worth across different domains, and as a diffused sense of social responsibility emanating from the market sphere — continue to construct a sociality that interweaves ties between the new middle class with people in lower socioeconomic groups. Global management techniques will have to contend with these knowledge workers, who are in an interstitial position to redefine economic practice and their moral worth in relation to other domains of values, shaping a practical reflexive subjectivity that is responsive to a sociality they call Confucian ethos.

The various trajectories and ethics of Chinese employees and cultural entrepreneurs show that there is no "Chinese soul" that can be easily reengineered by global business. Rather, there is selectivity and diversity in approach to business management, knowledge, and opportunities on Chinese terms, at both the individual and the national levels. Increasingly, unlike an earlier era of capitalist cosmopolitans, Chinese entrepreneurs and workers are now in the position to determine the goals of their employment, the form and meanings of work relationships, and the cultural configuration of their businesses. A tension thus emerges between global corporate norms that seek to develop team playing and firm loyalty, on the one hand, and the self-propelling ethic of Chinese employees seeking both individual benefits and to serve the motherland, on the other. The embedding of rational managerial practices in the corporation becomes entangled with situated ethics of guanxi. Chinese subjects constantly reflect on and reframe bureaucratic objectives and merit-based norms in guanxi terms that incorporate social claims from outside the corporate world. Such daily attempts to negotiate between corporate rules and guanxi ethics could be termed the mundane forms of "socialism with Chinese characteristics."

The Communist Party may appear to have ceded ground to global corporations and business knowledge for shaping the everyday thinking and practices of workers, but this is a strategic choice in the interest of nation building. Shanghainese actors demonstrate that, whether in foreign corporations or in their own entrepreneurial ventures, global management techniques are not incompatible with guanxi ethics, cross-cultural irony, and patriotism but in fact are tempered and transformed by them. As selective recipients and transformers of global business concepts and practices, urban Chinese show that they can operate effectively in a transnational, transcultural milieu without becoming truly "controllable" or "denationalized" by global capital.[31] The question is thus posed as to how neoliberal rationality and managerial knowledge makes an exception for situated ethics. Professionals and managers in Shanghai internalize managerial norms and yet deflect global corporate norms, display an ironic sense of cultural commercialization as well as nationalist capitalism, and are market savvy without giving up the claims of guanxi ethics. Will Shanghai soon reexport global business practices that rewire the Western business mentality for engaging Chinese markets? Is the global city fixed in a global grid, or is Shanghai an emergent exception? In a galaxy of ever shifting constellations, is the glittering metropolis a new planet swimming into view?

INTRODUCTION

1 See Ong, *Flexible Citizenship*, chap. 7.

2 Safire, "Inside a Republican Brain."

3 "Bush Pledges Broad Push."

4 For a class-based critique of early notions of citizenship based exclusively on the property-owning bourgeoisie, see Marx, "Jewish Question," 33–34.

5 Bush, "Inaugural Address."

6 Although some neoconservatives such as Irving Kristol maintain that extreme market rationality destroys American democratic morality. For a discussion of how such neoconservative claims about neoliberalism are echoed by feminist Wendy Brown, see Cruikshank, "Neopolitics."

7 Rose and Miller, "Political Power beyond the State."

8 Collier and Ong, "Global Assemblages, Anthropological Problems."

9 Collier, "Spatial Forms and Social Norms."

10 Foucault, "Governmentality."

11 Foucault, "Ethics of the Concern for Self," 300.

12 Barry, Osborne, and Rose, *Foucault and Political Reason*.

13 Schmitt, *Political Theology*, 13.

14 Agamben, *Homo Sacer*, 26–28.

15 Collier, "Spatial Forms and Social Norms."

16 Arendt, *Human Condition*.

17 See, e.g., Scott, *Seeing Like a State*; and Ferguson, *Anti-politics Machine*.

18 Sassen, *Global City*, and "Locating Cities," 2.

19 This ecology formulation is conceptually different from the "global city-region" model. See A. J. Scott, "Globalization and the Rise of City-Regions," *Research Bulletin* 26, July 19, 2000. Available online at www.lboro.ac.uk/gawc/.

20 Insiti and Levien, "Strategy as Ecology," 69.

21 Hardt and Negri, *Empire*.

22 Agamben, *Homo Sacer*, 170.

23 Polanyi, *Great Transformation*.

24 Nishiyama and Leube, *Essence of Hayek*.

25 Friedman, *Capitalism and Freedom*.

26 Becker, *Human Capital*.

27 The above summary of neoliberal policies draws on Peters, "Neoliberalism."

28 Pabst, "Immanence, Religion, and Neo-liberalism."

29 In 1996, Democratic president Bill Clinton signed the "Personal Responsibility and Work Opportunity Reconciliation Act," which ended "welfare as we know it" by requiring welfare recipients to participate in "workfare" programs.

30 Peters, "Neoliberalism."

31 Hall, *Hard Road to Renewal*.

32 The perspective is well presented in Gill, "Globalization, Civilization, Neoliberalism."

33 Comaroff and Comaroff, "Millennial Capitalism."

34 Harvey, "Neoliberalism," 11; my emphasis.

35 Geertz, *Interpretation of Cultures*, 24.

36 Paul Rabinow (*Anthropos Today*, 16–17) has noted that "the site of the trouble and of its resolution is the problematic situation."

37 Foucault, *Introduction*, 143, 139.

38 See Barry, Osborne, and Rose, *Foucault and Political Reason*; and Rose, *Powers of Freedom*.

39 Barry, Osborne, and Rose, introduction to *Foucault and Political Reason*, 64.

40 Von Hayek, *Political Order*.

41 Rose, *Powers of Freedom*, 27–28.

42 Gordon, "Governmental Rationality," 43–44.

43 Rose, "Governing 'Advanced' Liberal Democracies," 56.

44 For an analysis of how neoliberal calculations articulate postsocialist administrative practices in Russia, see Collier, "Spatial Forms and Social Norms."

45 See World Bank, *World Development Report*.

46 Arendt, *Human Condition*.

47 See, e.g., Bhabha and Coll, *Asylum Law*.

48 Marshall, *Class, Citizenship, and Social Class*.

49 See, e.g., Benhab, *Claims of Culture*.

50 Soysal, *Limits of Citizenship*.

51 Castles and Davidson, *Citizenship and Migration*, 18–19.

52 Bhabha, *Location of Culture*, 37.

53 Habermas, "Why Europe Needs a Constitution"; Delanty, *Citizenship in a Global Age*.

54 This is the evidence of an emerging cosmopolitical order pointed to in Held et al., *Global Transformations*.

55 See, e.g., Delanty, *Citizenship in a Global Age*.

56 For a discussion of the limits and dangers of cosmopolitanism, see Bowden, "Perils of Global Citizenship."

57 Ong, introduction to *Flexible Citizenship*.

58 Ruggie, *Constructing the World Polity*, 180.
59 Mamdani, *Citizen and Subject*, 16–18.
60 Roitman, "Garrison-Entrepot"; Ferguson, "Seeing Like an Oil Company."
61 Schmitt, *Political Theology*, 13.
62 Sack, *Human Territoriality*.
63 See Linklater, "Idea of Citizenship."
64 Some theorists claim that the analytical space of globalization is the region. See Ohmae, *End of the Nation State*.
65 Kelly and Olds, "Questions in a Crisis."
66 The need for conceptual caution is recognized by Brenner, "Limits to Scale?"
67 Harrison, Pile, and Thrift, *Patterned Ground*, 36, 40.
68 Hardt and Negri, *Empire*, 23, 328–29, 332, 210.
69 See Foucault, "Ethics of the Concern for Self," 282.
70 See Anderson, *Imagined Communities*.
71 Arendt, *Human Condition*, 7–9.
72 Agamben, *Homo Sacer*, 177, 180.
73 See Rabinow, "Midst Anthropology's Problems," 47–48.
74 Collier and Lakoff, "Regimes of Living," 23.
75 Agamben, *Homo Sacer*, 170–71.
76 Collier and Lakoff, "Regimes of Living," 29.
77 See Cohen, "Operability, Bioavailability, Exception."
78 Nguyen Vinh-kim, "Antiretroviral Globalism."

ONE Sisterly Solidarity

1 Agarwal, "Beijing Women's Conference."
2 Agarwal argues that the energy coming from the Beijing Platform will help Indian feminists challenge their government to put its "money and political backing where its words are" (ibid., 8–9).
3 For a skeptical view of a romantic global sisterhood, see Ong, "Gender and Labor Politics."
4 In this essay, I will be using the terms *Western* and *Northern* interchangeably, as I will the terms *Southern* and *non-Western*. They refer not so much to absolutely fixed geographical relations as to the relations of political and economic inequalities stemming from colonialism, imperialism, uneven capitalist development, and contemporary market forces.
5 In "Colonialism and Modernity," I argued that First World feminists defined themselves in opposition not to First World men, but to Third World women, whom they view as their social inferiors. We cannot talk about gender inequality in non-Western countries without situating our analyses in the context of cultural imperialism and the geopolitical ranking of nations.
6 See, e.g., Jayawardena, *Feminism and Nationalism*.

7 Chatterjee, *Nation and Its Fragments*, 147, 8, 13.

8 For an ethnographic study, see Ong, *Spirits of Resistance*.

9 For a brief historical account of Islamic gender cultures in insular Southeast Asia, see Reid, *Land below the Winds*.

10 Landes, *Women in the Public Sphere*.

11 Habermas, "Further Reflections on the Public Sphere."

12 Bhabha, *Location of Culture*, 24.

13 For a similar observation in another Muslim context, see Mernissi, *Beyond the Veil*, xxiv.

14 Sabbah, *Women in the Muslim Unconscious*, 17.

15 Malaysia has a population of 24 million. Most of the wealth has been produced by the expansion of manufacturing and from traditional sources like plantations, mining, and lumber extraction.

16 Often viewed as a paradigmatic "multiracial country," Malaysia has large minority populations of ethnic Chinese and ethnic Indians.

17 In the aftermath of the September 11, 2001, terrorist attacks on the United States, the Malaysian government took the opportunity to present itself as an antiterrorist ally of North America. There were some arrests of suspected Islamic terrorists who had been hiding in the country.

18 The ruling political party is called the United Malay Nation Organization (UMNO). It has been in power since independence in 1957 and is the leading faction in the multiethnic National Coalition that dominates the government.

19 For views of how Malay-Muslim cultures must be understood as a complex braiding of Islamic principles and *adat* beliefs and practices, see Peletz, *Reason and Passion*.

20 Williams, introduction to *Women Out of Place*, 21–22, 25.

21 For a discussion of regimes of localization, see Nonini and Ong, introduction to *Ungrounded Empires*.

22 Abdullahi Ahmed An-Na'im, "Towards an Islamic Reformation," 17.

23 Wadud-Muhsin, "Quran, Syariah, and Citizenship Rights," 78.

24 For more on passion and reason as gendered attributes in Muslim society, see Peletz, *Reason and Passion*; and Ong, "Japanese Factories, Malay Workers."

25 Such ideas about male rationality versus female passion pervade many agrarian cultures and are especially well represented in Islam, Christianity, and Buddhism. See a classic anthropological discussion in Ortner, "Is Male to Culture as Female Is to Nature?"

26 Kessler, *Politics and Islam*.

27 His views are summarized in a Sisters in Islam op-ed piece, "Nik Aziz's Putting Down Women Wrong."

28 "Time to Assert Women's Presence in Islam."

29 Sisters in Islam, "Spouses and Suitors."

30 Ibid.

31 The imposing of strict limitations on women in the public sphere by the Taliban in

Afghanistan is only the most recent example of such rigid assertions of masculine power in the name of postrevolutionary Islam.

32 See Asad, "Limits of Religious Criticisms."

33 Quoted in "Re-examining the Roles of Muslim Women."

34 Quoted in "Muslim Women's Movement Is Gaining Strength."

35 Quoted in "In Search of the Female Voice."

36 In many indigenous Southeast Asian societies, historically, social rank and age, rather than gender, have determined positions of authority. See Errington, introduction to *Power and Difference*.

37 Othman, "Sociopolitical Dimensions of Islamization," 140.

38 Othman, "Implementation of Syariah Criminal Law."

39 Sisters in Islam, *Muslim Women Speak*.

40 Sisters in Islam, "Nik Aziz's Putting Down Women Wrong."

41 Ibid.

42 Mernissi, *Veil and Male Elite*.

43 Sisters in Islam, "Nik Aziz's Putting Down Women Wrong."

44 Othman, "Sociopolitical Dimensions of Islamization."

45 "Of Dress and Muslim Women."

46 "Where Compulsion Is Obsession with Control."

47 "Islamic Dress Code Still a Major Issue."

48 Sisters in Islam, "Polygamy Not a Right Enshrined in the Quran."

49 Sisters in Islam, "Spouses and Suitors."

50 "Burden of Proof."

51 "Time to Assert Women's Presence in Islam."

52 "Polygamy Statement Made a Mockery of Women and Islam."

53 "Time to Assert Women's Presence in Islam."

54 In my own research, I have had many opportunities to observe sensual appreciation and activities in Malay villages. For instance, Malay women claim that the limited female circumcision they underwent as babies does not interfere with sexual pleasure, which they all agree is vitally important in marriage. See Ong, *Spirits of Resistance*.

55 Chatterjee, *Nation and Its Fragments*, is the most eloquent example of such a claim.

56 Othman, "Sociopolitical Dimensions of Islamization," 140.

57 Quoted in "Blame Men, Not Allah, Islamic Feminists Say."

58 Much of the country's development depends on foreign investment. The Islamic bank resolves the problem of Islam's prohibiting the collecting of interest by requiring "fees and commissions," so that the bank will be as profitable as any other commercial bank.

59 See Khoo, *Paradoxes of Mahathirism*, 159–97.

60 See "Blame Men, Not Allah, Islamic Feminists Say."

61 "In Search of the Female Voice."

62 The secular law on rape is derived from the old English penal code, which held that

there was no marital rape because wives did not have the right to withhold sex from their husbands. In Great Britain, the law was changed in 1991, when marital rape was legally recognized as an offense.

63 "Thorny Issue."

64 *Star* (Penang, Malaysia), July 10, 1996, 23.

65 *Star*, July 7, 1996, 18.

66 In Malaysia and Indonesia, cultural norms conspire to curb women's self-expression, especially in public speech. The good girl or woman is one who is silent and retiring. See, e.g., Ong, "Japanese Factories, Malay Workers: Industrialization and Sexual Metaphors in West Malaysia."

67 *Aurat* is the part of the body that must be covered under Islamic ruling. For women, the aurat includes the entire body except for the face and hands, while male aurat is between the navel and the knees.

68 "Rulers Agree." See also "K.L. Moving Cautiously."

69 Leggett, "Women Win New Rights."

70 Diverse moderate as well as radical Muslim movements are responding to deep yearnings for a resurgent Islamic sociality—an Umma—that ignores the man-made borders of nation-states. In Southeast Asia, the purported goals of the radical Islamic group Jemaah Islamiyah are to attack secular states and eventually to "restore" a regional caliphate state. See Ong, "Experiments with Freedom."

TWO Cyberpublics and Chinese Politics

1 The IMF imposed disciplinary conditions for loans, requiring the Indonesian state to cut subsidies for basic commodities such as flour and cooking oil. Millions of Indonesians driven to the edge of starvation turned their anger against the most visible target, ethnic Chinese shopkeepers.

2 For a brief historical view of anti-Chinese discrimination in Indonesia, see Skinner, "Chinese Minority." For a recent overview of the politics of Chinese economic domination, see Schwarz, *Nation in Waiting*.

3 Coppel, "Chinese Indonesians in Crisis."

4 At the 1998 Manila meeting of the Association of Southeast Asian Nations (ASEAN), Madeleine Albright, the U.S. Secretary of State, condemned the Burmese government for its mistreatment of opposition leader Aung San Suu Kyi, but she made no mention of the ongoing attacks on ethnic Chinese in Indonesia.

5 "Chinese Diaspora Using Internet to Aid Brethren."

6 The teach-in, organized by the Indonesian Chinese American Network (ICANET), and sponsored by San Francisco city councilman Leland Yee—one of two American Chinese councilmen in the United States' largest enclave of American Chinese—was dramatized by the personal accounts of the Jakarta riots by three Indonesians of Chinese descent, who spoke anonymously, behind a screen, to protect them from potential retaliation by the dark forces within the Indonesian government. This event was reported on www.huaren.org.

7   "Large Crowd Attends Teach-In."

8   "Tragedy and Technology Make Overseas Chinese UNITE."

9   "JT," "Our Shame for Failing to Help Huaren Refugee[s] in Vietnam and Cambodia in the Past." Available online at www.huaren.org.

10 "Dennis," "Re: Our Shame for Failing to Help Huaren Refugee[s] in Vietnam and Cambodia in the Past." Available online at www.huaren.org.

11 Cohen, "Cultural Strategies"; Wertheim, *East-West Parallels*.

12 Chirot and Reid, *Essential Outsiders*.

13 Reid, "Entrepreneurial Minorities," 40.

14 Skinner, "Chinese Minority."

15 Ghosh, "Diaspora in Indian Culture."

16 Gilroy, *Black Atlantic*.

17 Gilroy, *Small Acts*.

18 Tölölyan, "Rethinking Diaspora(s)."

19 Clifford, *Routes*, 36.

20 Clifford, "Indigenous Articulations," 482, 475.

21 Anderson, *Imagined Communities*.

22 Appadurai, *Modernity at Large*.

23 Ong and Nonini, *Ungrounded Empires*.

24 Anderson, "Long-Distance Nationalism," 74.

25 Pan, *Sons of the Yellow Emperor*, and *Encyclopedia of the Chinese Overseas*.

26 "Living Tree."

27 Chow, *Writing Diaspora*, 14, 99, 48, 118.

28 The literature is too extensive to be listed here. For a classic work, see Skinner, *Chinese Society in Thailand*; for a new ethnography of class, gender, and cultural diversity among diaspora Chinese in Southeast Asia, see Bao, *Marital Acts*.

29 Ong and Nonini, *Ungrounded Empires*.

30 E.g., Ong, *Flexible Citizenship*; McKeown, *Chinese Migrant Networks*; and Bao, *Marital Acts*.

31 Ong and Nonini, *Ungrounded Empires*.

32 Kwong, *Forbidden Workers*.

33 Ong, *Flexible Citizenship*, 139–84.

34 Williams, *Overseas Chinese Nationalism*, 128.

35 Tu, "Cultural China"; Liu, "Beijing Sojourners in New York."

36 Anderson, "Long-Distance Nationalism," 74.

37 Policy makers have stuck the label *Southeast Asian American* on all immigrants from mainland Southeast Asia. It has come to be an all-inclusive ethnic category for accessing major institutions and other resources. However, deep cultural, ethnic, and national differences persist among the variety of peoples from the region. See Ong, *Buddha Is Hiding*.

38 Hall, "Question of Cultural Identity."

39 Ibid., 630.

40 Sassen, "Digital Networks and Power," 62.

41 Coppel, "Chinese Indonesians in Crisis."

42 www.huaren.org.

43 Tay, "Global Chinese Fraternity."

44 Tens of thousands of Indonesian Chinese fled to surrounding countries. Some decided to settle in Perth, Australia, but many stayed with relatives or in hotels in Malaysia, Singapore, Hong Kong, and Thailand. The wealthy ones have since settled abroad, while others have returned permanently to Indonesia, their homeland and source of livelihood.

45 Prabowo was also involved in the disappearance of twenty-four activists earlier in the year. See reports in the *Jakarta Post* (July 14, 1998) and *APS* (Dec. 21, 1998).

46 In 1999, Wahid succeeded Habibie as president.

47 There is still disagreement as to whether there were 85 (verified) rapes during the riots, or 168, as many NGOs claim. Twenty of the rape victims subsequently died. See members.xoom.com.

48 For a UN fact-finding report on the May 1998 rapes of minority ethnic women in Java, Sumatra, and East Timor, see Coomaraswamy, "Report of UN Special Rapporteur."

49 See www.geocities.com/soekarno.

50 See ibid.

51 See www.geocities.com/Soho/Atrium/5140 (email message from soc@indonesia, August 10, 1998).

52 The dual categories of citizenship—which treat ethnic Chinese (citizens of foreign descent) as categorically different from indigenous Indonesians—date from the Dutch colonial era. See Coppel, "Chinese Indonesians in Crisis."

53 Held et al., *Global Transformations*, 81.

54 Tay, "Global Chinese Fraternity," 5.

55 Ang, "Indonesia on My Mind."

THREE Graduated Sovereignty

1 See Evans, "Eclipse of the State?"; Ruggie, *Constructing the World Polity*; and Ong, *Flexible Citizenship*.

2 Schmitt, *Political Theology*; Giddens, *Nation-State and Violence*.

3 Held, "Democracy," 32.

4 Foucault, *Power/Knowledge*.

5 Foucault, "Governmentality," 219.

6 Castells, *End of the Millennium*, 270–71.

7 See McVey, "Materialization of the Southeast Asian Entrepreneur."

8 The term *developmental state* originally referred to a massive state effort for the total economic transformation of the nation. The paradigmatic developmental state was the Soviet Union.

9 See, e.g., O'Donnell, "On the State," 1361.

10 Foucault, *Introduction*, 143, 199.

11 Castel, "Dangerousness to Risk," 294.

12 That is, compared to, say, advanced, neoliberal democracies like the United States and Great Britain, where a panoply of private agencies has become a much more important technology for the production of normativity, whereby individuals are encouraged to become rational, calculative, self-managing subjects. See Barry, Osborne, and Rose, *Foucault and Political Reason*.

13 Foucault, "*Omnes et Singulatim*," 300–303.

14 Anderson, *Imagined Communities*.

15 Ibrahim, *Asian Renaissance*.

16 Huntington, *Clash of Civilizations*.

17 Khoo, *Paradoxes of Mahathirism*, 65.

18 Khoo, *Paradoxes of Mahathirism*, 179, 181.

19 Jomo, "Malaysia Props Up Its Crony Capitalists."

20 See Ong, *Spirits of Resistance*.

21 Brosius, "Prior Transcripts."

22 Emilia, "Fired Female Worker Fights."

23 Li, "Articulating Indigenous Identity."

24 Lewis, *Empire of the East*, 223–31.

25 Peluso and Harwell, "Land Filled with Tears."

26 Samydorai, "Killing Fields of West Kalimantan."

27 Reuters, "Minister."

28 Aditjondro, "All in the Name of an ASEAN Solidarity."

29 Latour, *We Have Never Been Modern*, 134.

30 Bernard and Ravenhill, "Pursuit of Competitiveness in East Asia."

31 Jordan and Khanna, "Economic Interdependence and Challenges to the Nation-State."

32 Macleod and McGee, "Singapore-Johore-Riau Growth Triangle."

33 For a discussion of time-space mechanisms in flexible accumulation, see David Harvey, *The Condition of Postmodernity*. Oxford: Blackwell, 1989.

34 Macleod and McGee, "The Singapore-Johore-Riau Growth Triangle," 443.

35 "Region 3: Asia and the Pacific Rim: International Business Practices." Available at www.stat-usa.gov.

36 "Batam: Bigger and Better."

37 "Conduit to Fully Tap Creativity."

38 Ong, "Ecologies of Expertise . . ."

39 Wysocki, "Malaysia Is Gambling."

40 World Bank, *Sustaining Rapid Development*, 9, and *Indonesia*.

41 Quoted in "Currency Speculators."

42 "Towards a New Financial System."

43 Gill, "Globalization, Civilization, Neoliberalism," 214.

44 Karl Polyani (*Great Transformation*) maintains that in the unruly conditions pro-

duced by global markets in the 1930s, new forms of the state arose to assert social control over apparently natural laws of economic forces.

45 Attali, "Crash of Western Civilization."

46 Jomo, "Malaysia Props Up Its Crony Capitalists."

47 Robison and Goodman, "New Rich in Asia."

48 Tambiah, "Galactic Polity."

49 Stroper, "Resurgence of Regional Economies."

FOUR Zoning Technologies in East Asia

1 See, e.g., Kim, "Regionalization and Regionalism," 14.

2 Ohmae, *End of the Nation State*.

3 Weber, *Economy and Society*, 220.

4 Giddens, *Nation-State and Violence*, 172.

5 For a criticism of this model, see Taylor, "Beyond Containers."

6 See Johnson, MITI and the Japanese Miracle; and Evans, *Embedded Autonomy*.

7 Weiss, *Myth of the Powerless State*.

8 For a view of "social sovereignty" produced by a plurality of agents, such as the state, corporations, economic institutions, and expert systems, see Latham, "Social Sovereignty."

9 Rose, *Powers of Freedom*, 2.

10 Schmitt, *Political Theology*, 13.

11 Schwab, introduction to Schmitt, *Political Theology*, xxii–xxiii; xv–xix. The Schmittian concept of sovereign exception stirred criticism for his alleged support of the suspension of constitutional rights to protection under the Weimar Republic.

12 Ruggie, *Constructing the World Polity*, 172–73.

13 Krasner, *Problematic Sovereignty*.

14 Sassen, *Losing Control?*, xii.

15 Barry, *Political Machines*, 25–27.

16 UNIDO, "Industrial Free Trade Zones."

17 Ong, "Gender and Labor Politics of Postmodernity."

18 Tsuchiya, "Free Trade Zones in Southeast Asia," 280.

19 Zonings by urban authorities competing for investment resources have proliferated, but, since my focus is on the deployment of zoning from the national center, I will not discuss them here.

20 See www.wikipedia.org/wiki/Special_Economic_Zone.

21 Tatsuyuki Ota, "Role of Special Economic Zones," 4.

22 National People's Congress, People's Republic of China, "Regulations on Special Economic Zones in Guangdong Province," August 26, 1980. Available online at www.novexcn.com.

23 See Ong and Nonini, *Ungrounded Empires*.

24 Shek Ping Kwan, "China Country Report," Hong Kong Christian Industrial Committee (June 1995).

25 National People's Congress, "Regulations on Special Economic Zones."

26 For an account of the citizenship predicament of migrant workers, see Solinger, *Contesting Citizenship*.

27 Ong, *Flexible Citizenship*, 44.

28 Manuel Castells attributes the rising Hong Kong–centered metropolitan network to the building of regional infrastructure and flows, but he ignores other technologies of zoning and the transfer of business skills and practices. See Castells, *Rise of the Network Society*.

29 Lee, *Gender and the South China Miracle*.

30 Enright, Scott, and Dodwell, *Hong Kong Advantage*, 100.

31 Hsiung, *Making Capitalism in China*.

32 Law Siu Lan, "Lion and Dragon."

33 "Hong Kong Special Administrative Region." Available online at www.china. org.cn.

34 See Bradshore, "With Unrest Rising."

35 For specific details on Article 23 of the Basic Law, see www.answers.com/topic/ hong-kong-basic-law-article.

36 Krasner, *Sovereignty*.

37 Haacke, "ASEAN's Diplomatic and Security Culture."

38 Anderson, *Imagined Communities*.

39 See Dirlik, *What Is in a Rim?*

40 See Hong Liu, "Sino-Southeast Asian Studies."

41 Agamben, *Homo Sacer*.

FIVE Latitudes

1 This chapter has benefited from discussions at the Ethnohistory Workshop, University of Pennsylvania, Sept. 16, 2004. I thank David Ludden for his comments.

2 Hardt and Negri, *Empire*.

3 Kant, "Perpetual Peace."

4 Marx and Engels, *Communist Manifesto*.

5 Hardt and Negri, *Empire*, 332, 397.

6 Ibid., 23, 328–29, 332.

7 Saskia Sassen's claim that global cities are nodes in a "new geography of centrality" fails to recognize the existence of more variegated globalized spaces. See Sassen, *Global City*.

8 Saxenian, *Regional Advantage*.

9 Hardt and Negri, *Empire*, 23.

10 Foucault, "Governmentality," 201–22.

11 Deleuze, "Postscript on the Societies of Control."

12 Earlier geographies of Asian capital tended to be more regionalized, only weakly represented in the Western hemisphere. See Nonini and Ong, introduction to *Ungrounded Empires*.

13 Stark, "Value, Values, and Valuation."

14 Saxenian, *Silicon Valley's New Immigrant Entrepreneurs*.

15 Koslowski, "Intersections of Information Technology," 12.

16 Saxenian, *Silicon Valley's New Immigrant Entrepreneurs*.

17 Kwong, *Forbidden Workers*, 110–11.

18 "BCBG Names in Sweatshop Suit."

19 Beck, "Self-Dissolution and Self-Endangerment."

20 Lüthje, "Race and Ethnicity."

21 Ong, *Spirits of Resistance*.

22 Hukill, "When Unions Attempt to Organize."

23 "High Tech's Low Wages."

24 Lash, "Reflexivity and Its Doubles."

25 See Ong, *Spirits of Resistance*; and Lee, *Gender and the South China Miracle*.

26 Bluestone and Harrison, *Deindustrialization of America*.

27 Rose, "Governing 'Advanced' Liberal Democracies," 57.

28 "New California."

29 Rose, *Powers of Freedom*, 188.

30 Delanty, *Citizenship in a Global Age*, 106, 120.

31 Rose, *Powers of Freedom*, 167–76.

32 Davis, *Ecology of Fear*.

33 "San Jose Mayor Forms Housing Crisis Group."

34 "Mission District."

35 Lüthje, "Global Production and Electronics Manufacturing."

36 Lüthje, "Why China Matters in Global Electronics."

37 Lee, *Gender and the South China Miracle*.

38 Chen, "China Faces Rash of Protests."

39 Held et al., *Global Transformations*, 444–45, 449.

40 Hardt and Negri, *Empire*, 400.

41 Ibid., 397, 212.

42 Fong, "Chinese Puzzle."

SIX Higher Learning in Global Space

1 See, e.g., Gutmann, "Unity and Diversity."

2 "Economic action is primarily oriented to the problem of choosing the *end* to which a thing shall be applied; technology, to the problem, given the end, of choosing the appropriate *means*" (Weber, "Sociological Categories," 203).

3 For a view by a besieged humanist, see Miyoshi, "University in the 'Global' Economy."

4 See, e.g., Gutmann, *Multiculturalism*.

5 By "liberalism," I mean the basic ideals of democracy, equality, and political inclusion in the Western political tradition, and by "neoliberalism," I mean unregulated, borderless, and flexible market values.

6 Smith, *National Identity*.

7 Horsman, *Race and Manifest Destiny*.

8 Gellner, "Nationalism," 158–69; Anderson, *Imagined Communities*.

9 Emerson, *Selected Essays*.

10 Dewey, *Democracy and Education*.

11 Delanty, "University and Modernity," 35–37.

12 See Rodriguez, *Hunger of Memory*.

13 Shklar, *American Citizenship*, 3.

14 Bourdieu, *Distinction*.

15 Kaplan and Pease, *Cultures of United States Imperialism*.

16 Dirlik, *What Is in a Rim?*

17 See Cohen, *Asian American Century*.

18 Brubaker, introduction to *Immigration and the Politics of Citizenship*, 4–5.

19 For a discussion of the centrality of the civil rights movement to minority struggles, see Espiritu, *Asian American Pan ethnicity*.

20 Rosaldo, "Cultural Citizenship, Inequality, and Multiculturalism."

21 Lowe, *Immigrant Acts*.

22 Kymlicka, *Multicultural Citizenship*.

23 Taylor, "Politics of Recognition," 56–57.

24 Education Abroad Program, University of California, 2002.

25 www.nyu.edu/studyabroad.

26 Giddens, "Living in a Post-traditional Society," 59. See also Beck, *Risk Society*.

27 Olds and Thrift, "Cultures on the Brink."

28 See Ong and Nonini, *Ungrounded Empires*.

29 Six of my siblings were eventually educated in American universities.

30 Ong, *Flexible Citizenship*.

31 Saxenian, *Silicon Valley's New Immigrant Entrepreneurs*.

32 Marech, "Fremont's Little Asia."

33 Mitchell, "Education for Democratic Citizenship."

34 Ong, *Buddha Is Hiding*.

35 Miyoshi, "University in the 'Global' Economy," 36; Reich, *Work of Nations*.

36 Reich, *Work of Nations*.

37 Rose, "Governing the Enterprising Self," 142.

38 This is a term used by Great Britain's New Labor Party (Tony Blair's "Third Way" politics of globalization).

39 See, e.g., "Columbia and the World."

40 Hall, "Conclusion," 235, 236–37.

SEVEN Labor Arbitrage

1 Caller Kim, on *Forum*, KQED radio station, July 9, 2004, 9–10 a.m., San Francisco.

2 Caller Latisha on ibid.

3 Caller Miriam on ibid. A male caller raised the issue of "theft of American technol-

ogy" by Chinese companies in joint ventures with American firms, and the piracy of American intellectual properties in television and film products. A company representative on the show smoothly responded that American companies can work on their own in China, and that the Chinese workers are helping them develop technology. Also the Chinese government is cracking down on intellectual piracy in the consumer markets.

4 Latour, "Drawing Things Together," 26.

5 Marx, *Capital*.

6 For ethnographic studies of overseas manufacturing work, see Ong, *Spirits of Resistance*; and for off-shore data-entry jobs, see Freeman, *High Tech and High Heels*.

7 Reich, *Work of Nations*.

8 The concept of territorializations is from Deleuze and Guattari, *Thousand Plateaus*.

9 For one view of arbitrage in financial markets, see McKenzie, "Globalization, Efficient Markets, and Arbitrage."

10 A decade later, factory wages continue to fall with the expansion of alternative cheap labor markets, especially in China.

11 Eric Simonson, "Part I: What's Driving the Growth of BPO? The Impact of Labor Arbitrage." BPO Outsourcing Journal, November 2002. Available online at www. bpo-outsourcing-journal.com.

12 For an analysis of the systematic fragmentation and standardization of production processes, see Braverman, *Labor and Monopoly Capital*.

13 World Bank, *World Development Report*, 16.

14 "Another Lure of Outsourcing."

15 For an in-depth look at the rise of the high-tech industry in China, see Ross, *Fast Boat to China*.

16 "Teaching Tech."

17 Roach, "Global Labor Arbitrage."

18 The interview was conducted in the San Francisco Bay Area on September 18, 2002.

19 "Question of Fraud."

20 "Law Shouldn't Allow High-Tech Industry to Indenture Immigrants."

21 "U.S. Is Losing Its Dominance."

22 Reported in Schmid, "Chinese Engineers Its Next Great Leap."

23 For an account of Tata Consultancy activities in China, see Ross, *Fast Boat to China*.

24 "In India's Outsourcing Boom."

25 "Indians Go Home."

26 Peter Bendor-Samuel, "Three Kinds of Savings—Labor Arbitrage: How the Numbers Work." BPO Outsourcing Journal (Sept. 2003); see www.bpooutsourcing-journal.com/sep2003-everest.

27 "VC Firms Push for Outsourcing."

28 "Whole New World."

29 "Straight from the Mouth."

30 Ibid.

31 "We're from Bangalore."
32 Henderson, "America's Shortage."
33 But see Friedman, "It's a Flat World."
34 Ehrenreich, *Hearts of Men*.
35 Newman, *Falling from Grace*, 229–30.
36 Bush, "Inaugural Address."
37 Some American and European students have been hired by Indian call centers to fill gaps in linguistic and logistic skills. So young Americans are beginning to experiment with being workers in cheaper labor zones in order to serve the American customer.
38 "New Group Swells Bankruptcy Court."
39 Reich, *Work of Nations*.
40 Paul Craig Roberts, "Global 'Labor Arbitrage' Dismantling America." Available online at vdare.org.
41 Gordon, "Governmental Rationality," 43–44.
42 Weber, *Protestant Ethic*.
43 See Weber, "Sociological Categories," 199–200.

EIGHT Ecology, Citizenship

1 Goh Chok Tong, "New Singapore."
2 National resources were corralled (through an obligatory pension fund) to serve a coalition of government-led and multinational corporations. At the same time, foreign investors enjoyed tax exemptions of up to 90 percent on profits generated, making Singapore the leading recipient of foreign direct investment in the world.
3 Chan Heng Chee, "Singapore's Globalization Soiree."
4 Rose and Miller, "Political Power beyond the State," 196.
5 Rose, "Governing 'Advanced' Liberal Democracies."
6 See, e.g., Rabinow, *French DNA*.
7 Economic Development Board (EDB), *Into the Fifth Decade*, 9.
8 For a popular discussion of "the science of complexity," see Barabasi, *Linked*.
9 Iansiti and Levien, "Strategy as Ecology."
10 EDB, *Into the Fifth Decade*, 10.
11 Sole and Goodwin, *Signs of Life*, 199–200.
12 For reasons of confidentiality, names of interviewed subjects are not mentioned. All interviews with manpower officials were conducted in December 2001 in Singapore.
13 Sole and Goodwin, *Signs of Life*, 199–200.
14 Ong, "Ecologies of Expertise."
15 Available online at http://web.mit.edu/sma/.
16 Tan, keynote address.
17 "NUS Enterprise."
18 Liu, *Genome Institute of Singapore* (brochure).

19 Rose and Novas, "Biological Citizenship."

20 Rabinow, "Third Culture."

21 "Cloning Gets Nod."

22 Mui Teng Yap, "Singapore's 'Three or More' Policy."

23 Leete, "Continuing Flight from Marriage and Parenthood."

24 Heng and Devan, "State Fatherhood."

25 "It's Here!"

26 "Looming Clash."

27 "Foreign Talents Boosted GDP."

28 Tan Kong Yam et al., "Has Foreign Talent Contributed to Singapore's Economic Growth?"

29 Stark, "Value, Values, and Valuation."

30 Chan and Chiang, *Stepping Out*.

31 Lian, "Singapore."

32 George, *Singapore*.

33 Chang, "Human Resources for Technology and Innovation."

34 Contact Singapore advertisement. Available online at www.contactsingapore.org.sg/time.

35 EDB, "Responses to Recommendations on Housing."

36 Interview was conducted in September 2004, in Berkeley.

NINE A Biocartography

1 These accounts are abstracted from reports in the *Straits Times* (Singapore), the *New Straits Times* (Kuala Lumpur), and the *Wall Street Journal* (New York).

2 Jason Szep, "In Wealthy Singapore, Maids Push for Protection," March 19, 2004. Available online at www.netmaid.com.sg.

3 At the beginning of the twenty-first century, there were an estimated 10 million Asian migrant workers, half of whom were female; Asian Migrant Center (AMC), *Baseline Research*, 14.

4 Szep, "In Wealthy Singapore."

5 "Malaysia Maid Abuse Shocks PM," author's printout, July 7, 2004.

6 Hassan, "Maids as Slaves."

7 Kent, "Malaysia Angry at Maid Abuse."

8 Hassan, "Maids as Slaves"; Bowring, "Abuse Sheds Light."

9 Benhabib, *Claims of Culture*.

10 Agamben, *Homo Sacer*.

11 Balibar, "Outlines of a Topography of Cruelty"; Dauvergne, "Making People Illegal."

12 Agamben, *Homo Sacer*, 170–71, 179–80.

13 Ignatieff, "Human Rights," 318–19, 320.

14 See Castles and Davidson, *Citizenship and Migration*, chap. 8.

15   See, e.g., Held, *Democracy and the Global Order*.

16   For the trailblazing study of moral economy in Southeast Asia, see Scott, *Moral Economy of the Peasant*.

17   For specific case studies, see Ong, *Spirits of Resistance*; and Mills, *Thai Women*.

18   "Invest in the Philippines."

19   Guevarra, *Manufacturing the Ideal Work Force*.

20   Ibid., 164.

21   Rudnyckyj, "Technologies of Servitude."

22   Guevarra, *Manufacturing the Ideal Work Force*, 8.

23   Rudnyckyj, "Technologies of Servitude," 407.

24   The term "a biopolitical backwardness" is borrowed from Fassin, "Biopolitics of Otherness," 4.

25   Christine Chin (*In Service and Servitude*) has argued that in Malaysia, the demand for cheap foreign worker is so strong that it serves as a kind of "social contract" between the state and the middle classes.

26   Yeoh and Huang, "Spaces at the Margins," 1155.

27   Cited in ibid., 1156.

28   This new kind of household slavery is startlingly similar to the sexual slavery produced by the traffic of women in Asia. See Barry, Bunch, and Castley, *International Feminism*, 22.

29   Constable, *Maid to Order*.

30   Althusser, "Ideology and Ideological State Apparatuses," 174–75.

31   Yeoh and Huang, "Spaces at the Margins," 1156.

32   See Chin, *In Service and Servitude*, 109–11.

33   Interview with Tenaganita, June 2002, in Kuala Lumpur.

34   Although the Malaysian government does allow legal migrants temporary visa extensions in order to testify against an abuser, they are unable to work. In almost all cases, the worker settles for a sum of money and leaves the country. See Jones, *Making Money off Migrants*.

35   Constable, *Maid to Order*.

36   Aradau, "Beyond Good and Evil."

37   AMC, *Asian Migrant Yearbook*, 72.

38   "As Boom Fails."

39   "For Asia's Maids."

40   Jaschok, *Concubines and Bondservants*, 76–77.

41   Chin, *In Service and Servitude*, 144–45.

42   Constable, *Maid to Order*, 148–49.

43   Constable, *Maid to Order*, 71, 106–8.

44   Chin, *In Service and Servitude*, 144–45.

45   Ibid., 111.

46   For an instructive and poignant view of this transnational relay of family care, see Meerman, *Chain of Love*. See also Parrenas, *Servants of Globalization*.

47 Habermas, "Why Europe Needs a Constitution," 14.

48 Yeoh and Huang, "Spaces at the Margins."

49 See Collier and Lakoff, "On Regimes of Living."

50 See Ong, *Flexible Citizenship*, chap. 7.

51 Sassen, *Globalization and Its Discontents*; Hardt and Negri, *Empire*.

52 In December 1990, the United Nations passed the International Convention on the Protection of the Rights of All Migrant Workers and Members of Their Families, but it remains unratified by the majority of countries.

53 Foucault, *Power*, 319.

54 A Filipino priest quoted in Yeoh and Huang, "Spaces at the Margins," 1170.

55 Tenaganita, *Implications of the Economic Crisis*, 8.

56 Mydans, "Malaysia Upset."

57 Quoted in ibid.

58 Fassin, "Biopolitics of Otherness," 4.

59 Lee Ching Wern, "Not Slaves — Maids Speak Out against Unfair System," *Aware*, March 10, 2003, author's printout.

60 Hsiung, "Human Rights and International Relations," 185.

61 Interview with Tenaganita, July 18, 2002, in Kuala Lumpur.

62 This point is also made in Hsiung, "Human Rights and International Relations," 186.

63 Habermas, *Postnational Constellations*.

64 For a discussion of this case, see Rosca, "Mrs. Contemplacion's Sisters."

65 Anderson, "Cosmopolitanism," 267.

66 Agamben, *Homo Sacer*, 170–71.

67 Aradau, "Beyond Good and Evil."

TEN Reengineering the "Chinese Soul"

1 An exception is Guthrie, *Dragon in a Three-Piece Suit*.

2 Sassen, *Globalization and Its Discontents*, xx–xxviii.

3 Roberts, "Global Strategic Vision," 1–28.

4 Thrift, "Globalization of the System of Business Knowledge," 57, 59.

5 For a study of neoliberal practices in another Chinese city, see Hoffman, "Responsible Choices."

6 See Ross, *Fast Boat to China*.

7 Thrift, "Globalization of the System of Business Knowledge," 59.

8 "Embracing a New Culture."

9 Barboza, "Seven Habits of Highly Effective Cadres."

10 See Hammer and Champy, *Re-engineering the Corporation*.

11 Quoted in "Bigger Campus for Managers of the Future."

12 All names are pseudonyms. Interview was conducted May 30, 1999, in Shanghai.

13 Interview was conducted June 2, 1999, in Shanghai.

14 Interview was conducted June 3, 1999, in Shanghai.

15 Zhou, *Shanghai Baby*, 72.

16 See Hershatter, *Dangerous Pleasures*.

17 "City on the Make."

18 Since 1990, over one thousand skyscrapers have been built in Shanghai, a city of 13 million people; ibid.

19 Barlow, "Zhishifenzi [Chinese Intellectuals] and Power."

20 Mao, "Report on Peasant Classes in Hunan."

21 I first discussed self-orientalism by overseas Chinese in *Flexible Citizenship*, 81.

22 This sense of possibility has been part of China's historical attempt to grapple with Western technology without giving up Chinese culture. The early era of modernization was marked by "self-strengthening" societies that posited "Chinese learning as the fundamental structure, Western learning for practical use!"; Fairbank, *United States and China*, 143. In contemporary time, the interweaving of foreign and Chinese values is more complex and subtle, with the Chinese gaining control over global forms and making them their own.

23 It has been claimed that the rise of China's "business elite" has produced a new kind of state clientelism that is unlikely to promote "civil society," meaning democratization. See Pearson, *China's New Business Elite*, 4–5.

24 Interviewed June 22, 2004, in Shanghai.

25 For an analysis of the travails of masculinity in the transition to market reforms, see Zhang, "Impotence in the Making."

26 For a view of sexuality and foreign liaisons in other cities, see Ong, *Flexible Citizenship*, chap. 5.

27 This Hong Kong manager was interviewed in Shanghai, May 29, 1999.

28 Interviewed May 28, 1999, in Shanghai.

29 For different views on guanxi in contemporary China, see Yang, *Gifts, Favors, and Banquets*; and Guthrie, "Declining Significance of *Guanxi*."

30 Interviewed May 28, 1999, in Shanghai.

31 The claim that deregulation of markets leads to the "denationalization" of national territory is made in Sassen, *Globalization and Its Discontents*, xxviii.

Abdullahi Ahmed An-Nai'im. "Towards an Islamic Reformation: Islamic Law in History and Society Today." In *Syariah Law and the Modern Nation-State: A Malaysian Symposium*, ed. Noraini Othman. Kuala Lumpur: Sisters in Islam, 1994.

Aditjondro, George J. "All in the Name of an ASEAN Solidarity." *Sydney Morning Herald*, Nov. 14, 1996.

Agamben, Giorgio. *Homo Sacer: Sovereign Power and Bare Life*. Trans. Daniel Heller-Roazen. Stanford: Stanford University Press, 1998.

Agarwal, Bina. "Beijing Women's Conference: From Mexico '75 to Beijing '95." *Mainstream*, Oct. 8, 1995, 8–9.

Althusser, Louis. "Ideology and Ideological State Apparatuses." In *Lenin and Philosophy and Other Essays*, trans. Ben Brewster. London: New Left Books, 1971.

Amina Wadud-Muhsin. "The Quran, Syariah, and the Citizenship Rights of Muslim Women in the Umma." In *Syariah Law and the Modern Nation-State: A Malaysian Symposium*, ed. Noraini Othman. Kuala Lumpur: Sisters in Islam, 1974.

Anderson, Amanda. "Cosmopolitanism, Universalism, and the Divided Legacies of Modernity." In *Cosmopolitics: Thinking and Feeling beyond the Nation*, ed. Pheng Cheah and Bruce Robbins. Minneapolis: University of Minnesota Press, 1998.

Anderson, Benedict. *Imagined Communities*. 2nd ed. London: Verso, 1991 [1983].

———. "Long-Distance Nationalism." In *The Spectre of Comparisons: Nationalism, Southeast Asia, and the World*. London: Verso, 1998.

Ang, Ien. "Indonesia on My Mind." In *On Not Speaking Chinese: Living between Asia and the West*. New York: Routledge, 2001.

"Another Lure of Outsourcing: Job Expertise." *Wall Street Journal*, April 12, 2004.

Appadurai, Arjun. *Modernity at Large: Cultural Dimensions of Modernity*. Minneapolis: University of Minnesota Press, 1995.

Aradau, Claudia. "Beyond Good and Evil: Ethics and Securitization/Desecuritization Techniques." *Rubikon* (e-journal), Dec. 2001.

Arendt, Hannah. *The Human Condition*. Introduction by Margaret Canovan. 2nd ed. Chicago: University of Chicago Press, 1998 [1958].

Asad, Talal. "The Limits of Religious Criticisms in the Middle East: Notes on Islamic Public Argument." In *Genealogies of Religion*. Baltimore: Johns Hopkins University Press, 1993.

"As Boom Fails, Malaysia Sends Migrants Home." *New York Times*, April 9, 1998.

Asian Migrant Centre (AMC). *Asian Migrant Yearbook 2000*. Hong Kong: Asian Migrant Center, 1999.

———. *Baseline Research on Racial and Gender Discrimination towards Filipino, Indonesia, and Thai Domestic Helpers in Hong Kong*. Hong Kong, 2001.

Attali, Jacques. "The Crash of Western Civilization: The Limits of the Market and of Democracy." *Foreign Policy* 107 (Summer 1997): 54–64.

Balibar, Etienne. "Outlines of a Topography of Cruelty: Citizenship and Civility in the Era of Global Violence." *Constellations* 8 (2001): 581–83.

Bao, Jiemin. *Marital Acts: Gender, Sexuality, and Identity among the Chinese Thai Diaspora*. Honolulu: University of Hawai'i Press, 2005.

Barabasi, Albert-Laszlo. *Linked: How Everything Is Connected to Everything Else and What It Means for Business, Science, and Everyday Life*. New York: Plume, 2003.

Barboza, David. "Seven Habits of Highly Effective Cadres." *New York Times*, Feb. 19, 2005.

Barlow, Tani. "Zhishifenzi [Chinese Intellectuals] and Power." *Dialectical Anthropology* 16 (1991): 209–32.

Barry, Andrew. *Political Machines: Governing a Technological Society*. London: Athelone, 2001.

Barry, Andrew, Thomas Osborne, and Nikolas Rose. Introduction to *Foucault and Political Reason*, ed. Andrew Barry, Thomas Osborne, and Nikolas Rose, Chicago: University of Chicago Press, 1996.

———, eds. *Foucault and Political Reason*. Chicago: University of Chicago Press, 1996.

Barry, Kathleen, Charlotte Bunch, and Shirley Castley, eds. *International Feminism: Networking against Female Sexual Slavery*. New York: International Women's Tribune, Centre, 1984.

"Batam: Bigger and Better." Advertisement. *Far Eastern Economic Review*, Jan. 28, 1999, 32–33.

"BCBG Names in Sweatshop Suit." *Asianweek* (San Francisco), Aug. 1999.

Beck, Ulrich. *Risk Society*. London: Sage, 1992.

———. "Self-Dissolution and Self-Endangerment of Industrial Society: What Does This Mean?" In *Reflexive Modernization*, ed. Ulrich Beck, Anthony Giddens, and Scott Lash. Stanford: Stanford University Press, 1994.

Becker, Gary. *Human Capital: A Theoretical and Empirical Analysis — With Special Reference to Education*. New York: National Bureau of Economic Research, 1963.

Benhabib, Sela. *The Claims of Culture: Equality and Diversity in the Global Era*. Princeton: Princeton University Press, 2002.

Bernard, Mitchell, and John Ravenhill. "The Pursuit of Competitiveness in East Asia: The Regionalization of Production and Its Consequences." In *American Competitiveness, East Asia, and the World Economy: International Political Economy Yearbook*, ed. D. P. Rapkin. Vol. 8. Boulder, Colo.: Lynne Rienner, 1995.

Bhabha, Homi. *The Location of Culture*. London: Routledge, 1998, 23.

Bhabha, Jacqueline, and Geoffrey Coll, eds. *Asylum Law and Practice in Europe and North America*. Washington: Federal, 1992.

"Bigger Campus for Managers of the Future." *South China Morning Post* (Hong Kong), May 9, 1998.

"Blame Men, Not Allah, Islamic Feminists Say." *New York Times*, Oct. 10, 1996.

Bluestone, Barry, and Bennett Harrison. *The Deindustrialization of America*. New York: Basic, 1982.

———. *Distinction: A Social Critique of the Judgment of Taste*. Cambridge: Harvard University Press, 1985.

Bowden, Brett. "The Perils of Global Citizenship." *Citizenship Studies* 7.3 (2003): 349–62.

Bowring, Philip. "Abuse Sheds Light on Vulnerable Millions." *International Herald Tribune*, May 25, 2004.

Bradshore, Keith. "With Unrest Rising, Hong Kong and China Conclude an Agreement to Liberalize Trade." *New York Times*, June 30, 2003.

Braverman, Harry. *Labor and Monopoly Capital: The Degradation of Work in the Twentieth Century*. New York: Monthly Review Press, 1974.

Brenner, Neil. "The Limits to Scale? Methodological Reflections on Scalar Structuration." *Progress in Human Geography* 15.4 (2001): 525–48.

Brosius, Peter. "Prior Transcripts, Divergent Paths: Resistance and Acquiescence to Logging in Sarawak, East Malaysia." *Comparative Studies in Society and History* 39 (1997): 468–510.

Brubaker, William Rogers. Introduction to *Immigration and the Politics of Citizenship in Europe and North America*. Lanham, M.D.: University of America Press. 1989.

"The Burden of Proof in Hudud." *Star* (Malaysia), Nov. 27, 1993.

Bush, George W. "The Inaugural Address." *New York Times*, Jan. 21, 2005.

"Bush Pledges a Broad Push toward Market-Based Policies." *New York Times*, Nov. 4, 2004.

Castel, Robert. "From Dangerousness to Risk." In *The Foucault Effect: Studies in Governmentality*, ed. Graham Burchell, Colin Gordon, and Peter Miller. Chicago: University of Chicago Press, 1991.

Castells, Manuel. *The Rise of Network Society*. Vol. 1 of *The Information Age: Economy, Society, and Culture*. Oxford: Blackwell, 1992.

———. *End of the Millennium*. Vol. 3 of *The Information Age: Economy, Society, and Culture*. Oxford: Blackwell, 1998.

Castles, Stephen, and Alastair Davidson. *Citizenship and Migration: Globalization and the Politics of Belonging*. New York: Routledge, 2000.

Chan Heng Chee. "Singapore's Globalization Soiree." Singapore Ambassador to the United States, address at the Woodrow Wilson International Center for Scholars, April 25, 2001.

Chan Kwok Bun and Claire Chiang. *Stepping Out*. Singapore: Simon and Schuster, 1994.

Chang, Morris. "Human Resources for Technology and Innovation in Southeast Asia." Paper presented at the Singapore-MIT Alliance Symposium, Jan. 2002.

Chatterjee, Partha. *The Nation and Its Fragments: Colonial and Postcolonial Histories*. Princeton: Princeton University Press, 1993.

Chen, Kathy. "China Faces Rash of Protests." *Wall Street Journal*, Nov. 5, 2004.

Chin, Christine. *In Service and Servitude: Foreign Domestic Workers in Malaysia*. New York: Columbia University Press, 2000.

"Chinese Diaspora Using Internet to Aid Plight of Brethren Abroad." *Wall Street Journal*, July 23, 1998.

Chirot, Daniel, and Anthony Reid, eds. *Essential Outsiders: Chinese and Jews in the Modern Transformation of Southeast Asia and Central Europe*. Seattle: University of Washington Press, 1997.

Chow, Rey. *Writing Diaspora: Tactics of Intervention in Contemporary Cultural Studies*. Bloomington: Indiana University Press, 1993.

"City on the Make." *Time* (international ed., Hong Kong), Sept. 18, 1998.

Clifford, James. *Routes: Travels and Translation in the Late Twentieth Century*. Cambridge: Harvard University Press. 1997.

———. "Indigenous Articulations." *Contemporary Pacific* 13.2 (2001): 468–90.

"Cloning Gets Nod from Singapore." *Straits Times* (Singapore), Jan. 4, 2002.

Cohen, Abner. "Cultural Strategies in the Organization of Trading Diasporas." In *The Development of Indigenous Trade and Markets in West Africa*, ed. Claude Meillassoux. London: Oxford University Press, 1971.

Cohen, Lawrence. "Operability, Bioavailability, and Exception." In *Global Assemblages: Technology, Politics and Ethics as Anthropological Problems*, ed. Aihwa Ong and Stephen J. Collier. Malden, Mass.: Blackwell, 2005.

Cohen, Warren I. *The Asian American Century*. Cambridge.: Harvard University Press, 2002.

Collier, Stephen J. "The Spatial Forms and Social Norms of 'Actually Existing Neoliberalism': Toward a Substantive Analytics." Unpublished manuscript.

———, and Andrew Lakoff. "On Regimes of Living." In *Global Assemblages: Technology, Politics and Ethics as Anthropological Problems*, ed. Aihwa Ong and Stephen J. Collier. Malden, Mass.: Blackwell, 2005.

———, and Aihwa Ong. "Global Assemblages, Anthropological Problems." In *Global Assemblages: Technology, Politics and Ethics as Anthropological Problems*, ed. Aihwa Ong and Stephen J. Collier. Malden, Mass.: Blackwell, 2005.

"Columbia and the World." Special issue of *Columbia: The Magazine of Columbia University*, Winter 2004–5.

Comaroff, Jean, and John L. Comaroff. "Millennial Capitalism: First Thoughts on a Second Coming." *Public Culture* 12.2 (2000): 291–343.

"Conduit to Fully Tap Creativity." *New Straits Times* (Kuala Lumpur), July 30, 1997.

Constable, Nicole. *Maid to Order in Hong Kong*. Ithaca, N.Y.: Cornell University Press, 1997.

Coomaraswamy, Radhika. "The Report of UN Special Rapporteur on Violence against Women." Report presented at the Fifty-fifth session of the UN High Commission on Human Rights, Geneva, March 22–April 30, 1999.

Coppel, Charles. "Chinese Indonesians in Crisis: 1960s and 1990s." Paper presented at the workshop "Chinese Indonesians: The Way Ahead," Australian National University, Canberra, Feb. 14–16, 1999.

Cruikshank, Barbara. "Neopolitics: Policy Decentralization and Governmentality." Paper presented at the conference "Professionals between Policy and People," Amsterdam/Utrecht, Oct. 7–8, 2004.

"Currency Speculators Out to Undermine Asian Economies." *New Straits Times* (Kuala Lumpur), July 25, 1997.

Dauvergne, Catherine. "Making People Illegal." In *Critical Beings: Law, Nation, and the Global Subject*, ed. Peter Fitzpatrick and Patricia Tuitt. London: Ashgate, 2003.

Davis, Mike. *Ecology of Fear: Los Angeles and the Imagination of Disaster*. New York: Vintage, 1999.

Delanty, Gerard. *Citizenship in a Global Age: Society, Culture, Politics*. Buckingham, UK: Open University Press, 2000.

——. "The University and Modernity: A History of the Present." In *The Virtual University? Knowledge, Markets, and Management*, ed. Kevin Robins and Frank Webster. New York: Oxford University Press, 2002.

Deleuze, Gilles. "Postscript on the Societies of Control." *October* 59 (Winter 1992): 3–7.

——, and Félix Guattari. *A Thousand Plateaus: Capitalism and Schizophrenia*. Trans. Brian Massumi. Minneapolis: University of Minnesota Press, 1987.

Dewey, John. *Democracy and Education*. New York: MacMillan, 1924.

Dirlik, Arif, ed. *What Is in a Rim? Critical Perspectives on the Pacific Rim Idea*. 2nd ed. Rowman and Littlefield, 1998.

Economic Development Board. "Responses to Recommendations on Housing." Concept Plan Committee. Unpublished manuscript. 2000.

——. *Into the Fifth Decade*. Singapore Economic Development Board, 2001.

Ehrenreich, Barbara. *The Hearts of Men: American Dreams and the Flight from Commitment*. Garden City, N.J.: Anchor, 1983.

"Embracing a New Culture." *South China Morning Post* (Hong Kong), June 14, 1998.

Emerson, Ralph Waldo. *Selected Essays*. Harmondsworth, UK: Penguin, 1985.

Emilia, Steve. "Fired Female Worker Fights for Better Labor Conditions." *Jakarta Post*, Aug. 25, 1996.

Enright, Michael J., Edith E. Scott, and David Dodwell. *The Hong Kong Advantage*. Hong Kong: Oxford University Press, 1997.

Errington, Shelly. Introduction to *Power and Difference: Gender in Island Southeast Asia*, ed. Jane Atkinson and Shelly Errington. Stanford: Stanford University Press, 1990.

Espiritu, Yen. *Asian American Pan-ethnicity*. Philadelphia: Temple University Press, 1992.

Evans, Peter. *Embedded Autonomy: States and Industrial Transformation*. Princeton: Princeton University Press, 1995.

——. "The Eclipse of the State? Reflection on Stateness in an Era of Globalization." *World Politics* 50 (Oct. 1997): 67–87.

Fairbank, John K. *The United States and China*. New York: Viking, 1958.

Fassin, Didier. "The Biopolitics of Otherness." *Anthropology Today* 17.1 (2001): 3–23.

Ferguson, James. *The Anti-politics Machine: "Development," Depoliticization, and Bureaucratic Power in Lesotho*. Cambridge: Cambridge University Press, 1990.

——. "Seeing Like an Oil Company: Space, Security, and Global Capital in Neoliberal Africa." *American Anthropologist* 107.3 (2005): 377–82.

"For Asia's Maids, Years of Abuse Spill into the Open." *Wall Street Journal*, Feb. 19, 2004.

"Foreign Talents Boosted GDP by 20% in Last Decade: SM Lee." *Straits Times* (Singapore), Oct. 30, 2001.

Foucault, Michel. *Power/Knowledge: Selected Interviews and Other Writings, 1972–1977*. New York: Vintage, 1977.

——. *An Introduction*. Vol. 1 of *The History of Sexuality*. Trans. M. Hurley. New York: Pantheon, 1978.

——. "The Ethics of the Concern for Self as a Practice of Freedom." In *Ethics*, Vol. 1 of *Essential Works of Foucault, 1954–1984*, ed. Paul Rabinow. Translated by Robert Hurley and others. New York: New Press, 1994.

——. "Governmentality." In *Power*. Vol. 3 of *Essential Works of Foucault, 1954–1984*, ed. James Faubion. Ser. ed. Paul Rabinow. New York: New Press, 2000.

——. "*Omnes et Singulatim*: Toward a Critique of Political Reason." In *Power*. Vol. 3 of *Essential Works of Foucault, 1954–1984*, ed. James Faubion. Ser. ed. Paul Rabinow. New York: New Press, 2000.

——. *Power*. Vol. 3 of *Essential Works of Foucault, 1954–1984*, ed. James Faubion, Ser. ed. Paul Rabinow. New York: New Press, 2000.

Freeman, Carla. *High Tech and High Heels: Women, Work, and Pink-Collar Identities in the Caribbean*. Durham, N.C.: Duke University Press, 1999.

Friedman, Milton. *Capitalism and Freedom*. With the assistance of Rose D. Friedman. Chicago: University of Chicago Press, 1962.

Friedman, Thomas. "It's a Flat World, After All." *New York Times Magazine*, April 3, 2005, 33–37.

Geertz, Clifford. *The Interpretation of Cultures: Selected Essays*. New York: Basic, 1973.

Gellner, Ernst. "Nationalism." In *Thought and Change*. London: Weidenfeld and Nicholson, 1964.

George, Cherian. *Singapore: The Air-Conditioned Nation*. Singapore: Landmark, 2000.

Ghosh, Amitav. "Diaspora in Indian Culture." *Public Culture* 2.1 (1989): 73–78.

Giddens, Anthony. *The Nation-State and Violence*. Vol. 2 of *A Contemporary Critique of Historical Materialism*. Berkeley: University of California Press, 1987.

——. "Living in a Post-traditional Society." In *Reflexive Modernization*, ed. Ulrich Beck, Anthony Giddens, and Scott Lash. Stanford: Stanford University Press, 1994.

Gill, Stephen. "Globalization, Market Civilization, and Disciplinary Neoliberalism."
    Millennium: Journal of International Studies 24.3 (1995): 399–423.
Gilroy, Paul. *The Black Atlantic: Double Consciousness and Modernity*. Cambridge: Har-
    vard University Press, 1993.
———. *Small Acts: Thoughts on the Politics of Black Culture*. London: Serpent's Tail, 1993.
Goh Chok Tong. "New Singapore." National Day Rally 2001 Speech by the Prime Min-
    ister at the National University of Singapore, Aug. 19, 2001. Singapore: Ministry of
    Information and the Arts.
Gordon, Colin. "Governmental Rationality: An Introduction." In *The Foucault Effect:
    Studies in Govermentality*, ed. Graham Burchell, Colin Gordon, and Peter Miller.
    Chicago: University of Chicago Press, 1991.
Guevarra, Anna. "Manufacturing the Ideal Work Force: The Transnational Labor Bro-
    kering of Nurses and Domestic Workers from the Philippines." PhD diss., Univer-
    sity of California, San Francisco, 2003.
Guthrie, Douglas. "The Declining Significance of *Guanxi* in China's Economic Transi-
    tion." *China Quarterly* 154 (1998): 31–62.
———. *Dragon in a Three-Piece Suit: The Emergence of Capitalism in China*. Princeton:
    Princeton University Press, 2001.
Gutmann, Amy. "Unity and Diversity in Democratic Multicultural Education: Creative
    and Destructive Tensions." In *Diversity and Citizenship Education*, ed. James A.
    Banks. New York: J. Wiley, 2003.
———, ed. *Multiculturalism: Examining the Politics of Recognition*. Princeton: Princeton
    University Press, 1994.
Haacke, Jürgen, "ASEAN's Diplomatic and Security Culture: A Constructivist Assess-
    ment." *International Relations of the Asia-Pacific* 3 (2003): 57–87.
Habermas, Jürgen. "Further Reflections on the Public Sphere." In *Habermas and the
    Public Sphere*, ed. Craig Calhoun. Cambridge: MIT Press, 1992.
———. *Postnational Constellations*. Cambridge: MIT Press, 2001.
———. "Why Europe Needs a Constitution." *New Left Review* 11 (Sept.–Oct. 2001):
    5–26.
Hall, Stuart. *The Hard Road to Renewal*. London: Verso, 1988.
———. "The Question of Cultural Identity." In *Modernity: An Introduction to Modern
    Societies*, ed. Stuart Hall, David Held, Don Hubert, and Kenneth Thompson.
    Oxford: Blackwell, 1996.
———. "Conclusion: The Multi-cultural Question." In *Un/Settled Multiculturalisms:
    Diasporas, Entanglements, "Transruptions,"* ed. Barnor Hess. London: Zed, 2000.
Hammer, Michael, and James Champy. *Re-engineering the Corporation: A Manifesto for a
    Business Revolution*. New York: HarperCollins, 1993.
Hardt, Michael, and Antonio Negri. *Empire*. Cambridge: Harvard University Press,
    2000.
Harrison, Stephan, Steve Pile, and Nigel Thrift, eds. *Patterned Ground: Entanglements of
    Nature and Culture*. London: Reaktion, 2004.

Harvey, David. "Neoliberalism and the Restoration of Class Power." Unpublished manuscript. CUNY Graduate Center, fall 2004.

Hassan, Hazlin. "Maids as Slaves: Asia's Hidden Shame." *Manila Times*, June 3, 2004.

Hayek, Friedrich von. *The Political Order of a Free People*. Vol. 3 of *Law, Legislation, and Liberty*. London: Routledge and Kegan Paul, 1979.

Held, David. "Democracy: From City-States to a Cosmopolitan Order?" In *Prospects for Democracy: North, South, East, West*, ed. David Held. Stanford: Stanford University Press, 1993.

——. *Democracy and the Global Order: From the Modern State to Cosmopolitan Governance*. Stanford: Stanford University Press, 1995.

——, Andrew McGrew, David Goldblatt, and Jonathan Perraton. *Global Transformations: Politics, Economics and Culture*. Stanford: Stanford University Press, 1999.

Henderson, William D. "America's Shortage of Quality Jobs." Letter to the Editor, *New York Times*, July 25, 2004.

Heng, Geraldine, and Janadas Devan. "State Fatherhood: The Politics of Nationalism, Sexuality and Race in Singapore." In *Bewitching Women, Pious Men*, ed. Aihwa Ong and Michael Peletz. Berkeley: University of California Press, 1995.

Hershatter, Gail. *Dangerous Pleasures: Prostitution and Modernity in Twentieth-Century Shanghai*. Berkeley: University of California Press, 1997.

"High Tech's Low Wages: Two Silicon Valley Firms Sued over Alleged Labor Violations." *Asianweek* (San Francisco), Dec. 23, 1999.

Hoffman, Lisa. "Responsible Choices: Patriotic Professionalism and Hong Liu. "Sino-Southeast Asian Studies: Towards an Alternative Paradigm." *Asian Studies Review* 25.3 (2001): 259–84.

Horsman, Reginald. *Race and Manifest Destiny: The Origins of American Racial Anglo-Saxonism*. Cambridge: Harvard University Press, 1981.

Hsiung, James C. "Human Rights and International Relations: Morality, Law, and Politics." In *Human Rights of Migrant Workers: Agenda for NGOs*, ed. Graziano Battistella. Quezon City: Scalabrini Migration Center, 1993.

Hsiung, You-tien. *Making Capitalism in China: The Taiwan Connection*. New York: Oxford University Press, 1998.

Hukill, Traci. "When Unions Attempt to Organize Silicon Valley's Growing Vietnamese Labor Force, They Find Custom, Language, and History Standing in the Way." *Metro: Silicon Valley's Weekly Newspaper,* Sept. 16, 1999.

Huntington, Samuel. *The Clash of Civilizations and the Remaking of World Order*. New York: Simon and Schuster, 1996.

Iansiti, Marco, and Roy Levien. "Strategy as Ecology." *Harvard Business Review*, March 2004, 68–78.

Ibrahim, Anwar. *The Asian Renaissance*. Kuala Lumpur: Times, 1997.

Ignatieff, Michael. "Human Rights." In *Human Rights in Political Transitions: Gettysburg to Bosnia*, ed. Carla Hesse and Robert Post. New York: Zone, 1999.

"In India's Outsourcing Boom, GE Played a Starring Role." *Wall Street Journal*, March 23, 2005.

"Indians Go Home, But Don't Leave the U.S. Behind." *New York Times*, July 24, 2004.

"In Search of the Female Voice." *Star* (Malaysia), Sept. 5, 1996.

"Invest in the Philippines: Home of the Great Filipino Worker." Advertisement. *Far Eastern Economic Review*, June 13, 2002.

"Islamic Dress Code Still a Major Issue." *New Straits Times* (Kuala Lumpur), Dec. 3, 1991.

"It's Here!" *Manpower News*. Singapore: Manpower Ministry, Sept. 2001.

Jaschok, Maria. *Concubines and Bondservants: The Social History of a Chinese Custom*. London: Zed, 1998, 76–77.

Jayawardena, Kumari. *Feminism and Nationalism in the Third World*. London: Zed, 1986.

Johnson, Chalmers. *MITI and the Japanese Miracle*. Stanford: Stanford University Press, 1982.

Jomo, K. S. "Malaysia Props Up Its Crony Capitalists." *Asian Wall Street Journal*, Dec. 21, 1998.

Jones, Sydney. *Making Money off Migrants: The Indonesian Exodus to Malaysia*. Hong Kong: Asia 2000 Ltd., 2000.

Jordan, Amos A., and Jane Khanna. "Economic Interdependence and Challenges to the Nation-State: The Emergence of Natural Economic Territories in the Asia-Pacific." *Journal of International Affairs* 48.2 (1995): 433–62.

Kant, Immanuel. "Perpetual Peace: A Philosophical Sketch." In *Political Writings*, ed. Hans Reiss. Cambridge: Cambridge University Press, 1991.

Kaplan, Amy, and Donald Pease, eds. *Cultures of United States Imperialism*. Durham, N.C.: Duke University Press, 1993.

Kelly, Philip, and Kris Olds. "Questions in a Crisis: The Contested Meanings of Globalization in the Asia-Pacific." In *Globalization and the Asia-Pacific*, ed. K. Olds, P. Dicken, P. F. Kelly, L. Kong, and H. W.-C. Yeung. London: Routledge, 1999.

Kent, Jonathan. "Malaysia Angry at Maid Abuse." *BBC News*, May 21, 2004.

Kessler, Clive. *Politics and Islam in a Malay State*. Ithaca, N.Y.: Cornell University Press, 1978.

Khoo Boo Teik. *Paradoxes of Mahathirism*. Kuala Lumpur: Oxford University Press, 1995.

Kim, Samuel S. "Regionalization and Regionalism in East Asia." *Journal of East Asian Studies* 4.1 (2004): 39–67.

"K.L. Moving Cautiously on Islamic Dressing Code." *New Straits Times* (Kuala Lumpur), Aug. 8, 1997.

Koslowski, Rey. "Intersections of Information Technology and Human Mobility: Globalization vs. Homeland Security." Paper presented at St. Hugh's College, University of Oxford, March 25–28, 2004.

Krasner, Stephen D. *Sovereignty: Organized Hypocrisy*. Princeton, NJ: Princeton University Press, 1999.

———, ed. *Problematic Sovereignty: Contested Rules and Political Possibilities*. New York: Columbia University Press, 2001.

Kwong, Peter. *Forbidden Workers: Illegal Chinese Immigrants and American Labor*. New York: Free Press, 1997.

Kymlicka, Will. *Multicultural Citizenship: A Liberal Theory of Minority Rights*. Oxford: Oxford University Press, 1995.

Landes, Joan B. *Women in the Public Sphere*. Ithaca, N.Y.: Cornell University Press, 1988.

"Large Crowd Attends Teach-In on Indonesia Crisis in SF." *San Francisco Chronicle*, Aug. 1, 1998.

Lash, Scott. "Reflexivity and Its Doubles: Structure, Aesthetics, Community." In *Reflexive Modernization*, ed. Ulrich Beck, Anthony Giddens, and Scott Lash. Stanford: Stanford University Press, 1994.

Latham, Robert. "Social Sovereignty." *Theory, Culture, and Society* 17.4 (2000): 1–18.

Latour, Bruno. "Drawing Things Together." In *Representation in Scientific Practice*, ed. Michael Lynch and Steve Woolgar. Cambridge: MIT Press, 1990.

——. *We Have Never Been Modern*. Trans. Catherine Porter. Cambridge: Harvard University Press, 1993.

"Law Shouldn't Allow High-Tech Industry to Indenture Immigrants." *San Francisco Chronicle*, Sept. 9, 2000.

Lee, Ching Kwan. *Gender and the South China Miracle*. Berkeley: University of California Press, 1998.

Leete, Richard. "The Continuing Flight from Marriage and Parenthood among the Overseas Chinese in East and Southeast Asia: Dimensions and Implications." *Population and Development Review* 20.4 (1994): 811–29.

Leggett, Karby. "Women Win New Rights in Morocco by Invoking Islam." *Wall Street Journal*, Aug. 10, 2004.

Lewis, Norman. *An Empire of the East: Travels in Indonesia*. New York: Henry Holt, 1994: 223–31.

Li, Tania M. "Articulating Indigenous Identity in Indonesia: Resource Politics and the Tribal Slot." *Comparative Studies in Society and History* 42.1 (2000): 149–79.

Lian, Daniel. "Singapore: New Economy Proletariat or Bourgeoisie?" Morgan Stanley Global Economic Forum, Jan. 16, 2001.

Linklater, Andrew. "The Idea of Citizenship and the Development of the Modern State." In *European Citizenship, Multiculturalism, and the State*, ed. Urlich K. Pruess and Ferran Requejo. Baden-Baden, Germany: Nomos, 1998.

Liu, Lydia. "Beijing Sojourners in New York: Postsocialism and the Question of Ideology in Global Media Culture." *positions* 7.3 (1999): 763–97.

"The Living Tree." Special issue of *Daedalus* 120.2 (1991).

"Looming Clash over Foreign Talents." *Straits Times* (Singapore), Oct. 24, 2001.

Lowe, Lisa. *Immigrant Acts: On Asian American Cultural Politics*. Durham, N.C.: Duke University Press, 1996.

Lüthje, Boy. "Race and Ethnicity in 'Post-Fordist' Production Networks: Silicon Valley and the Global Information Technology Industry." Unpublished manuscript. Department of Social Sciences, University of Frankfurt, 1998.

———. "Why China Matters in Global Electronics." *International Occupational and Environmental Health* 9.4 (2003): 345–46.

———. "Global Production and Electronics Manufacturing in China." Paper presented at the Institute of Industrial Relations, University of California, Berkeley, Sept. 9, 2004.

Macleod, Scott, and T. G. McGee. "The Singapore-Johore-Riau Growth Triangle: An Emerging Extended Metropolitan Region." In *Emerging World Cities in Pacific Asia*, ed. Fu-chen Lo and Yue-man Yeung. Tokyo: United Nations University Press, 1996.

Mamdani, Mahmood. *Citizen and Subject: Contemporary Africa and the Legacy of Late Colonialism*. Princeton: Princeton University, 1996.

Mao Tse-Tung. "Report on Peasant Classes in Hunan." *Quotations from Chairman Mao Tse-Tung (The Little Red Book)*. Beijing: Foreign Language Press, 1967.

Marech, Rona. "Fremont's Little Asia." *San Francisco Chronicle*, May 17, 2002.

Marshall, Thomas H. *Class, Citizenship, and Social Class*. New York: Doubleday, 1963.

Marx, Karl. *Capital*. Vol. 1. New York: International, 1967 [1867].

———. "The Jewish Question." In *The Marx-Engels Reader*, ed. Robert C. Tucker. 2nd ed. New York: W. W. Norton, 1978.

———, and Friedrich Engels. *The Communist Manifesto*, ed. Gareth Jones. New York: Penguin Classic, 2002 [1848].

McKenzie, Donald. "Globalization, Efficient Markets, and Arbitrage." Paper presented at the SERC/SSRC colloquium "Money and Migration after Globalization," St. Hugh's College, Oxford University, March 25–28, 2004.

McKeown, Adam. *Chinese Migrant Networks and Cultural Change: Peru, Chicago, Hawaii, 1900–1936*. Chicago: University of Chicago Press, 1999.

McVey, Ruth. "The Materialization of the Southeast Asian Entrepreneur." In *Southeast Asian Capitalists*, ed. Ruth McVey. Ithaca, N.Y.: Southeast Asia Program, Cornell University, 1992.

Meerman, Marika. *The Chain of Love*. Documentary film, Icarus Films, Brooklyn, N.Y., 2001.

Mei Fong. "A Chinese Puzzle: Surprising Shortage of Workers." *Wall Street Journal*, Aug. 16, 2004.

Mernissi, Fatima. *Beyond the Veil: Male-Female Dynamics in Modern Muslim Society*. Rev. ed. Bloomington: Indiana University Press, 1987.

———. *The Veil and the Male Elite: A Feminist Interpretation of Women's Rights in Islam*. Reading, Mass.: Addison-Wesley, 1991.

Mills, Mary Beth. *Thai Women in the Global Labor Force*. New Brunswick, NJ: Rutgers University Press, 1999.

"Mission District Fights Case of Dot-Com Fever." *New York Times*, Nov. 5, 2000.

Mitchell, Katharyne. "Education for Democratic Citizenship: Transnationalism, Multi-culturalism, and the Limits of Liberalism." *Harvard Educational Review* 72 (Spring 2001): 51–78.

Miyoshi, Masao. "The University in the 'Global' Economy." In *The Virtual University? Knowledge, Markets and Management*, ed. Kevin Robins and Frank Webster. New York: Oxford University Press, 2002.

Mui Teng Yap. "Singapore's 'Three or More' Policy: The First Five Years." *Asia-Pacific Population Journal* 10.4 (1996): 39–52.

"Muslim Women's Movement Is Gaining Strength." *New York Times*, May 12, 1996.

Mydans, Seth. "Malaysia Upset at Treatment of Maids." *New York Times*, Feb. 20, 2000.

"A New California." *San Francisco Examiner*, Feb. 20, 2000.

"New Group Swells Bankruptcy Court: The Middle-Aged." *Wall Street Journal*, Aug. 6, 2004.

Newman, Katharine. *Falling from Grace: The Experience of Downward Mobility in the American Middle Class*. New York: Vintage, 1989.

Nguyen Vinh-kim. "Antiretroviral Globalism, Biopolitics, and Therapeutic Citizenship." In *Global Assemblages: Technology, Politics, and Ethics as Anthropological Problems*, ed. Aihwa Ong and Stephen J. Collier. Malden, Mass.: Blackwell, 2005.

Nishiyama, Chiaki, and Kurt R. Leube, eds. *The Essence of Hayek*. Stanford: Hoover Institution Press, Stanford University.

Nonini, Donald, and Aihwa Ong. "Introduction: Chinese Transnationalism as an Alternative Modernity." In *Ungrounded Empires: The Cultural Politics of Modern Chinese Transnationalism*, ed. Aihwa Ong and Donald Nonini. New York: Routledge, 1996.

"The NUS Enterprise: A Hotbed for Entrepreneurship." *Alumnus* (National University of Singapore), no. 48 (Jan. 2002): 15.

O'Donnell, Guillermo. "On the State, Democratization and Some Conceptual Problems: A Latin American View with Glances at Some Postcommunist Countries." *World Development* 21.8 (1993): 1355–69.

"Of Dress and Muslim Women." *New Straits Times* (Kuala Lumpur), Nov. 14, 1991.

Ohmae, Kenichi. *The End of the Nation State: The Rise of Regional Economies*. New York: Free Press, 1995.

Olds, Kris, and Nigel Thrift. "Cultures on the Brink: Re-engineering the Soul of Capitalism on a Global Scale." In *Global Assemblages: Technology, Politics and Ethics as Anthropological Problems*, ed. Aihwa Ong and Stephen J. Collier. Malden, Mass.: Blackwell, 2005.

Ong, Aihwa. *Spirits of Resistance and Capitalist Discipline: Factory Women in Malaysia*. Albany, NY: State University of New York Press, 1987.

——. "Colonialism and Modernity: Feminist Re-presentations of Women in Non-Western Societies. *Inscriptions*, no. 3/4 (1988): 79–93.

——. "Japanese Factories, Malay Workers: Industrialization and Sexual Metaphors in West Malaysia." In *Power and Difference: Gender in Island Southeast Asia*, ed. J. Atkinson and S. Errington. Stanford: Stanford University Press, 1990.

——. *Flexible Citizenship: The Cultural Logics of Transnationality*. Durham, N.C.: Duke University Press, 1999.

——. Introduction to *Flexible Citizenship: The Cultural Logics of Transnationality*. Durham, N.C.: Duke University Press, 1999.

——. "The Gender and Labor Politics of Postmodernity." In *Globalization and the Challenges of a New Century: A Reader*, ed. P. O'Meara, H. D. Mehlinger, and M. Krain. Bloomington: Indiana University Press, 2002.

——. *Buddha Is Hiding: Refugees, Citizenship, the New America*. Berkeley: University of California Press, 2003.

——. "Ecologies of Expertise: Governmentality in Asian Knowledge Societies." In *Global Assemblages: Technology, Politics and Ethics in Anthropological Problems*, ed. Aihwa Ong and Stephen J. Collier. Malden, Mass.: Blackwell, 2005.

——. "Experiments with Freedom: Milieus of the Human." *American Literary History* (forthcoming).

——, and Donald Nonini, eds. *Ungrounded Empires: The Cultural Struggles of Modern Chinese Transnationalism*. New York: Routledge, 1997.

Ortner, Sherry. "Is Male to Culture as Female Is to Nature?" In *Gender, Culture, and Society*, ed. Louise Lamphere, Michelle Rosaldo, and Sherry Ortner. Stanford: Stanford University Press, 1976.

Othman, Noraini. "Implementation of Syariah Criminal Law in Modern Society: Some Sociological Questions." Paper presented at the ISUD Women's Affairs Forum on Women and the Syariah Criminal Bill (II), Kelantan, Kuala Lumpur, Nov. 10, 1993.

——. "The Sociopolitical Dimensions of Islamization in Malaysia: A Cultural Accommodation of Social Change." In *Syariah Law and the Modern Nation-State: A Malaysian Symposium*. Kuala Lumpur: SIS Forum (Malaysia) Berhad, 1994.

Pabst, Adrian. "Immanence, Religion, and Neo-liberalism." Paper presented at the University of Bologna, Sept. 25–27, 2004.

Pan, Lynn. *Sons of the Yellow Emperor: A History of the Chinese Diaspora*. Boston: Little, Brown, 1990.

——. *The Encyclopedia of the Chinese Overseas*. Cambridge: Harvard University Press, 1999.

Parrenas, Rhacel Salazar. *Servants of Globalization: Women, Migration and Domestic Work*. Stanford: Stanford University Press, 2001.

Pearson, Margaret M. *China's New Business Elite: The Political Consequences of Reform*. Berkeley: University of California Press, 1997.

Peletz, Michael. *Reason and Passion: Representations of Gender in a Malay Society*. Berkeley: University of California Press, 1996.

Peluso, Nancy, and Emily Harwell. "Territory, Custom, and the Cultural Politics of Ethnic War in West Kalimantan Indonesia." In *Violent Environments*, ed. Nancy Peluso and Michael Watts. Ithaca: Cornell University Press, 2001.

Peters, Michael. "Neoliberalism." In *Encyclopedia of Philosophy of Education*. London: Routledge, 1999.

Polanyi, Karl. *The Great Transformation: The Political and Economic Origins of Our Time*. Boston: Beacon, 1957 [1944].

"Polygamy Statement Made a Mockery of Women and Islam." Letter to editor. *New Straits Times* (Kuala Lumpur), Dec. 3, 1996.

"Question of Fraud: Silicon Valley Pushes for More Foreign Workers Despite Federal Probes." *San Francisco Chronicle*, Sept. 21, 2000.

Rabinow, Paul. "The Third Culture." *History of the Human Sciences* 7.2 (1994): 53–64.

——. *French DNA: Trouble in Purgatory*. Chicago: University of Chicago Press, 1999.

——. *Anthropos Today: Reflections on Modern Equipment*. Princeton: Princeton University Press, 2003.

——. "Midst Anthropology's Problems." In *Global Assemblages: Technology, Politics and Ethics as Anthropological Problems*, ed. Aihwa Ong and Stephen J. Collier. Malden, Mass.: Blackwell, 2005.

"Re-examining the Roles of Muslim Women." *New Straits Times* (Kuala Lumpur), Jan. 8, 1990.

Reich, Robert. *The Work of Nations: Preparing Ourselves for Twenty-first Century Capitalism*. New York: Alfred A. Knopf, 1991.

Reid, Anthony. *The Land below the Winds*. Vol. 1 of *Southeast Asia in an Age of Commerce, 1450–1680*. New Haven, Conn.: Yale University Press, 1988.

——. "Entrepreneurial Minorities, Nationalism, and the State." In *Essential Outsiders: Chinese and Jews in the Modern Transformation of Southeast Asia and Central Europe*, ed. Daniel Chirot and Anthony Reid. Seattle: University of Washington Press, 1997.

Reuters. "Minister: Fires out of Control in Indonesia." April 14, 1998.

Roach, Stephen. "The Global Labor Arbitrage." *Global Economic Forum*. Morgan Stanley, Oct. 6, 2003.

Roberts, Susan. "Global Strategic Vision: Managing the World." In *Globalization under Construction: Governmentality, Law, and Identity*, ed. Richard Perry and Bill Maurer. Minneapolis: University of Minnesota Press, 2004.

Robison, Richard, and David S. G. Goodman. "The New Rich in Asia: Economic Development, Social Status, and Political Consciousness." In *The New Rich in Asia*, ed. Richard Robison and David S. G. Goodman. London: Routledge, 1996.

Rodriguez, Richard. *Hunger of Memory: The Education of Richard Rodriguez—An Autobiography*. Boston: D. R. Godine, 1981.

Roitman, Janet. "The Garrison-Entrepot: A Mode of Governing in the Chad Basin." In *Global Assemblages: Technology, Politics and Ethics as Anthropological Problems*, ed. Aihwa Ong and Stephen J. Collier. Malden, Mass.: Blackwell, 2005.

——. "Cultural Citizenship, Inequality, and Multiculturalism." In *Race, Identity, and Citizenship*, ed. Rodolfo D. Torres, Louis F. Mirón, and Jonathan Xavier Inda. Boston: Beacon, 1997.

Rosca, Ninotchka. "Mrs. Contemplacion's Sisters: The Philippines' Shameful Export." *Nation*, April 17, 1995.

Rose, Nikolas. "Governing the Enterprising Self." In *The Values of the Enterprise Culture*, ed. Paul Heelas and Paul Morris. London: Routledge, 1992.

———. "Governing 'Advanced' Liberal Democracies." In *Foucault and Political Reason*, ed. Andrew Barry, Thomas Osborne, and Nikolas Rose. Chicago: University of Chicago Press, 1996.

———. *Powers of Freedom: Reframing Political Thought*. Cambridge: Cambridge University Press, 1999.

———, and Peter Miller. "Political Power beyond the State: Problematics of Government." *British Journal of Sociology* 43.2 (1992): 1–19.

———, and Carlos Novas. "Biological Citizenship." In *Global Assemblages: Technology, Politics and Ethics in Anthropological Problems*, ed. Aihwa Ong and Stephen J. Collier. Malden, Mass.: Blackwell, 2005.

Ross, Andrew. *Fast Boat to China: Corporate Flight and the Consequences of Free Trade*. New York: Pantheon, 2006.

Rudnyckyj, Dar. "Technologies of Servitude: Governmentality and Indonesian Transnational Labor Migration." *Anthropology Quarterly* 77.3 (2004): 407–34.

Ruggie, John. *Constructing the World Polity*. London: Routledge, 1998.

"Rulers Agree: Standardised Islamic Laws for All States, Says Dr. Mahathir." *Star* (Malaysia), Aug. 1, 1997.

Sabbah, Fatna. *Women in the Muslim Unconscious*. New York: Pergamon, 1984.

Sack, Robert D. *Human Territoriality: Its Theory and History*. Cambridge: Cambridge University Press, 1986.

Safire, William. "Inside a Republican Brain." *New York Times*, July 21, 2004.

"San Jose Mayor Forms Housing Crisis Group." *San Francisco Chronicle*, Sept. 14, 2000.

Sassen, Saskia. *The Global City: New York, London, Tokyo*. Princeton: Princeton University Press, 1991.

———. *Losing Control? Sovereignty in an Age of Globalization*. New York: Columbia University Press, 1996.

———. *Globalization and Its Discontents*. New York: New Press, 1998.

———. "Digital Networks and Power." In *Spaces of Culture: City, Nation, World*, ed. M. Featherstone and S. Lash. London: Sage, 1999.

———. "Locating Cities on Global Circuits." In *Global Networks, Linked Cities*. New York: Routledge, 2002.

Saxenian, AnnaLee. *Regional Advantage: Culture and Competition in Silicon Valley and Route 128*. Cambridge: Harvard University Press, 1994.

———. *Silicon Valley's New Immigrant Entrepreneurs*. San Francisco: Public Policy Institute of California, 1999.

Schmid, John. "China Engineers Its Next Great Leap." *Milwaukee Journal Sentinel*, December 31, 2003.

Schmitt, Carl. *Political Theology: Four Chapters on the Concept of Sovereignty*. Intro. and trans. George Schwab. Cambridge: MIT Press, 1987.

Schwab, George. Introduction to *Political Theology: Four Chapters on the Concept of Sovereignty*. Intro. and trans. George Schwab. Cambridge: MIT Press, 1987.

Schwarz, Adam. *A Nation in Waiting: Indonesia in the 1990s*. Sydney: Allen and Unwin, 1994.

Scott, James C. *The Moral Economy of the Peasant*. New Haven, Conn.: Yale University Press, 1976.

——. *Seeing Like a State*. New Haven, Conn.: Yale University Press, 1998.

Shklar, Judith N. *American Citizenship: The Quest for Inclusion*. Cambridge: Harvard University Press, 1991.

Sinapan Samydorai. "The Killing Fields of West Kalimantan." *Human Rights Solidarity* (Hong Kong) 7.2 (1997): 5–7, 29.

Sisters in Islam. "Polygamy Not a Right Enshrined in the Quran." *New Straits Times* (Kuala Lumpur), August 20, 1990.

——. "Nik Aziz's Putting Down Women Wrong." *New Straits Times* (Kuala Lumpur), Jan. 17, 1991.

——. "Spouses and Suitors: States Differ on Approach to Polygamy." *Far Eastern Economic Review*, Aug. 22, 1991.

——. *Muslim Women Speak*. Pamphlet. SIS Forum (Malaysia) Berhad, 2000–2005.

Skinner, G. William. *Chinese Society in Thailand*. Ithaca, N.Y.: Cornell University Press, 1957.

——. "The Chinese Minority." In *Indonesia*, ed. Ruth McVey. New Haven, Conn.: Human Relations Area Files, 1963.

Smith, Anthony D. *National Identity*. Reno: University of Nevada Press, 1993.

Sole, Ricard, and Brian Goodwin. *Signs of Life: How Complexity Pervades Biology*. New York: Basic, 2000.

Solinger, Dorothy J. *Contesting Citizenship in Urban China: Peasant Migrants, the State, and the Logic of the Market*. Berkeley: University of California Press, 1999.

Soysal, Yasemin. *The Limits of Citizenship: Migrants and Postnational Membership in Europe*. Chicago: University of Chicago Press, 1994.

Stark, David. "Value, Values, and Valuation: Work and Worth in the New Economy." Paper presented at the Social Science Research Council conference "The New Global Economy," Emory University, April 13–14, 2001.

"Straight from the Mouth: Executives Speak Out." *San Francisco Chronicle*, March 7, 2004.

Stroper, Michael. "The Resurgence of Regional Economies, Ten Years Later." *European Urban and Regional Studies* 2.3 (1995): 191–221.

Takeo Tsuchiya. "Free Trade Zones in Southeast Asia." In *International Capitalism and Industrial Restructuring*, ed. Richard Peet. Boston: Allen and Unwin, 1997.

Tambiah, Stanley. "The Galactic Polity: The Structure of Traditional Kingdoms in Southeast Asia." *Ann. New York Academy of Sciences* 293 (1977): 69–97.

Tan Kong Yam et al. "Has Foreign Talent Contributed to Singapore's Economic Growth? An Empirical Assessment." Singapore Ministry of Trade and Industry, 2002.

Tan, Tony. Keynote address at the Singapore-MIT Alliance Symposium, January 2002.

Tatsuyuki Ota. "The Role of Special Economic Zones in China's Economic Development as Compared with Asia's Export Processing Zones, 1979–1995." *Asia in Extenso*, March 2003: 4.

Tay, Elaine. "Global Chinese Fraternity and the Indonesian Riots of May 1998: The Online Gathering of Dispersed Chinese." *Intersections*, no. 4 (Sept. 2000).

Taylor, Charles. "The Politics of Recognition." In *Multiculturalism*, ed. Amy Gutmann. Princeton: Princeton University Press, 1994.

Taylor, P. J. "Beyond Containers: Internationality, Interstateness, Interterritoriality." *Progress in Human Geography* 18 (1995): 151–62.

"Teaching Tech." *Wall Street Journal*, Sept. 27, 2004.

Tenaganita. *Implications of the Economic Crisis on Migrant Workers*. Kuala Lumpur: Tenaganita, 1998.

"Thorny Issue of Whether Marital Rape Is an Offence." *New Straits Times* (Kuala Lumpur), Aug. 7, 1994.

Thrift, Nigel. "The Globalization of the System of Business Knowledge." In *Globalization and the Asia-Pacific: Contested Terrains*, ed. K. Olds, P. Dicken, P. F. Kelly, L. Kong, and H. W.-C. Yeung. London: Routledge, 1999.

"Time to Assert Women's Presence in Islam." *New Straits Times* (Kuala Lumpur), Jan. 18, 1990.

Tölölyan, Khachig. "Rethinking Diaspora(s): Stateless Power in the Transnational Moment." *Diaspora* 5.1 (1996): 3–36.

"Towards a New Financial System: The Perils of Global Capital." *Economist*, April 11, 1998.

"Tragedy and Technology Make Overseas Chinese UNITE." *Straits Times* (Singapore), Aug. 20, 1998.

Tu, Wei-ming. "Cultural China: The Periphery as the Center." *Daedalus* 120, no. 2 (1991): 1–32.

United Nations Industrial Development Organization (UNIDO). "Industrial Free Trade Zones as Incentives to Promote Export-Oriented Industries." ID/WG, 112/3, Oct. New York: UNIDO, 1971.

"U.S. Is Losing Its Dominance in the Sciences." *New York Times*, May 3, 2004.

"VC Firms Push for Outsourcing." *San Francisco Chronicle*, March 7, 2004.

Weber, Max. *Economy and Society*. Berkeley: University of California Press, 1978.

——. *The Protestant Ethic and the Spirit of Capitalism*. London: Routledge, 1992.

——. "Sociological Categories of Economic Action." In *Essays in Economic Sociology*, ed. Richard Swedberg. Princeton: Princeton University Press, 1999.

Weiss, Linda. *The Myth of the Powerless State*. Ithaca, N.Y.: Cornell University Press, 1998.

"We're from Bangalore (But We're Not Allowed to Tell You)." *New York Times*, March 21, 2001.

Wertheim, W. P. *East-West Parallels: Sociological Approaches to Modern Asia*. The Hague: Van Hoeve, 1964.

"What Really Happened?" *Straits Times* (Singapore), Nov. 8, 1998.

"Where Compulsion Is Obsession with Control." *New Straits Times* (Kuala Lumpur), Nov. 25, 1991.

"A Whole New World." *Wall Street Journal*, Sept. 27, 2004.

Williams, Brackette F. "Introduction: Mannish Women and Gender after the Act." In *Women out of Place: The Gender of Agency and the Race of Nationality*, ed. Brackette F. Williams. New York: Routledge, 1996.

Williams, Lea. *Overseas Chinese Nationalism: The Genesis of the Pan-Chinese Movement in Indonesia, 1900–1916*. Cambridge: Center for International Studies, Massachusetts Institute of Technology, 1960.

World Bank. *Sustaining Rapid Development in East Asia and the Pacific*. Washington: World Bank, 1993, 9.

———. *Indonesia: Sustaining Development*. Washington: World Bank, 1994.

———. *World Development Report 1998/99: Knowledge for Development*. Washington: World Bank, 1999.

Wysocki, Bernard, Jr. "Malaysia Is Gambling on a Costly Plunge into a Cyber Future." *Wall Street Journal*, June 10, 1997.

Yang, Mayfair. *Gifts, Favors, and Banquets: The Art of Guanxi in Chinese Society*. Ithaca, N.Y.: Cornell University Press, 1994.

Yeoh, B. S. A., and S. Huang. "Spaces at the Margin: Migrant Domestic Workers and the Development of Civil Society in Singapore." *Environment and Planning A* 31.7 (1999): 1149–67.

Zhang, Everett Yue-hong. "Impotence in the Making: An Illness of Chinese Modernity." PhD diss., University of California, Berkeley, 2003.

Zhou Wei Hui. *Shanghai Baby*. New York: Washington Square, 1999.

index

Chapter 1 reworks material from "'Strategic Sisterhood' or Sisters in Solidarity? Questions of Communitarianism and Citizenship in Asia," *Indiana Journal of Global Legal Studies* 4.1 (1997): 107–35, and "Muslim Feminists in the Shelter of Corporate Islam," *Citizenship Studies* 3.3 (1999): 355–71.

Earlier versions of other chapters appeared in different places. Chapter 2 appeared as "Chinese Diaspora Politics and Its Fallout in a Cyber Age," in *Encyclopedia of Diasporas*, ed. Melvin Ember (New Haven, Conn.: Human Relations Area Files, 2005). Reprinted with permission of Springer Publishing Company. Chapter 3 appeared as "Graduated Sovereignty in Southeast Asia," *Theory, Culture, and Society* 17.4 (Aug. 2000): 55–75. Reprinted by permission of Sage Publications Ltd. © Theory, Culture, and Society Ltd., 2000. Chapter 4 appeared as "The Chinese Axis: Zoning Technologies and Variegated Sovereignty," *Journal of East Asian Studies* 4 (2004): 69–96. © 2004 by the East Asia Institute. Used with permission of Lynne Rienner Publishers. Chapter 5 appeared as "Splintering Cosmopolitanism: Techno-Migrants in the American West," in *Sovereign Bodies*, ed. Thomas Hansen and Finn Stepputat (Princeton: Princeton University Press, 2005). Reprinted with permission. Chapter 6 appeared as "A Higher Learning: Educational Availability and Flexible Citizenship in Global Space" in *Diversity and Citizenship Education*, ed. James A. Banks (New York: J. Wiley, 2003), 49–70. Reprinted with permission of Jossey-Bass Publishers. Chapter 8 appeared as "Intelligent Island, Baroque Ecology," in *Beyond Description*, ed. R. Bishop, J. Philips, and Yeo Wei Wei (London: Taylor and Francis, 2004), 176–89.

AIHWA ONG is a professor of anthropology and
Southeast Asian studies at the University of
California, Berkeley. She is the author of several
books, including *Global Assemblages: Technology,
Politics, and Ethics as Anthropological Problems*
(coedited with Stephen J. Collier); *Buddha Is Hiding:
Refugees, Citizenship, the New America*; and *Flexible
Citizenship: The Cultural Logics of Transnationality*,
winner of the Association for Asian American
Studies' Cultural Studies Book Award and also
published by Duke University Press.

Library of Congress Cataloging-in-Publication Data
Ong, Aihwa.
Neoliberalism as exception : mutations in citizenship
and sovereignty / Aihwa Ong.
p. cm.
Includes bibliographical references and index.
ISBN 0-8223-3736-3 (cloth : alk. paper)
ISBN 0-8223-3748-7 (pbk. : alk. paper)
1. Autonomy. 2. State, The. 3. Citizenship. 4. Self-
determination, National. 5. Culture and globalization — China. 6. China — Politics and government —
2002– 7. China — Economic conditions — 2000–
I. Title.
JC327.O54 2006
323.601 — dc22   2005036015